EVERYDAY
ETHICS
AND
SOCIAL
CHANGE

EVERYDAY ETHICS AND SOCIAL CHANGE

The Education of Desire

ANNA L. PETERSON

COLUMBIA UNIVERSITY PRESS / New York

COLUMBIA UNIVERSITY PRESS

Publishers Since 1893

New York   Chichester, West Sussex

Copyright © 2009 Columbia University Press

Library of Congress Cataloging-in-Publication Data

Peterson, Anna Lisa, 1963–

  Everyday ethics and social change : the education of desire / Anna L. Peterson.

    p. cm.

  Includes bibliographical references (p.   ) and index.

  ISBN 978-0-231-14872-6 (cloth : alk. paper)—ISBN 978-0-231-14873-3 (pbk. : alk. paper)—
ISBN 978-0-231-52055-3 (ebook)

  1. Ethics. 2. Values. 3. Social change. I. Title.

  BJ37.P48 2009

  170—dc22
                             2009003313

Columbia University Press books are printed on permanent and durable acid-free paper.

This book is printed on paper with recycled content.

Printed in the United States of America

c 10 9 8 7 6 5 4 3

References to Internet Web sites (URLs) were accurate at the time of writing.
Neither the author nor Columbia University Press is responsible for URLs that may
have expired or changed since the manuscript was prepared.

Our original guiding stars are struggle and hope.

But there is no such thing as a lone struggle, no such thing as a lone hope.

—PABLO NERUDA, *TOWARD THE SPLENDID CITY*

CONTENTS

ACKNOWLEDGMENTS

My first acknowledgment, and this book's dedication, goes to my oldest friends and comrades, with whom I have shared so many good fights over the years. In particular I thank Jane Fischberg, in the hopes that she might know how much her friendship and moral compass have meant over the years. Many other old friends have been on my mind as I have worked on this book, especially Jane Appling, Kristen Bole, Gloria Carranza, Toby Hecht, Sarah Lawton, Dan Robinson, Yolanda Rodríguez, Sam Schuchat, Jeb Sharp, Judy Shevelev, Nico van Aelstyn, and Francisca Velásquez. They have all meant a great deal to me over the past two decades or more; they have helped me be, on occasion, my best self. *La lucha continúa.*

Many other people have helped me think through these issues. Special thanks must go to my husband, Manuel Vásquez, and my brother, Brandt Peterson, both constructive thorns in my intellectual side. I cannot imagine my thinking or my life without them.

It is a special pleasure—surely an immanent utopia—to have good colleagues who are also good friends. In particular, I thank Nora Alter, David Hackett, LoraKim Joyner, Vasu Narayanan, Les Thiele, Philip Williams, and the Sustainable Seven: Martha Monroe, Whitney Sanford, Katie

Sieving, and Sam Snyder. I am grateful also to Kay Read for her friendship and for thinking with me about children and the common good. I am fortunate as well to be able to talk about these issues with smart, thoughtful, and committed graduate students; special thanks to those who took my fall 2007 course on Environmental Values and Practices.

I must also thank the participants in the April 2007 conference on "Walking the Talk" in Gainesville, which was supported by the University of Florida School for Natural Resources and the Environment. I benefited greatly from conversations with all the people at that unusual meeting, too many to list here, who sharpened my thinking about values and practices. I presented early versions of parts of this book at several other campuses, including the Transdisciplinary Theological Colloquium at Drew University School of Theology in October 2005; a workshop on the environmental politics of sacrifice at Allegheny College in September 2007; and lectures at the University of Illinois-Urbana/Champaign and Kalamazoo College, both in April 2008. I am grateful for stimulating conversations at all those places, and especially for the help and ideas I received from Carol Anderson, Shreena Gandhi, Laurel Kearns, Catherine Keller, Mike Maniates, Jay McDaniel, Robert McKim, John Meyer, Tom Princen, Michael Scoville, and Dan Spencer.

In writing this book, I have returned to some of my earliest intellectual concerns, and in so doing I realize again my debts to the teachers who first helped me think about ethics, theology, and social change. I am indebted to Robert Bellah, John Coleman, Jean Comaroff, Robin Lovin, Hal Sanks, David L. Smith, and Mark Taylor. What a privilege to have teachers like these introduce me to Marx, Weber, Tillich, E. P. Thompson, Habermas, Gramsci, Gustavo Gutiérrez, and so much more. Their impact on my thinking grows stronger over the years. I also remember with gratitude the late Anne Carr, for her pioneering work on both feminist theology and theological anthropology and her gentle, uncompromising commitment to a better world.

I owe much, also, to Wes Jackson and Sharon Welch, without whose work I could not have conceived of this project. They put together ethics, activism, and everyday life with brilliance, persistence, and grace.

I do not think that my family suffered as I wrote this book, or at least no more than usual. I am grateful, however, for tolerance and support from

Manuel, Brandt, Casey Williamson, and Judith Peterson. My children, Gabriel, Eva, and Rafael, bring great joy as well as great complication into my life. So too do my nonhuman companions—Tozi, Libby, and Thunder, Devo and Missy, and even the chickens, Mora and Fluffy Hawk. As I was finishing this book, my long-time canine friends Inti and Balo died two weeks apart. I miss them tremendously and am thankful for all that I learned from them in our years together. I am also grateful for the mixed community in which I participate through my fortuitous engagement at Mosswood Farm and for the local foodshed to which I am connected through the efforts of Rose Koenig and Plowshares CSA.

It has been a great pleasure to work with the staff at Columbia University Press, especially Wendy Lochner. I am thankful also for a Humanities Enhancement Grant from the University of Florida during summer 2005, which helped me get a start on several chapters of this book.

EVERYDAY
ETHICS
AND
SOCIAL
CHANGE

1 / A PRESENCE AND A BEGINNING

We live in difficult times. We face social and environmental problems that are massive in scope, for which effective solutions are elusive, at best. These problems are well symbolized by global warming, which threatens nonhuman species, unique ecosystems, and human communities equally. Climate change is so disturbing that my twelve-year-old son, who is passionately interested in public affairs in general and the environment in particular, refuses to discuss it. It is too depressing, he says; he cannot see a way out; he cannot bear to think about what it means for his future. His despair breaks my heart, but I have no comforting words to offer. I feel depressed and overwhelmed as well. I am tempted to retreat into a more comfortable and manageable universe, to shrink the world into something I can control.[1]

I know that I am far from alone in feeling this. It is hard to look at the world outside and not find reasons for discouragement and motivation to retreat. As the bumper sticker says, "If you're not worried, you're not paying attention." Any of us who love something in this threatened world—our children, our students, wild nature, humanity in general—are right to worry. What is much less sure is whether we are right to hope. This book is a reflection on where we might direct our attention to uncover reasons to hope.

Perhaps reason is not the right word, insofar as it suggests rational arguments and evidence. I suspect that the grounds for hope are more akin to what Saint Paul expressed in his letter to the Romans: "In hope he believed against hope" (Romans 4:18). One of my favorite theologians, Paul Tillich, quoted this line at the start of an essay on "The Right to Hope." For Tillich, believing against hope meant going "ever again through the narrows of a painful and courageous 'in-spite-of.' For hope cannot be verified by sense experience or rational proof."[2] Tillich's "in spite of" rests on the "ground of being," the God whose existence we trust not because of rational proofs but because we experience existential courage. "There are no valid arguments for the 'existence' of God," explains Tillich, "but there are acts of courage in which we affirm the power of being, whether we know it or not."[3] Nor are there valid arguments to justify moral and political hope. In place of rational arguments, we know acts of hopefulness in which we affirm the possibility of something better. We hold fast to visions of this something better even when nothing in our world indicates progress is possible. This hope is utopian: utopia means, literally, "no place," and our hope rests in no place we can know for sure.

Utopias are always transcendent, beyond the here and now. Some utopias, however, are also immanent. They already exist, albeit in partial and embryonic form. We know relations of love and solidarity, even if these are fragile and fragmentary. We know connectedness with other people and with members of other species. We play freely and joyfully. We find satisfaction in taking care of those who need us and in being cared for. In these moments we glimpse what Tillich calls "the seed-like presence of that which is hoped for. In the seed of a tree, stem and leaves are already present, and this gives us the right to sow the seed in hope for the fruit." Here we find, if not reasons, then a right to hope: the seed that might develop into something bigger, that has no guarantee but which represents "a presence, a beginning of what is hoped for." This presence makes hope possible: "We hope for the fulfillment of our work, often against hope, because it is already in us as vision and driving force. We hope for a lasting love, because we feel the power of this love present. But it is hope, not certainty."[4]

This book is about the connection between the presence of "that which is hoped for" in our everyday lives and the possibility of this good on a larger and more lasting scale. Hope may or may not be justified in the end, but it is real. It is real because it is rooted in something that exists here and now. Without this presence and beginning, "hope is foolishness," as Tillich insists.[5] We must know love, fulfillment, peace, or any other good in some way in order to ground larger hopes. We find the presence and beginning of hope for a better world in loving friendships, family ties, encounters with nonhuman creatures, and ventures into wild nature. These relationships and experiences give meaning and value to our lives. They find us at our best: relating to human and nonhuman others in nonutilitarian ways, sacrificing for larger goods, finding satisfaction in experience and relationship rather than consumption and calculation. Because they embody not only alternative values but also alternative sources of joy, these experiences constitute the immanent utopias of everyday life.

I am interested in these moments of grace not only in themselves but also for their potential and actual connections to the public sphere and to large-scale social change. I believe that some of these relationships, experiences, and practices embody not just private but public hopes and values. To fulfill their political potential, however, we face uphill battles, sacrifices of time, convenience, and perhaps more, risks of failure and disappointment. We have to resist the lure of retreat into private pleasures, avoiding the temptation to keep our hope small and private—which in the end, as Tillich asserts, is "a poor and foolish hope."[6] We need to hope together, for each other: to connect our private hopes and dreams to the common good.

A vital tool in any process of social change is what English Marxist historian E. P. Thompson calls "the education of desire." Thompson describes hopes that "teach desire to desire, to desire better, to desire more, and above all, to desire in a different way."[7] This, according to Thompson, is the "proper and new-found space" of Utopia. Rather than a utopia that is "no place," Thompson proposes one intimately connected to ordinary lives and aspirations. This utopia entails a vision of a qualitatively different and better life without which we cannot think about creating better societies. As feminist poet Adrienne Rich puts it, "If the imagination is to transcend and transform experience it has to question, to challenge, to conceive of alternatives, perhaps to the very life you are living at that moment."[8] These alternatives, however, must not seem utterly disconnected from the lives we are currently living. Utopian ideas have power only if they resonate with the people who need them. Impossible dreams, extraterrestrial fantasies, and descriptions of societies unimaginably far removed from our own might help spark imagination and critique, but they do not generate sustained energy for resistance and construction. The education of desire, like the right to hope, must be rooted in the soil of everyday life.

I argue in this book that the education of desire begins with the realization that the experiences that give meaning and value to our personal lives are not random or isolated exceptions to "the way things really are." Rather, they reflect an alternative ethic, in operation only in fragmented, fleeting instances. This ethic assumes that human nature can be social and cooperative, not only individualistic and competitive. People can relate to each other in unselfish, mutually responsive ways. They can seek common goods and not only private benefits. People can also relate to nonhuman nature with wonder and respect, seeking understanding without exploiting every resource for personal gain. If this sounds as fantastic as any work of science fiction, consider that most of us embody these qualities and live by these values every day of our lives, at least momentarily. In family life, with friends, with companion animals, in wild places, we find countless occasions to live according to a moral system that differs radically from the voluntaristic, individualistic, and utilitarian assumptions that rule most of our lives.

We cannot easily expand this alternative morality to all facets of our lives, all or even most of the time. However, I believe that we can benefit from recognizing this ethic, analyzing and appreciating it more fully, even in its present constrained circumstances. If we can identify the contents of this ethic and the circumstances under which it operates, we might even expand it into parts of our shared public life. This means understanding the relations between values and politics in a way that has not yet been done very systematically.

This effort must begin with the acknowledgment that most of our everyday lives are far from utopian. The fragmentary and rare moments when it all works illuminate the flip side, the more frequent times when things fall apart. Family life, for example, is stressful and hard just as often as it is joyous and comforting. As fallible and limited creatures, humans will probably always experience conflict and misunderstandings in our interpersonal relationships. We will always be prone to illness, pain, conflicts, and disappointments. These existential challenges are compounded by political and

economic ones. Stress, overwork, social violence, and ecological damage
all make it impossible for even the most fortunate and caring of families to
make the good a permanent condition. Poverty further constrains the efforts of many more parents. Popular culture and media reinforce negative
ways of interacting with others, often making our private lives just as competitive, utilitarian, exploitative, or shallow as the larger world from which
we want to escape.

I have no illusions of an end to conflict, suffering, or unpleasantness.
As some humanist revisers of Marx, including Tillich, have pointed out,
even the end of capitalism would not eliminate all forms of existential, physical, and emotional suffering. With our limitations firmly in mind, however, I am convinced we can do better. To do so, we need to distinguish
more clearly between the obstacles that are existential and ineradicable and
those that are socially imposed and open to transformation. This process of
discernment leads not to "the naive denial of any genuine limits," as feminist ethicist Sharon Welch explains, but rather to "a sophisticated questioning of what a social system has set as 'genuine limits.'" Such questioning
can expand the "boundaries of human hope," expanding our dreams beyond what we have been taught to expect—educating us, in short, to desire
more and better.[9] I am convinced that we can achieve this education and that
the immanent utopias of everyday life are crucial not only to the education
of desire but also to the development of effective practices of social change.
These mundane utopias—the moments when we experience something
qualitatively different from utilitarian calculus and consumption—provide
embodied proof that a different, better life is possible.

These utopian moments, however, are also fleeting, fragmentary, and
embattled. Their fragility has long been recognized in Christian understandings of the reign of God. This reign is already here and now—"in the
midst of you," as Jesus told the Pharisees (Luke 17:20–21)—at the same
time it is never full realized, always "not yet." What makes the world into
the reign of God, or any community a utopia, is its capacity to embody
ultimate hopes and values, to live "the kingdom as social ethic."[10] The "already not yet" of the Christian tradition is the immanent utopia most familiar to me, but it is far from the only one. Buddhism teaches that enlightenment and nirvana are achieved not by leaving the physical world
behind but rather by understanding, and living in, this world differently.[11]

Nonattachment is an immanent utopia insofar as it is an embodied way of being differently here and now. Other traditions also have visions and experiences that help flesh out the many possible immanent utopias we might encounter or build in our various places on Earth. The grounded messianism of Judaism reveals Israel as a state that is both earthly and spiritual, utopian insofar as its hopes must always transcend any concrete embodiment. The recognition of this transcendence is crucial, or there is a risk of "idolatry," of making a particular institution or experience into an end in itself. We might here invoke Tillich's "Protestant principle," which protests "against every power that claims divine character for itself."[12] This is a danger for many forms of utopianism, religious and secular, which risk "absolutizing what is not absolute" as they look toward radically different values and ways of living.[13] Despite the dangers, many religious traditions, as well as other philosophical and cultural streams, offer insights and models that can help flesh out, in particular times and places, what a better world should and might be.

In this book I want, first, to identify the sources of meaning and joy that constitute the kingdoms in our midst, the utopias that we already live. I hope then to tease out these fragments, to identify experiences and practices that challenge destructive social patterns and especially the habitual emphasis on individual self-interest at the cost of larger goods. I want to build on these ideas in order to explore the different values we live by, constituting different worlds, experienced and embodied in the moments of everyday grace. Finally, I explore the ways these beginnings can educate our desires so that we might expand them into our collective lives.

PRIVATE AND PUBLIC LIFE

This hope might seem foolish given the decidedly nonutopian character of everyday life in the contemporary United States. North American society is characterized by growing political and cultural polarization, social inequalities, poverty, environmental destruction, and endless war. Related to these problems is the fact that we are increasingly cut off from other people and from a larger public sphere. The decline of connectedness, of community, and of "social capital" in the United States has been well documented in recent decades, most notably in *Habits of the Heart* (first published in

1985) by sociologist Robert Bellah and four coauthors and in *Bowling Alone*
(1995) by political scientist Robert Putnam. These and other studies offer
extensive evidence that both private and public relationships have declined
in the past several decades. Formal public sphere organizations, such as
political parties and trade unions, have lost participation and membership,
as have charitable and volunteer groups, from parent-teacher associations
to bridge clubs.

The authors of *Habits of the Heart* note in particular the increasing scar-
city of what they term "communities of memory," in which people know
themselves "as social selves . . . members of a people, inheritors of a history
and a culture that we must nurture through memory and hope." The community is held together by a constitutive narrative and by "examples of the
men and women who have embodied and exemplified the meaning of the
community. For Bellah and his colleagues, this points to a more general
definition of community, which "is not a collection of self-seeking individuals, not a temporary remedy, like Parents without Partners, that can be
abandoned as soon as a partner has been found, but a context within which
personal identity is formed, a place where fluent self-awareness follows the
currents of communal conversation and contributes to them."[14] They give
examples of such communities, which range from a traditional Protestant
church to people held together by labor union activism. What these ideo-
logically and demographically diverse groups hold in common is that for
each, civic engagement is not simply a voluntary choice but a complex
identity, a heritage carried from the past that demands a response in the
present. Activism that is not tied in this way to participants' identities and
histories, reinforced by overlapping formal and informal social connections,
is unlikely to endure for the necessary long haul.

Civic engagement must not only be rooted in a common history but also
look toward the future. Often overlooked in readings of *Habits of the Heart*
is the authors' insistence that while communities of memory tie members
to the past, they also point to the future as "communities of hope" that can
"allow us to connect our aspirations for ourselves and those closest to us
with the aspirations of a larger whole and see our own efforts as being in
part contributions to the common good."[15] Some innovative cultural and
political groups today might qualify as communities of hope or expectation
in this sense, united by a sense of possibility, a commitment to a common

good, by shared moral and social values, even if their collective memories do not reach far into the past.

The emergence of new social movements and networks counterbalances, to some extent, the decline in communities of memory and traditional organizations that Bellah, Putnam, and others lament. Some new groups rely heavily on new media, compensating for the loss of economic and geographic ties by finding other ways to build relationships and accomplish goals. Many of these movements consist of "'invisible' networks of small groups submerged in everyday life," as the Italian sociologist Alberto Melucci contends. They rarely participate directly in the public sphere, focusing instead on "new forms of everyday life" that embody their values and goals in the present.[16] Such movements are formed not because of a shared heritage or material interests but rather through the recognition of common values and orientations. By embodying these values in its own organization and practices, a movement helps constitute and reinforce an identity for the participants. The movement itself, as Melucci argues, becomes the message; it is not simply an instrument for achieving a separate end.[17]

This point is echoed by another scholar of new social movements, the Spanish sociologist Manuel Castells, who describes contemporary urban movements as expressions of a new way of doing politics, rooted in everyday life experiences and embodying personal identity and values as much as explicitly public commitments.[18] As examples of this sort of movement, Castells mentions environmental, feminist, gay rights, and urbanist groups, among others. All are concerned primarily with the quality of their everyday lives and with the expression of personal identity, especially identities that are not valued by larger cultural and social institutions. Other examples of new social movements might include those focused on local food, neighborhood revivals, or alternative approaches to parenting, among many others. All of these are relevant to this book, insofar as their values and their social ties are rooted in alternative forms of relationship that are, or at least can be, embodied in everyday life.

The values and relationships embodied in everyday life are not limited to humans. Neither humanistic social scientists such as Bellah and Putnam nor new social movement theorists like Melucci and Castells have paid much attention to social connections between human and nonhuman animals, what philosopher Mary Midgley calls "mixed communities." Midgley points out that human social groups have long included other species, even though scholars have rarely noticed. "Man does not naturally exist in species-isolation," as Midgley puts it.[19] Humans coevolved with countless other species, domestic and wild, and we would not be who we are, biologically or socially, otherwise. Taking the mixed community seriously challenges our understanding of community and even of human nature itself. "Species interdependence is the name of the worldling game on earth," writes feminist theorist Donna Haraway, "and that game must be one of response and respect. That is the play of companion species learning to pay attention."[20] The challenge of meeting other species in respectful and mutual encounters can lead to joyful and meaningful expansion of the boundaries of hope and of love.

Mixed communities, new social movements, and other contemporary social networks provide real alternatives to the traditional forms of community mourned by Putnam, Bellah, and others. Still, I do not dismiss their worries as unfounded. There seems to be real evidence that social engagement is changing, at the least, and the verdict is open as to what those changes mean for public and private life. It is far from clear that declining participation in public and semipublic institutions is counterbalanced by expanding informal networks, or even by ties among relatives, neighbors, and friends. For many people today, permanence and emotional closeness are limited to fewer relationships, primarily those between spouses, parents and children, and other close relatives. The nuclear family appears to be the last repository for values of personal communication and care, unqualified affection, and long-term commitment. This is reinforced by a June 2006 study showing that "Americans have fewer confidants and those ties are also more family-based than they used to be," as one of the study's authors, Lynn Smith-Lovin, puts it. The new survey data show that the number of people who talk only to family members about important matters increased from 57 percent to 80 percent between 1985 and 2006, and the number who depend totally on a spouse rose from 5 percent to 9 percent. Americans now list an average of two "close friends," down from an average of three in 1985.[21] Putnam cites similar surveys showing that fewer people invite friends over, go out to dinner together, or participate in leisure and athletic activities with others than twenty-five years ago.

These changes may well indicate "something that's not good for our society," as Smith-Lovin and her coauthors suggest. "Ties with a close network of people create a safety net. These ties also lead to civic engagement and local political action."[22] People who do not know their neighbors, their children's teachers, or local business owners may not have a community of interweaving, overlapping relationships, especially if they do not find or create alternative communities based on shared values or goals. Informal social networks and relationships provide a foundation for efforts to solve common problems. Studies show that efforts at social change are most likely to succeed when they are rooted in already existing networks such as neighborhoods, workplaces, schools, or religious congregations *and* when they make explicit the connections between local problems and larger structures. Thus the most effective movements bring communities together around common concerns and seek to identify the causes of problems and realistic ways to address them.

This insight has been central to my thinking about social change. I first began reflecting seriously about, and experiencing, this approach to social change when I worked for Oregon Fair Share in the early 1980s. Fair Share went into neighborhoods, canvassing door-to-door and holding meetings, to learn about residents' concerns and develop effective ways to address these. Organizing often began around a local problem, such as neighborhood safety or amenities, or around "bread-and-butter" issues such as utility costs or education. The goal was to educate people about the larger context of such issues—unequal distributions of power and undemocratic political institutions—and to help working- and middle-class people feel empowered to address these issues effectively. This approach came from the theory of Saul Alinsky, who had begun his career working with industrial laborers in Chicago in the 1930s. As Castells notes, Alinsky's central principle was that poor and powerless people had one real resource: their organizational capacity. Groups like Fair Share can develop this capacity by organizing people around a clear-cut issue with identifiable and achievable goals. The aim was to seek victory on small demands, not just to improve people's lives, but to provide people with power. Once educated and empowered, ordinary people are more willing and able to confront powerful institutions and negotiate with them, from a position of strength, in order to increase their share in distribution of wealth and decision-making. Alinsky insisted that the goals and direction of the movement had to come from people themselves, based on their daily practices.[23]

The notion that efforts at large-scale social change could and should begin close to home has remained central to my scholarship and my political activism ever since. After working with Fair Share and similar community organizations in the United States, I began learning about social movements in Latin America. As a college student, I came across Phillip Berryman's book *The Religious Roots of Rebellion*, about the role of progressive Catholics in Central American opposition movements.[24] I was hooked by the book's preface, in which Berryman described a grassroots Christian community (*comunidad eclesial de base*, or CEB) in Solentiname, Nicaragua. The members of the community, all poor fishers and farmers, met weekly, beginning in the late 1960s, to discuss gospel passages in light of their own experiences. Their conversations related their evolving understanding of Christianity to family and local concerns and, eventually, to their country's increasingly tense political situation. While the community in Solentiname had been founded by the eminent Nicaraguan poet and priest Ernesto Cardenal, in other ways it resembled other CEBs that had emerged in many poor communities throughout Latin America following the Second Vatican Council (1962–65). The communities shared a common defining activity, group reading and discussion of biblical passages in the light of their everyday lives. Through this process of *reflexión*, they developed both strong social bonds and ethical analyses of common problems they faced.

In politically polarized settings such as Nicaragua, El Salvador, and Brazil, CEBs and other progressive Catholic initiatives became important players in opposition movements. Their political efficacy was rooted in their capacity to achieve both *concientización* (consciousness raising) and community building among impoverished and disempowered people. Like Alinsky-style organizations in the United States, CEBs helped people discover common concerns, connect those concerns to larger political and economic structures, and develop strategies for addressing their problems effectively. None of the groups achieved all their goals. However, in the United States and in Latin America, community-based organizations have made life measurably better for millions of people. This success rests, I believe, on their basic insight that people will work for social change if they feel two kinds of connection: first, the link between "politics" and their real lives, and second, the bonds between people who face similar problems and seek similar goods.

Such movements are much weaker when people are disconnected from each other, as recent studies of declining social capital suggest. If people do not spend time with their neighbors and coworkers, if neighborhoods are merely "lifestyle enclaves,"[25] then it is nearly impossible to mobilize them around common values and goals. As informal and semipublic networks and bonds decline, then, so does the possibility of making real changes in our political system, from local to larger levels. The possibility of social change is also weakened by changes in the quality, as well as the quantity, of our social relationships. While in the past many U.S. institutions, both formal and informal, connected people to each other and to the larger society's activities and purposes, today many serve mainly private, individual purposes. These transformations are clearly evident in marriage, which was traditionally viewed as a foundation not only for families but for wider communities. The marital bond linked people to larger cultural, religious, and economic institutions. Today, however, most people see matrimony as a route to individual fulfillment and happiness. These goals are not trivial, but something has been lost. Similar changes have affected other social relations, including friendships, neighborhoods, and, perhaps most notably, nuclear and extended families. Not only are families smaller today, but their character has changed, with less emphasis on participation in group purposes and more on individual choice and satisfaction. For the most part, families no longer form integral parts of a larger moral ecology, tying individual to community, church, and nation. Family remains the core of the private sphere, as it has always been, but today it does not link its members to the public, symbolically or practically. Instead, the family seems opposed to the public sphere, a refuge from it rather than a medium for participating in it. And even as families bear a growing burden for people's social and emotional lives, the studies cited earlier show that family members spend less time together and engage less often in shared activities, ranging from sit-down dinners to vacations.[26]

We can recognize the loss of particular kinds of social ties without romanticizing everything about them. Traditional models of marriage and the nuclear family carry their own limitations and problems. Far too many women, for a start, have been damaged by marriages that may have provided stability but lacked many other qualities, including mutual respect, equal treatment, and even noninstrumental affection. Far too many people, especially those in love with someone of the same gender or a different color, have been unable to live freely with their partner of choice, and thus unable to help create alternative communities and a new kind of public sphere. The sort of marriage, or romantic partnership more generally, that nurtures public commitments need not and indeed should not be equated with "one woman + one man" (as my neighbor's bumper sticker proclaims). As someone married across ethnic, national, and religious lines, I look for models of marriage and family that do not reinforce narrow notions of community and morality. My children are multiethnic, binational, and religiously undefined. I hope for them and for myself a community in which they can be full citizens, with whatever partnerships and families they form as adults. These partnerships and families should not, however, exist only as expressions of free, individual choice, calculated to serve private ends. All relationships benefit from the wider social networks that ground and support them, and that they should, in turn, support, reinforce, and also challenge and transform.

Within the family, values of loyalty, mutual care, and even self-sacrifice may rule, as members take care of "their own," but less often do these values extend to larger communities. Few families and couples today frame their commitments to each other in light of larger commitments to public goods or goals. This lack of public engagement is tied to a strongly voluntaristic understanding of even the most intimate relationships. Today connections with spouses, friends, parents, and children are frequently seen as contracts, in which autonomous, equal persons choose to participate in a particular kind of relationship because it serves their purposes at a particular time; when those purposes are no longer met, either can withdraw, leaving every commitment unstable. This perspective "seems to undercut the possibility of other than self-interested relationships," resembling contracts which individuals enter freely and which they end when they do not serve their purposes.[27] This utilitarian, contractual perspective defines the good life in terms only of individual choice, preference, and personal satisfaction, without binding commitments or substantive shared values.

There is no single source or cause of these social trends, of course. One major factor is the modern Western notion of the autonomous self, which has roots in both Enlightenment philosophy and Protestant Christianity. Both these traditions of thought have contributed to an image of humans as self-defined and largely self-sufficient rational creatures, who enter into relationships with other people only voluntarily and in their own self-interest. This vision does not acknowledge humans as social animals, mutually constituted in and through interactions and relationships with other beings. Social relationships and larger collectives are seen as external to personal identity, and often threatening or oppressive to it. These ideas are reinforced by political and economic developments, including social contract models of government and free market economic systems. There has been no conspiracy to reinvent human nature but rather a series of elective affinities, to use Max Weber's term, in which cultural, political, and economic forces have reinforced each other, often inadvertently. The end result is what *Habits of the Heart* calls the "unencumbered" self, "suspended in glorious, but terrifying, isolation."[28]

Countless articles, books, and blogs have analyzed ramifications of these trends. I have discussed their implications for environmental attitudes and behavior myself at some length in previous work. In the present book I am interested in the ways that the unencumbered self becomes a particular sort of moral and political actor, one whose private and public lives are mostly separate while sharing contractual, utilitarian assumptions. In public and in private, ethical debates and decisions are understood largely within the framework of individual choice, in which "morality" is something that individuals freely exercise, usually when faced with a clear-cut choice between two options. This approach brings issues such as abortion, euthanasia, gun control, and even gay marriage to the fore, while erasing or ignoring the ways they are embedded in complex, collective histories and economic processes. Structural problems related to the distribution of wealth, employment, social security, the use of public land and natural resources, and the character and function of political institutions seem ideological rather than ethical in nature. This definition of morality became especially evident after the 2004 elections, when pundits and surveys declared that moral issues were crucial to voters' decisions, while defining these issues in extremely narrow terms, primarily in relation to gay marriage and abortion. Progressives declared that their challenge was to present their concerns, including the environment, unemployment, and health care, as moral issues.

The redefinition of moral politics is impossible as long as private meaning and satisfaction are separate from public goods. Bringing the two back together will not be easy, since their separation has deep roots, going back to the division of labor that accompanied industrialization and urbanization in the modern West. The private sphere, usually defined as the family and other interpersonal relationships, includes frequent face-to-face contact, mutual dependence, and long-term ties that give precedence to values of nurture, altruism, and loyalty. Feminist scholar Nel Noddings has characterized the primary values of the private sphere with the term "caring-for," which encompasses the qualities of nurture, attentive love, and support for personal development and growth.[29] These values are especially associated with women and their nurturing activities in the family.

In contrast, the modern public sphere of work and politics gives precedence to values such as individualism, free choice, and equal exchange as the basis of contractual relationships, and instrumentalism. Unlike the long-term commitment, empathy, and altruism that are valued, if not always fully realized, in the private realm, public-sphere values are impersonal and voluntaristic. Their validity comes from their applicability to a host of situations regardless of the persons involved and their relationships. Such impersonal values become primary, both historians and philosophers have argued, when most interactions are with people we do not know and with whom we have no ongoing relationship. In turn, more abstract moralities may reinforce impersonal relationships, insofar as they shape how we think about and treat others even in our immediate circle.

For many philosophers, the distinction of values corresponding to public and private spheres is both appropriate and necessary. In particular, the activities, roles, and values of the private sphere should not enter into the public sphere, as they are associated with irrational emotion, parochialism, and sentimentality, rather than with the impartial and universalistic perspective needed for political deliberation and decisions. Public decisions should be made in isolation from social relationships, cultural history, and anything that makes a person particular. Immanuel Kant most famously expressed this approach. For Kant and his followers, ethics must be universalizable, abstract, generic, and thus eminently impersonal. The strong feelings and loyalties of the private sphere are rightly excluded from ethics and politics. Personal relationships between men and women or adults and children may require the application of moral principles, such as equal justice or human rights, but personal experiences do not help determine those principles. For Kant, the public square is the place for ethical discussions, while private life is the realm of partial, biased relations.

This modern dualism parallels certain religious views of the relations between public and private values. The twentieth-century Protestant theologian Reinhold Niebuhr described a dichotomy between "moral man and immoral society." For individuals, being moral means "that they are able to consider interests other their own in determining problems of conduct, and are capable, on occasion, of preferring the advantages of others to their own."[30] This capacity for unselfishness, even self-transcendence, defines the Christian value of unselfish *agape* love or charity. However, this ethic cannot be applied widely beyond intimate personal relationships, Niebuhr believes, because social groups lack individuals' capacity for unselfish behavior. Power relations and interests, both among and within groups, prevent altruism, rationality, and conscience from determining behavior. Thus, Niebuhr concludes, the best we can hope for in the public sphere is some form of justice to reduce abuses of power and moderate social and economic inequities.[31] In a sense, Niebuhr's ethic represents the other side of Kant's: Niebuhr individualized and privatized affect, while Kant universalized rationality.

What they agreed on was a sharp distinction between public and private values. In recent decades, feminists and others have challenged this distinction. It often has entailed, as for Kant and his Enlightenment colleagues, devaluing interpersonal relationships and domestic goods. Or this public-private split can lead to the sort of political cynicism of which Niebuhr is often accused. Realistic political hope is compatible neither with the rationalist dismissal of personal life as sentimental and trivial nor with the idealization of the private sphere as a rarified space that must be insulated from politics. My aim in this book is to identify ways in which everyday life, including many dimensions of the private sphere and interpersonal relations, can nurture qualities that rarely thrive elsewhere—qualities that we need in order to create a better society. In this perspective, we have reason to worry about the expansion of instrumental, utilitarian, and voluntaristic patterns into personal life, just as we should worry about the shrinking of interpersonal networks and the decline of social trust. It means something for political ethics that families are smaller and more separate from each other, neighbors are not as likely to know each other well or to engage in shared activities, and private-sphere values of intimacy, mutual care, and emotional depth characterize fewer and fewer relationships.

One result of these changes, as sociologist Stacey Oliker explains, is that "communal sentiment and responsibility contract from a wider circle of kin, neighbors, and friends to the realm of the household. Secondary institutions such as the guild, church, and civic council lose their moral hold. The public sphere of sociality and community disappears; deep lasting friendship, communal exchange, and ritual are replaced by shallow instrumental sociability and neighborliness."[32] The values of the public sphere, in other words, influence semipublic settings and, increasingly, private ones. Shallow and utilitarian public values displace, and even make obsolete, contrasting values that traditionally have been associated with family life and also with neighborhoods, congregations, and other intermediate communities. Displaced private values include "virtue-based concepts such as friendship, love, respect, care, concern, gratitude, community and compassion," as Australian philosopher Val Plumwood notes, all of which "are in conflict with the rational instrumentalism of the public sphere, in which they have no place."[33] These noninstrumental values correspond to a different conception of moral life, now excluded from the public sphere and mostly confined to private relations.

Perhaps the most influential analyst of this process is German social theorist Jürgen Habermas, who describes and criticizes what he calls the invasion or colonization of the "lifeworld" (which includes the private spheres of home and neighborhood) by the "system" (the market economy and the state).[34] The system is dominated by an instrumental rationality that opposes the more egalitarian and communicative culture of the lifeworld, encompassing household, neighborhood, religion, and other private and semiprivate realms. Habermas worries that the system and its instrumental language and values are displacing the characteristic discourse, values, and practices of the lifeworld. This displacement yields troubling consequences not only for everyday life but for democracy itself, he argues, insofar as the latter requires practices nourished by the lifeworld, including communication oriented toward understanding (not just profit) and willingness to set aside self-interest for larger goods.

Habermas aims at a new definition of morality, in which "communication oriented toward understanding" provides a basis for an open, egalitarian democratic politics. While I differ with Habermas on many points, I find his work very helpful in thinking about how we might bridge the divide between public and personal life. How might we not only defend the values of the lifeworld in their home space but also reconsider their place in the public sphere? How do developments in the market and politics impinge on our ability to enact nonutilitarian values even in our most intimate relationships? Such questions can help us understand that individual moral choices are not isolated from social structures or economic systems. Ethics is not just about making good choices on narrowly defined questions but about envisioning and working toward a common good, contributing to a larger whole, and playing a meaningful part in a movements toward a better society. This understanding of morality challenges mainstream understandings of both ethics and politics in the United States. Resources for these challenges, far from being limited to marginal political perspectives, may lie in some of the most important and common practices and values of our ordinary lives.

Despite ambivalence, frustration, and disappointment, for most people, interpersonal relationships and experiences give life meaning and happiness. These private joys, however, are largely separate from, even opposed to, larger patterns and institutions. I aim here to examine the possibility of connection. Instead of separating us from the world beyond our everyday lives, I propose, our private experiences and relationships can link us to it and offer visions of how it should look. These visions take a particular form, including a more relational sense of self and a different understanding of politics and the common good. Enacting these visions, even in part, will require transformations of everyday life and identity as well as structural, institutional, and legal changes. In the pursuit of this social change, our domestic relationships, personal experiences, and encounters with nonhuman nature can provide social, logistical, and ideological resources that can help us build a better world.

These issues have been central to my thinking and my life for as long as I can remember. They have been crystallized and often reformulated by various experiences, by relationships with friends and with adversaries, and by public events that have forced me to reflect on my own commitments, priorities, and trajectory. One recurring theme throughout has been the relationship between personal loyalties and political activism. This issue was posed very clearly for me more than twenty years ago, when I went with my friend Jane Fischberg to see *The Good Fight*, a documentary about the Abraham Lincoln Brigade, U.S. citizens who had volunteered to fight on the side of the republic in the Spanish Civil War in the 1930s. The film recounted not only the brigade's experiences in that war but also the ways the surviving veterans continued throughout their lives to struggle against fascism in Italy and Germany during World War II, against racism during the civil rights movement, against U.S. involvement in the Vietnam War. At the time the documentary was made, in the early 1980s, the Veterans of the Abraham Lincoln Brigade were raising funds for ambulances to be used by the Sandinista government in Nicaragua, then fighting the U.S.-backed contras. Brigade members' solidarity with the oppressed did not come without costs. A number were killed or wounded in Spain, and more died fighting Nazism after World War II began. After their return home, many were harassed by the U.S. government, which considered them "premature antifascists" for opposing Franco while the United States was still officially neutral.

As we left the theater, Jane and I were both thinking hard. I was full of awe at the dedication of these women and men fifty years my senior. I was also full of self-doubt: would I have gone to Spain? What should I do now? Could I measure up to their selflessness? What had they sacrificed in order to fight the good fight for so many decades? Jane must have been posing similar questions to herself, for after a time, she asked, "Which do you think is more important, relationships or politics?" While I have forgotten exactly how our conversation went after that, I remember hoping that politics and relationships need not be mutually exclusive, that the two could even strengthen each other. That hopeful synergy seemed far from certain, however. Finite beings with limited time, energy, and, perhaps, imagination might not be able to juggle such weighty balls successfully.

In the decades since I watched *The Good Fight*, the question about the priorities and relations between political commitment and personal happiness has never been too far from my mind. At times I have agonized over the pulls between commitments and desires, and at other times I have rejoiced in the complexities. Over the years, I have chewed over the issues with Jane many times, as well as with other friends, who have challenged and supported my relationships and my politics and shared their own struggles. As many of us are now raising children, we add new complexities to the mix: how to find time for activism, for parenting, for earning a living, and for being a friend as well. Children, like friends, change our senses of ourselves and what we value most, at the same time as they make us "more ourselves." My life would be so much poorer—it would not be my life—without the enduring friendships that are so much a part of what I am. These friendships themselves would be impoverished without a shared sense of commitment to bigger goals, to a good fight. Aristotle, Cicero, and other classical philosophers of friendship were on to something when they insisted that shared values and pursuit of the good are as necessary to friendship as are mutual enjoyment and benefit.

Not long after I saw *The Good Fight*, I watched *The Kiss of the Spider Woman*, made in Brazil from a novel by Argentine writer Manuel Puig. Puig's work sheds light on the ambiguous potential of connecting the personal and the political. It features two men who share a cell—Valentín, a political prisoner, and Molina, a gay window dresser. Both have dreams that are impossible to achieve in the society in which they live—Molina's hope for a loving, lifelong relationship with another man no less than Valentín's vision of socialist revolution. However, in their everyday interactions and deepening relationship, the two catch glimpses of what they desire. "Here we are," Valentín reflects in the novel, "all alone, and when it comes to our relationship . . . we could make any damn thing out of it we want. . . . In a sense we're perfectly free to behave however we choose with respect to one another. . . . It's as if we were on some desert island. An island on which we may have to remain alone together for years. Because, well, outside of this cell we may have our oppressors, yes, but not inside."[35]

We are all inside a cell, insofar as we have some small, limited space in which we can enact qualities that do not seem possible outside—equality, kindness, unself-interested love. We all face the same dilemma that Valentín encountered: understanding what these values have to do with the world outside, where we cannot avoid oppressive structures, where we experience ourselves as much less free to choose. Manuel Castells describes the challenges facing contemporary social movements in similar terms. Such movements address real issues, he argues, but not on the scale or the terms adequate to the task. They have no choice, however, because they are fighting a rear-guard battle against economic and political changes that draw both power and meaning from their lives. Thus, Castells writes, "When people find themselves unable to control the world, they simply shrink the world to the size of their community."[36] Like Valentín and Molina in their cell, local activists attempt, on small scales, to embody the principles by which whole societies should live. In the face of encroaching power structures, they struggle for local autonomy, for cultural and moral meaning, and for human connections.

The community-based organizations I discussed earlier, including Fair Share and Latin American *comunidades de base*, respond to these struggles by making explicit the connections among local problems and political structures. They also try to bring the goods that people value and seek in their everyday lives—cultural identity, personal meaning, mutual support—into political contexts. Thus they pose the question of the relationship between smaller communities, in which egalitarian and noninstrumental values often operate, and the outside world dominated by power inequities and utilitarianism. In *The Kiss of the Spider Woman*, a prison cell offers, paradoxically, utopian moments that sustain both main characters. In his relationship with Valentín, Molina wants to be and ultimately is accepted for himself, loved by another man without being exploited or humiliated. Valentín finds that it is hard, but worthwhile, to live by his revolutionary political ethic of mutual respect and free sharing. Both educate and expand their hopes, as well—they educate their desire, learn to desire better. Molina learns to respect himself, to take himself as he is, and to seek an autonomy that is neither lonely isolation nor selfish separation but instead the strength to extend beyond himself and his private dreams, an extension made possible in and through relationship. For his part, Valentín finds that the revolutionary solidarity and equality to which he has dedicated himself, at no small cost to his private happiness, has important commonalities with the intense interpersonal bonds at the center of Molina's life.

Valentín's commitment to equality, to dignity for all, takes on new meanings in the context of his relationship with the other man. Molina, in turn, finds that his love for Valentín gives rise to a desire to serve the political cause for which Valentín has sacrificed his personal happiness. The complex friendship that Valentín and Molina forge across their many differences enables both to experience expanded forms of love, empathy, and solidarity. Molina's spontaneous generosity offers an unexpected glimpse of an alternative to "everything that's wrong with the world." For Molina, in turn, Valentín offers the possibility of a different kind of relationship between men. "If I'm nice to you," he tells Valentín,

> it's because I want to win your friendship, and, why not say it? . . . your affection. Same as I want to be good to my mom, because she's a nice person, who never did anybody any harm, because I love her, because she's nice, and I want her to love me. . . . And you too are a very nice person, very selfless, and you've risked your life for a very noble ideal. . . . And because you're that way . . . I respect you, and I'm fond of you, and I want you to feel the same about me, too. . . . Because, just look, my mom's affection for me is, well, it's the only good thing that's happened to me in my whole life, because she takes me for what I am, and loves me just that way, plain and simply. And that's like a gift from heaven, and the only thing that keeps me going, the only thing.[37]

In and through their love for each other, both men change their vision of what is desirable and possible. The relationship between Molina and Valentín offers a model of what Tillich terms "the meaning of ethics"—"to express the ways in which love embodies itself and life is maintained and saved."[38] In this kind of ethic, love is both a human emotion and a political principle. Loyalty to causes and loyalty to persons are woven together, and people become willing to act politically when their values are reinforced by personal bonds. In this way, the utopian moments of private life help give rise to and sustain public commitments. Experiencing a relationship in which neither is humiliated or used as a means to another's end, they learn to desire similar qualities in other aspects of their lives—and, Valentín might add, in the world outside. Puig's fictional revolutionary would resist the notion that his small utopia is simply a symbolic last stand against oppression, a retreat from real confrontation with oppressive political and economic institutions. Rather, the small-scale, mundane utopias created in interpersonal relationships might function like the urban movements described by Castells: "They are symptoms of our contradictions, and therefore potentially capable of superseding these contradictions."[39] By pretending to build, on a small scale, a type of community they know to be unattainable—a utopia— such efforts contribute to a larger political struggle.

This is the argument of my book *Seeds of the Kingdom*, which described two types of religiously based utopian communities: Amish agrarians in the midwestern United States and progressive Catholic peasants in northern El Salvador. The book explored the intentional communities created in both places by people who sought to make real their distinctive visions of the Christian reign of God on Earth. While finding much that is relevant to my own life in these experiences, I also realize that these small, rural, religiously and culturally homogeneous communities are distant from the experiences of most people today, in the United States and elsewhere. This book responds to this dilemma, by turning to ordinary experiences and relationships in my own society.

The search for utopian moments in this society is far from easy or self-evident. For many people, noninstrumental values, interpersonal trust, and spontaneous generosity are vanishingly rare even in private life. While we might hope for, and even expect, these qualities in our most intimate personal relationships, expanding them to the public sphere seems unthinkable. However, even though interpersonal connections have diminished in frequency and extent, they are still a large part of what makes people's lives meaningful and satisfying. My goal in this book is to reflect on the ways we might we try to reconceive our lives, public and private, to make room for these values and the practices that embody them. Just as certain communities harbor alternative values that provide moral and emotional depth, historical and spatial connectedness, so, I argue, might we find some of these values in smaller and less formal settings. I look for the everyday utopian moments—the experiences in which we find the most meaning, happiness, and sense of connection—as the necessary starting point for making political hope real.

This connection is possible only if the apparently hard-and-fast line between personal and political loyalties turns out to be a blurry frontier that is both porous and shifting. While women and men alike might have good reasons for retreating to the private sphere and rejecting the difficulties and disappointments of public engagement, there is also a possibility that interpersonal love can nurture activism and incubate public goods. I hold out hope that the challenges of mutual care and respect can expand and give new meaning to political commitment, that interpersonal relationships can give us models of empathy, solidarity, courage, and a willingness to put others first, necessary political qualities that have depth and staying power only if they are experienced in the flesh.

This idea of values in the flesh is increasingly connected to my thinking about ethics. In ethnographic and also more philosophical writing, I have looked at the ways that people interpret and act out moral traditions. I believe that ethical systems emerge out of continuous interplay between individuals and structures, as well as between ideas and practical experiences. Much of my scholarship so far has examined the ways ethical systems are lived out, especially by religious people who strive to embody their values in political activism and community building. This is what I have called "lived ethics," which I defined in an earlier book as "an approach to ethics that attends to the moral assumptions, principles, and ideals that shape, implicitly or (perhaps less often) explicitly, the ways individuals and groups make decisions, set and pursue goals, in short, live their lives. To speak of lived ethics points to the mutual shaping of ideas and real life and hints, at least, at the concern that moral systems be not simply applied to concrete situations and problems but rather applicable to and livable in them."[40] Lived ethics is different from the well-established model of "applied ethics," I argue, insofar as the latter refers to established moral systems that are identified and then applied to practical problems. Unlike lived ethics, applied ethics does not assume mutual shaping between morality and real life; it remains a top-down approach in which values descend to shed light on dilemmas that have emerged prior to the process of moral discernment and deliberation. In contrast, my thinking about ethics has always been part of my larger concern for the interactions between large structures and everyday life, as well as between values and practices, and between individuals and institutions.

Without abandoning my interest in the ways that ethical systems are worked out in real life, I am increasingly interested in how practical experiences reveal values that may not be consciously expressed but that are embodied and made real in acts and structures. In other words, in addition to receiving moral principles and ideas that are then enacted and transformed in everyday life, people also enact moral values that they have not consciously reflected on or articulated. These are not just lived but embodied ethics. Attending to the values embodied, often unacknowledged, in everyday life requires us also to look for the ways political and economic institutions are embodied in that life, to see the structural in the everyday. I return to these ideas, and some of their theoretical implications, in the last chapters of this book.

While I find fascinating the theoretical dimensions of the relations between values and behavior, or between ideas and structures, what is most important is eminently practical. We desperately need to change the way we live, now. We will not achieve this if we wait until we have the right ideas. It is not, in this case at least, the thought that counts. Rather than more good ideas, we need good practices and experiences. We need to identify the kind of practices that we want and need, for a better world; we need to understand what values these practices embody; and we need to learn how to expand them.

2

LOVE AND POLITICS

How many times have I asked myself whether it was possible to tie oneself to a mass without even having loved anyone . . . whether one could love a collectivity if one hadn't loved deeply some single human beings. . . . Wouldn't that have made barren my qualities as a revolutionary, wouldn't it have reduced them to a pure intellectual fact, a pure mathematical calculation?

—ANTONIO GRAMSCI

After more than twenty years, I remember *The Good Fight* and *The Kiss of the Spider Woman* not so much for their narrative power as for the issues they raised about the relationship between love and politics. Those questions continue to challenge me now, at a very different stage of my life. Is it possible—can one person have time and energy enough—to dedicate oneself to making the world a better place and also to have healthy, fulfilling personal relationships? If it is possible to live fully in both public and private spheres, how do the commitments, practices, and emotions generated in each realm relate to each other? Do the meaning and joy experienced in friendships and family life have anything to do with political activism and social change? For over two decades I have considered these as personal, eminently practical, issues. I turn to them now as intellectual problems as well, in search of philosophical and historical resources to make sense of the complex and not always comfortable relationship between personal and public commitments.

The relationship between love and politics occurred as a potential problem to the Italian communist Antonio Gramsci, who asked about the relationship between deep love for "single human beings" and deep love for collectivities in a letter to his wife, Giulia, shortly before he was imprisoned by Mussolini. Gramsci asserts not just that the two may be combined but even that love for collectivities may require more personal forms of love. This affirmation may be among the most revolutionary words that Gramsci wrote because it challenges our whole way of thinking about politics—and with it, the way we view love and human nature as well. Gramsci's insistence that personal love and political commitment require each other undermines a host of assumptions that help define mainstream politics, philosophy, and popular culture. Among these are the common convictions that private and public spheres operate according to different logics and different moralities; that we cannot bring the values of one sphere into the other; and that we must settle for less of certain goods (such as generosity or justice) in one sphere or the other. As a result of these assumptions, very often "love is identified with a resignation of power and power with a denial of love," as Tillich summarized.[1] This identification underlies the common, rarely questioned assumptions that interpersonal relationships inevitably draw us inward, away from the *polis*; that we must choose between private and public commitments; and that the values, attitudes, and practices of loving personal relationships are distinct from, even opposed to, those of public life. If these assumptions are true, if interpersonal love merely distracts us from politics, or vice-versa, then the utopias of everyday life have nothing to do with social change.

If, on the contrary, Gramsci is correct in asserting that intimate commitments can deepen political commitments, then a whole world of possibility opens up. We might begin to desire, and even to demand, much more from both our personal lives and our politics. The subversive possibility that Gramsci affirms is vital to my hope that everyday relationships and experiences can contribute to progressive politics. This possibility was embodied, for me, in the lives of many political activists in El Salvador and Nicaragua during the 1980s and 1990s. Many of the activists I knew took up difficult and dangerous political activities with their love for particular people front and center. It was not that they did not care about larger principles or causes, but those causes took on flesh and urgency in the bodies of people they loved. Again and again, people told me that the example of a spouse, friend, sibling, or child encouraged them to act—sometimes in order to be physically with the loved one, often to emulate him or her; if someone had died, to make sure their sacrifices were not in vain; and even to assert a kind of moral equality: if he could do it, how can I hold myself apart? These themes are echoed in the recollections of a young Salvadoran woman who became an activist after her husband was murdered. "I had to continue what my husband did, and not just because he was my husband. . . . He respected his brother's property, he was humble and affectionate with the children, with the communities. . . . With a man like that, living seven years together, I saw I had to continue doing what he was doing when they killed him. His courage gave me strength to continue."[2] While North American activists often experience the relationship between love and politics as permanently conflicted, many of the Salvadorans and Nicaraguans I knew seemed to weave them together—not always easily, but in a way that did not assume an either-or choice between public commitments and private happiness.

Underlying the differences in activism are understandings of personhood, love, and politics that diverge radically from those that dominate even progressive sectors in the United States. In an overly simple summary, we could say that the Central American activists do not always assume that they or other people are self-interested individuals; that love is only an exclusive, inward-looking relationship between two such individuals; or that politics is something that happens far from home. The roots of these different worldviews lie in political institutions, religious history, family structure, and a host of other factors. Without elaborating on the genealogy of different political cultures, we can see one result: an experience of both love and politics as concrete realities in the everyday practices of political organizations, in which intimacy, family life, and political activism intermingle freely. Activism, in these circumstances, is as much about love, about concrete relationships with "single human beings," as it is about abstract principles and sweeping social transformations. Anthropologist Roger Lancaster made similar observations in Nicaragua, where, he argues, people often entered politics not because of abstract ideals but rather out of "love of real concrete persons," families, spouses, lovers, and friends.[3]

The fact that a political commitment is deeply personal does not make it unstable, shallow, or compromised. In fact, the intertwining of love and power, of relationality and citizenship, may constitute their most revolutionary aspect. Activism is about love, at least in part, because the desired social change is also about love. The aim is a society defined by solidarity and brotherhood, what Martin Luther King Jr. called the "beloved community."[4] In pursuit of this goal, activism is defined not by the strategic mobilization of resources or utilitarian calculation of risks and benefits but rather by the effort to embody, here and now, the qualities that characterize the good society. Certainly Central American activists are shrewd and practical, sometimes ruthless—they could not have succeeded as well as they did otherwise. However, both their goals and their methods point toward a qualitatively different kind of politics than what is dominant either in their societies or in our own, one in which love and power are not opposed but rather intertwined.[5]

It is important not to romanticize; certainly these social movements are not free of inequities, rivalries, hierarchies, or disagreements. However, they contain countless moments of grace, when love is a lived reality, when solidarity takes precedence over ideological abstractions. The movement becomes the message, in Melucci's terms. The structural changes that activists seek are embodied in their everyday interactions and relationships.[6] The relationships within the political organization offered alternative values and expectations that educated participants' public desires. I look to my experiences in Central America for hints at what people in a nonrevolutionary setting might do to transform the relationship between love for single persons and love for collectivities.

We face real, practical challenges in this task: it is genuinely hard to balance competing claims, to do justice to all our commitments. Limitations of time, energy, and money make it feel easier to manage the private responsibilities, whose scale is more manageable and closer to home. Further, private concerns often feel most urgent to us: the pressing demands of children, loved ones, domestic chores, and livelihoods. What is important here is not that we should abandon these demands but rather that we might stop seeing them in a vacuum. We see them in a vacuum in part because our culture systematically separates private and public, love and politics. This makes it seem necessary to choose between competing demands, and impossible to do justice to both. What Gramsci's letter to Giulia hints at, and what I hope to elaborate in what follows, is the possibility that what happens in our personal lives is inextricably tied to politics and the polis. In the rest of this chapter, I begin exploring this possibility in relation to two of our most basic interpersonal relationships: friendship and marriage.

Friendship is both a microcosm of and a model for other kinds of interpersonal relationships, revealing their positive as well as negative potentials. Although it receives little scholarly attention today, friendship was by far the most important relationship in classical Greek and Roman philosophy. Aristotle devotes a substantial section of *Nichomachean Ethics* to friendship, including categorizations of different kinds of friendship and reflections on the meaning and purpose of these relationships. Friendship gives pleasure to both parties, he writes, but true friendship rests not simply on mutual enjoyment or on the desire for personal advantage or profit, but rather on virtue, including appreciation of the ends and interests of the other. "Perfect friendship," writes Aristotle, "is the friendship of men who are good, and alike in virtue; for these wish well alike to each other qua good, and they are good in themselves. Now those who wish well to their friends for their sake are most truly friends; for they do this by reason of their own nature and not incidentally; therefore their friendship lasts as long as they are good—and goodness is an enduring thing."[7]

Friends, for Aristotle, are "the greatest of external goods," necessary even for the man who appears "supremely happy and self-sufficient."[8] Since humans are social animals, the right sort of social relationships are necessary for human happiness and morality. Here friendship, for classical thinkers, is far more significant than marriage. Friendship undergirds the virtuous *polis* that is the overarching theme of classical political philosophy. Close relationships between mutually respectful, loving persons who share a commitment to a common good are both a necessary building block for a good society and a microcosm of it, a model of a virtuous and just community.

About three hundred years after Aristotle, Cicero summarized many classical ideas about friendship in his treatise *On Friendship* (*De Amicitia*). Echoing Aristotle and other earlier Greek philosophers, Cicero writes that "it is virtue itself that produces and sustains friendship, not without virtue can friendship by any possibility exist."[9] Virtuous friendship may not always be easy, but it is well worth pursuing since it "is to be regarded as the best and happiest possible, inasmuch as it leads to the highest good that nature can bestow."[10] Humans are social animals, who can pursue and achieve the highest moral and political goods only in the company of people who share their values and goals—true friends.

Both Aristotle and Cicero recognize complexities and possible problems. First, not every relationship that is called friendship meets the requirements of virtue and shared commitment to the good. They call these false friendships because they are based on selfishness and the thoughtless pursuit of pleasure. In the classical accounts, these are the main complications in the relationship between friendship (or any close personal tie) and larger political goods. There is little if any concern that intense personal relationships might pull people away from their public commitments. Perhaps because of the sort of virtue involved in classical definitions of "true friendship," these accounts take for granted a relative harmony between private and public commitments.

The possibility of mutual reinforcement rather than irreconcilable contradiction between eros and agape is central to the twelfth-century classic *On Spiritual Friendship*, by the Cistercian monk Aelred of Rievaulx. Building on Cicero, Aelred begins with the classical conviction that friendship based in mutual respect, love, and understanding is central to the good life, both for individuals and for the larger society. For Aelred, loving personal relationships characterize a good and joyous human existence, in this life and the next. Spiritual friendship is thus both a model of the ultimate heavenly community and an aid to Christian life on Earth. So closely is spiritual friendship linked to religious virtue, for Aelred, that "he that abides in friendship abides in God, and God in him."[11] The divine and the mundane, the personal and the transcendent, intermingle.

The kind of friendship of interest to Aelred—what he calls true, genuine, or spiritual friendship—requires not just virtue in general or even love of God, but rather appreciation for friends as ends in themselves. "For spiritual friendship, which we call true, should be desired, not for consideration of any worldly advantage or for any extrinsic cause, but from the dignity of its own nature and the feelings of the human heart, so that its fruition and reward is nothing other than itself." Aelred criticizes a utilitarian view of friendship, according to which "men love their friends as they do their cattle, from which they hope to derive some good. They, indeed, lack genuine and spiritual friendship, which ought to be sought on account of God and for its own sake."[12] True friendship rests not on individual self-interest or the fulfillment of contractual assumptions but rather on appreciation for the friend's own nature and on the affection and joy inherent to the relationship. This nonutilitarian regard for the significant other is tied to the friends' shared commitment to a common good—they live out in their own friendship the goods that they most value in the larger society.

Aelred reminds us that not just any interpersonal relationship is potentially virtuous, let alone utopian. We need to be specific about what qualities are desired. Friendship must be both reciprocal and egalitarian. "How beautiful it is that the second human being was taken from the side of the first," Aelred writes, "so that nature might teach that human beings are equal and, as it were, collateral, and that there is in human affairs neither a superior nor an inferior, a characteristic of true friendship."[13] True friendship is made possible by the virtue of both parties and specifically by their commitment to treat each other in egalitarian and noninstrumental ways, to be honest and loyal to each other, and to seek together a higher good. This good is unity with Christ, glimpsed on Earth and culminating in an eternal life characterized by harmonious, loving community between people and God. "True and eternal friendship," for Aelred, "begins in this life and is perfected in the next. . . . here [it] belongs to the few where few are good, but there belongs to all where all are good."[14] Spiritual friendship is both the highest form of human relationship and a divine gift, offering a glimpse of the eternal joy promised by God. His conviction that true friendship represents the highest human good is crystallized in a lovely passage from *Spiritual Friendship*, in which he recalls his dear friend and fellow monk Ivo:

> He was, therefore, as it were, my hand, my eye, the staff of my old age. He was the refuge of my spirit, the sweet solace of my griefs, whose heart of love received me when fatigued from labors, whose counsel refreshed me when plunged in sadness and grief. He himself calmed me when distressed, he soothed me when angry. Whenever anything unpleasant occurred, I referred it to him, so that, shoulder to shoulder, I was able to bear more easily what I could not bear alone. What more is there, then, that I can say? Was it not a foretaste of blessedness thus to love and thus to be loved; thus to help and thus to be helped . . . ?[15]

Aelred connects the deep mutual love and companionship he felt with Ivo to his religious and moral aspirations. Not only did their friendship help him be a better person—more patient, less angry—but the relationship itself showed him "a foretaste of blessedness," a hint of the ultimate good toward which his faith and vocation pointed.

Like earlier philosophers such as Aristotle and Cicero, Aelred considered the bond between two persons a social institution as well as a private pleasure, an important contributor not just to private happiness but also to the common good. This conviction is foreign to contemporary U.S. culture. Few of us think of our friendships in terms of efforts to improve the larger society or even to be better people. Friends are about private pleasures—sharing our innermost thoughts, enjoying common interests or leisure pursuits, having company in the course of everyday activities. They are not, for most of us, about politics or ethics. Scholars, likewise, spend little time on the role that friendship might play in the formation of good persons or good societies. A few have linked the privatization of friendship to larger trends in U.S. culture, most notably in *Habits of the Heart*. For the most part, however, the moral and political dimensions of friendship receive little attention. I think this fails to do justice to what is really going on in many of our friendships. Like Aelred and Ivo, sometimes our friendships can help us be better persons and also help us realize some of our highest social, as well as personal, goals. Certainly this is true in my own life: bereft of friends, I would be not only infinitely less happy but also poorly equipped to enter the public sphere as an activist and citizen.

At its best, friendship is a microcosm both of desirable human community and of the utopia of eternal life. It is indeed both an experience of blessedness here and now and a path to larger blessings, a "school of love," in the words of contemporary theologian Paul Wadell.[16] Wadell argues that intimate relationships, especially friendship, need not detract from or contradict the Christian ideal of agape, as some theologians have feared. Instead, friendship can be the relationship in which agape is learned and mastered, and thus a school for other forms of love, literally an education of desire. In friendship, good people practice the virtues that are necessary both for personal moral development and for a larger good society. "Friendship is the crucible of the moral life, the relationship in which we come to embody the good by sharing it with friends who also delight in the good."

Friendship teaches virtues and enables people to practice them; it also provides mutual satisfaction and pleasure, making life not only morally good but also meaningful and worthwhile. This suggests a new politics and a new polis, in which the good does not have to be barren of joy and interpersonal warmth. Religious or secular, the good society cannot be utopian if it is not full of the encounters that make ordinary life meaningful and satisfying.

One of the lessons taught in the school of friendship is the degree to which people depend upon each other, not just for daily sustenance but for their very identities. Relationships teach a relational understanding of the self, the necessary grounds for wider love and care. As Wadell notes, "Friendship is a model for the moral life which insists that the self is social and relational, not autonomous and solitary." According to this view, "relationships are not external to the self but constitutive of the self. . . . we stand not apart from or over against others, but in deep connection with them and all of life, a connection we rarely perceive and only dimly appreciate. That our relationships constitute our self is why friendships have such grand moral importance, whether that friendship be with God or a soulmate of many years."[17] This echoes classical philosophical reflections on friendship, virtue, and human nature and also complements the relational understanding of the self common to many Native American and Asian traditions, against the individualism emphasized in mainstream Western philosophy.

A relational model of personhood also has roots in Western religion and philosophy. Aelred insisted that people are social beings, implanted by God and nature "from the very beginning" with "the desire for friendship and charity."[18] Like many premodern Western thinkers, he assumed what philosophers call "internal relatedness," according to which relationships literally make people who they are. We are all born into a web of relationships that are neither chosen nor dispensable and that make us who we are at every point along the way: "Actual encounters are what make beings," as Donna Haraway puts it.[19] This contrasts with the voluntaristic understanding of relationality, predominant in our present culture, according to which interpersonal relationships are "external" to some preformed essence that defines the individual. In this model, persons choose to engage with others because of the benefits they expect to accrue, and they can withdraw from relationships at will, without fundamentally changing who they are. Internal relatedness suggests, rather, that persons are literally made in and by their relationships; there is no freestanding self that can enter and leave social interactions unchanged.

A relational understanding of selfhood grounds a distinctive view of ethics. In this model, as Wadell writes, "The moral life is what happens to us in relationship with others." We cannot be moral alone, *pace* the autonomous, rational moral agent of Enlightenment philosophy. Instead, "all morality begins in and is an elaboration of the discovery that something other than ourselves is real—whether it is nature, another person, or God—and the moral life is the ongoing attempt to understand, deepen, and apply that discovery."[20] The reality and value of other beings is discovered in concrete practice, specifically in relations with others. Haraway call this "encounter value," an addition to Karl Marx's categories of use and exchange value. Haraway's felicitous concept of encounter value illuminates the goods that emerge from relationships not only with other people but also with nonhuman "significant others."[21]

We cannot encounter others and value them only at the level of theory. Encounter value is practical; it must be lived. In concrete interactions, friends treat each other as real, as valuable, as ends in themselves, and not, as Aelred put it, like "cattle, from which they hope to derive some good." (A better appreciation for nonhuman others suggests that not even cattle should be treated only as means to ends, or in Marxist terms simply as sources of use or exchange value.) Friendships and other valuable encounters decenter the self, so that the individual can no longer be his or her only reality, the sole sun of a personal universe.[22] Encounters make beings real, in Haraway's words. As the history, interests, needs, and concerns of another become part of our worldview, we come to value the friend's values and also her good. Our vision of and commitment to a common welfare expands as a consequence of the encounters and affections we share.

Friendships and encounters can also help us realize our own best selves, as Aelred's recollection of Ivo underlines. Sociologist Stacey Oliker finds this potential particularly in women's friendships. Such friendships may embody an egalitarian understanding of relationship as well as a relational view of selfhood. They do not deny individuality but rather acknowledge interdependence as a condition of independent striving. Friends can encourage each other to be their best selves without denying their unique identities. They do so by exercising a "practice of constraint" and "a communal ethic of interdependence."[23] What Oliker describes echoes, in sociological language, what Aelred noted many centuries ago: good friends help us be our best selves; they help us restrain our excesses and sometimes subordinate our private interests for a larger good; they tie us to communities that we want not only to participate in but to make better.

Few of us reflect on these processes often or at length. When we stop to think, however, it seems obviously true that relationships with friends and peers contribute to our own moral development. For example, desire for our friends' respect and anticipation of their reactions to our decisions can guide ethical choices, in matters both big and small. In a class on environmental values and practices, for example, several students explained that they chose "greener" options in transportation, food, and other areas, at least in part because they wanted their friends to think well of them. If all my friends bicycle to campus, one student said, I feel self-conscious and guilty if I drive. Guilt may not be the most sustainable motivation, but what is really going on here might just as well be described as good examples, the ways that watching a friend's practice can inspire our own attempts. This works even for not-so-close relationships. A number of parents I know only in passing have told me they started bicycling to school with their kids after watching me do it day in and day out. If she can do it, they reasoned, so can I. The same logic worked in the much more dramatic setting of wartime El Salvador, where many activists explained their political work by reference to the examples of others. Someone else's committed action can make us think twice about doing the same act, even if it previously seemed impossible. Good behavior close to home (or work, or school) makes us feel accountable in ways that distant examples do not. The fact that Mahatma Gandhi was a vegetarian means little to my everyday life; the fact that my best friend is one (and her reasons for it) may be momentous.

Ethicists need to pose the sociological question of what kind of selves and relations people need in order to hold each other accountable, to help each other live by our own highest values and be our own best selves. Friendships can nurture creativity and self-expression while offering communal support and constraint; they serve as microcosms of a moral polis.

Like the communities of memory described in *Habits of the Heart*, these friendships both support expressive individualism and offer communal support and constraint. They diverge from the voluntaristic, exchange-based model of friendship suggested by utilitarian individualism. Certain friendships provide a model of a community that maintains the distinct values of individual expression and aspiration, on the one hand, and communal accountability and mutual interdependence, on the other. Drawing on these relationships, Oliker proposes a new "ideal-type of community" that connects personal ties and public responsibilities: "Shared moral values enable people to identify with and invest themselves in others and thus to build commitment; they deepen and extend relationships beyond self-interest. Moral bonds cognitively anchor emotional ones, steadying otherwise volatile attachments."[24]

Friendship, in this feminist perspective, provides a school not only for expansive forms of love but also for political resistance and activism, encouraging people to connect their lives to a larger social world and to collective action. If personal relationships can provide models for larger public relations and values, perhaps we do not have to choose between unlimited individualism and oppressive collectivism. We may be able to find, in relationships that already exist, models for an alternative kind of human society: one in which people are accountable to and dependent upon each other while also supporting personal expression and achievement. This vision, central to classical Western philosophies from Aristotle onward, may be reclaimed today in an explicitly progressive way. Friendship can be not only a training ground for the moral life but also a model or microcosm of that life, a way in which "men and women live now, however incompletely, the wholeness human life is given to achieve."[25] Not all, but some friendships offer a hint of the "already" of the reign of God, the ideal form for which human life is ultimately intended.

MARRIAGE

In contrast to friendship, that other intense and nearly universal human dyad, marriage seems to have inspired relatively little serious philosophical and ethical reflection.[26] Given the centrality of marital relationships not only for families but also for many economic and political institutions, the lack of systematic attention may stem from assumptions that we know what marriage is rather than from lack of interest. The attention that has been given to marriage as a political and moral issue in the United States in recent years only confuses the philosophical issues at stake. Debates over legal unions between lesbians or gay men and, more broadly, "family values" have (along with discussions of abortion and childcare) explicitly raised the issue of how personal and public ethics relate to each other. Without getting into the details of these controversies, it is worth noting that they include foundational assumptions not only about what marriage means but also about the social functions of the married couple and the institution itself. Underlying these debates is the usually unexplored conviction that marriage is a foundation of both private and public spheres, simultaneously the core relationships of the domestic sphere and "our smallest and most enduring of social institutions."[27] A great deal is at stake, then, when we consider redefining marriage. It may help to recognize that marriage has changed many times in the course of our own culture's history (and, of course, in countless other societies), and that mainstream assumptions about what marriage means have a particular and relatively short history.

While classical philosophers like Aristotle devoted little attention to heterosexual marriage, Christian theology and ethics do offer systematic reflection on its character and social roles. This reflection has been markedly ambivalent, especially about the relations between marriage and religious values. On the one hand, marriage is a sacrament, blessed by God and the church, and is the foundation for the family, which in turn makes possible congregational life. On the other hand, theologians have worried that marriage can distract people from larger social and religious goods. The intense, mutual love known as eros is often irreconcilable with agape, the expansive, unself-interested love of God and others demanded by Christian morality. This concern helps justify the requirement of clerical celibacy in Roman Catholicism. The rule stems less from contempt for sexuality than from an assumption that a person cannot give himself or herself fully to God and the church, on the one hand, and equally to spouse and family, on the other. A priest, monk, or nun should be, as the old phrase puts it, married to the church. "Just as marriage is the total gift of self to another," a Catholic journalist explains, "the priesthood requires the

total gift of self to the Church. A priest's first duty is to his flock, while a
husband's first duty is to his wife."[28] Celibacy is required, in this perspective, because the roles of husband and priest will often collide, and one commitment or the other will suffer. As one Catholic priest puts it, "Celibacy enables the priest to focus entirely on building up the kingdom of God here and now."[29] This assumes that the kingdom of God is the exclusive business of, and modeled only by, the institutional church. Other forms of community, including family and friends, are at best peripheral and at worst contradictory to the primary religious obligation to "build up the kingdom." This Catholic view of religious vocation parallels Valentín's initial (pre-Molina) understanding of political activism in *The Kiss of the Spider Woman*: intimate and domestic ties undermine commitment to a larger cause and community.

These claims are not without foundation. It is undeniably difficult to devote oneself fully, at the same time, to more than one consuming passion. At the same time, some thinkers have seen the possibility of a mutual reinforcement between friendship and love of God. In many religions, the experience of romantic and family relationships can nurture and support faith and provide necessary skills, as well as support, for building religious community. The sacrifices and also the joys of marriage and family life, in this perspective, provide a valuable and perhaps necessary foundation for effective ministry. Intense love for particular persons can nurture and deepen commitment to God, "the people," or another community. This love, and the lasting, committed relationships it makes possible, can in fact not only serve as the foundation for the activism of individuals but also connect individuals and families to the larger society. This social function is central to traditional Roman Catholic understandings of marriage, but it has declined as personal satisfaction has become the main motivation for and perceived benefit of marriage.

In addition to changes in its social roles, marriage today, especially but not only in the United States, is an increasingly stressed and fragile institution. Contemporary marriages carry more of the emotional burdens of both partners, as their other relationships and communities contract. Marriage is vulnerable to the economic and logistical stresses of everyday life, at the same time it is supposed to serve as a buffer from these stresses. The nuclear family, and especially married life, is often seen as a sanctuary for pleasures and values that cannot survive in the public sphere, a means to individual satisfaction rather than an institution connecting private and public life. Increasingly, marriage is called on to fulfill needs that in other times and places have been spread among a range of relations, practices, and communities. This affects not only the internal dynamics of married couples but also the larger community to which they belong.

Women bear most of the emotional and logistical burdens created by matrimony. Studies consistently show that men have fewer friends and that their friendships do not involve the same kind of emotional intimacy and sharing as female friendships. Many men believe themselves independent and autonomous while actually depending on their relationships with women whose work is rarely acknowledged.[30] Many people, especially men, have a false sense of self-sufficiency, which rests on a failure to appreciate and often even to recognize the emotional, logistical, and productive labor of women that makes possible male illusions of independence. The difficulty many men have in seeing or admitting their dependence places an emotional burden on the women who keep things going, often generating stresses and strains within heterosexual relationships. This false autonomy is damaging for both parties in the relationship, especially for the women whose unappreciated emotional and domestic labor makes men's public lives possible. It is also damaging for the polis, in practical ways—such as keeping women out of public life—and also in philosophical ways. Men's false sense of self-sufficiency may shape their larger worldviews, leading them, for example, to despise interdependence as weakness. Striving for separate autonomy tends to make people self-centered, according to philosopher Richard Schmitt. They want to "be their own man," not beholden to anyone, but in reality they depend on others (often women), whose contributions they ignore or devalue. Assertions of independence often deny the contributions of others as well as our own need for them. Thus separateness, Schmitt contends, "is rarely a morally admirable quality."[31]

Separateness may be not only immoral but largely impossible. Humans' social nature has strong biological and evolutionary roots. People necessarily depend on each other, at the very least for physical survival during vulnerable periods of our lives. This physical dependency accompanies emotional dependency. People care for babies, sick children and adults, and old people because they care about them. Without, at the minimum, parental bonds of affection, humans, like most other mammals and birds, would not survive. The issue is not whether we are in relation, then, but what kind of relations we create, and how we view them. If our unceasing need for other people and for nonhuman others can provide a foundation not for selfishness and exploitation but for humility and openness, then our polis, as well as our private lives, will look very different. Acknowledging our need for others makes us vulnerable and thus likely, at some point, to experience pain; to avoid this kind of love in order to avoid suffering, however, would be a moral as well as an emotional disaster. Those who deny fragility both miss out on much of the meaning and joy possible in human life and place an unfair and immoral burden on others. The belief that autonomy is both possible and good can lead people to shirk physical and emotional labor, to hurt other people, and to miss a great deal of joy and meaning.[32]

Marriages often suffer from carrying such a weight, so many of our most precious eggs in one charged and fragile basket. Power imbalances from the outside world intrude, people expect too much of each other, and daily domestic duties can be hard to balance with deep emotional fulfillment. Despite the challenges, and amidst both inevitable and transient imperfection, many marriages contain moments of grace. The greatest virtue of marriage, as Lis Harris puts it, "may be that it offers two people a chance to create a sustaining context, a world that is infinitely larger and richer than anything that either could invent alone—and one that draws on the deepest human capacities."[33] The everyday practices of marriage—cooperation in pursuit of a common goal, shared sacrifices and also shared triumphs, emotional negotiations, and intellectual challenges—can strengthen both individuals and their relationship. It can also link individuals, together, to larger institutions in transformative ways.

Interracial relationships offer a suggestive example of this possibility. In a racist society, love between people of different races is not only a private choice but a potentially radical public act—"love's revolution," as Maria Root calls it. Interracial marriage, Root argues, "gives us hope that love can transcend some of the barriers that legislation has not. Its power to transform us, one at a time, cannot be underestimated, allowing us to release the hate, fear, and guilt of the past and move into the future with love as a political device . . . love has the capacity to erode . . . fear and hate."[34] Root's optimism has been matched by some civil rights activists, for whom interracial relationships constitute "a symbol of the integrated world they were seeking to create."[35] Studies of interracial couples show that the desire to rebel or make a political statement hardly ever motivates people to marry, but in a divided and race-conscious society, interracial relationships cannot be other than transgressive. In this they resemble the longing of Molina, in *The Kiss of the Spider Woman*, for a committed permanent relationship with the man he loves—so traditional and yet so revolutionary in the homophobic society he inhabits. Even if the partners see their relationship as a matter of love and not political protest, mixed marriages challenge, de facto, many categories and properties of mainstream society.

Interracial relationships, especially relationships as serious and (in principle) permanent as marriage, show that it is possible to put egalitarian values into practice, to begin creating the beloved community even in the midst of a racist and divided nation. Such relationships can serve as microcosms of the virtuous polis, as friendship does for Aristotle and other classical philosophers. Similar potential may come from lesbian and gay relationships; simply being together in a committed, public way can be a revolutionary act. By demonstrating the possibilities and real fruits (as well as hazards and dangers) of integration, interracial couples may live according to their own deepest principles and at the same time contribute to the new society they desire.

Like utopian communities, these relationships provide both a seed and a model of a better world: they help build it here and now while also pointing toward future possibilities. Also like utopian experiments, interracial relationships show some of the limitations of creating a microcosmic better world in the midst of a real world that has very far to go. As historian Renee Romano cautions, celebrations of "love as the answer to racial problems" can become "a convenient way to discount the continued significance of institutionalized forms of racism." The idea that racial progress can best be achieved through individual relationships and bonds between blacks and whites, Romano contends, simplifies, depoliticizes, and downplays the continued significance of race in American society. It suggests that "racism is the work of isolated racists rather than something systemic or structural." While appreciating the real significance of interracial marriage, Romano concludes that "it will take more than love to break down those

barriers. Old hierarchies must be dismantled for new attitudes about interracial love and marriage to flourish."[36]

Interracial marriage, and marriage in general, provides a helpful lens for exploring the values and challenges of a social ethics that begins with practice. They can help us see how structural factors such as racism, inequality, and privatization are embodied in everyday life. They push us to learn from and about the real experiences of people living according to a different morality, a second language. We can explore the obstacles that these people face, how they overcome them (if at all), and what sustains them, brings them meaning and joy. Their experiences can tell us a great deal about how we all might connect their private pleasures and challenges to the larger public spheres, first and foremost by underlining the fact that private choices and relationships always take place within social contexts. This does not erase the significance of small-scale, personal acts, but it reminds us that such acts must be connected to others in a larger pattern if institutional change is to occur. We need to see how big structures, even national politics and economies, are present in everyday life. We can see structures in the everyday in diverse ways. One of the clearest is in consumption patterns and the environmental consequences of our choices regarding food, transportation, housing, and so forth. I will return in later chapters to consumption in particular and, more generally, to the ways that we might learn better to see—and transform—the big structures that shape the most intimate dimensions of our lives.

THE PERSONAL IS POLITICAL

I first heard the claim that "the personal is political" in the context of second-wave feminism. I took it to mean, at first, mainly that what happens in the private sphere is shaped by the power dynamics and institutions of the "outside" world of politics. For example, the power inequities of the public sphere, including emotional as well as practical dimensions, find expression in the home and family life. Feminists often illustrate this by pointing to domestic violence, in which (usually) men enforce their physical and economic power over women and children. What many people may see as a purely personal issue—the relationship between husband

and wife or boyfriend and girlfriend—turns out to be strongly influenced by the institutions and laws, as well as the cultural values, of the larger society. Another issue connecting the political and the personal is child care. The need for reliable, nurturing supervision of children so that women can enter the public sphere for education, work, and civic engagement is not simply a private dilemma to be negotiated within the family but a problem with public causes and consequences. What happens in women's—and men's and children's—personal lives has political implications, and the dilemmas of personal life often require political solutions.

This is not all that it means to say that the personal is political, however. It also means that the very existence of a private sphere, what constitutes it, and what can happen within it are all decided in the public arenas such as courts, legislatures, and workplaces. Marriage, for example, traditionally serves as a haven for men who can enter and succeed in economic and political endeavors because of the unremunerated work of women who maintain the household and family. Women's efforts in the domestic sphere, including the education of children into both private and public moralities, enable the public work of men to take place and in fact make it possible for the public sphere to flourish. This is not only a feminist point: Marx and Engels analyzed the ways that private reproduction both enabled and replicated the exploitative patterns of capitalist economic production. Feminists have illuminated the ways that women's private work taking care of children and the home, and related tasks such as volunteering in schools and religious congregations and caring for the elderly and sick, enable men to do their work "in the world." The personal is political, in this sense, because personal life makes politics possible.

In reflecting on the personal as political, feminist scholars regularly and rightly point out how the hierarchies and injustices of the public sphere enter into family life. Less attention has been turned to the flip side of this insight: the dynamics and events of private life reverberate throughout the public sphere as well. On the one hand, the power relations of the family influence how people face the larger world. On the other hand, in domestic life we can learn ways of acting and thinking that challenge the public status quo—and we might also develop the courage, imagination, and perseverance necessary to make this challenge explicit. Thus a third, and for my purposes the most significant, meaning of "the personal is political" is the fact that in personal, especially domestic, life, we develop fundamental political attitudes and practices. This begins in families, which, as philosopher Paul Ginsborg notes, "are the principal institutions which form individuals in the modern world." More specifically, families are *"agents* of everyday politics, pre-eminent sites not only of emotions and affections, intimacy and dependency, but also of education, socialisation, and the construction of opinion. To a large extent they shape the way in which individuals connect to the wider world."[37]

Gender roles, perhaps most obviously, are produced and reproduced in our families. However, so are attitudes about race, nature, work, and many other crucial political categories. Any political theory or movement that ignores the various roles played by family life, continuing not only in childhood but throughout our lives, will fall flat. More broadly, political and moral attitudes are affected by relationships not only with family members but with a range of people, as well as nonhuman animals, places, and social institutions. All these relationships help shape our constantly developing selves, as do our responses to them. In personal life, we learn to cope (or not) with inconsistency, ambivalence, and changes and to make choices about which values to prioritize, which relationships to nurture, and which goals to pursue.[38]

Thus "the personal is political" is not simply a feminist battle cry but also a philosophical claim of some complexity. One issue toward which it points is the possibility of bringing together the public and private spheres. Such a possibility has little precedence, in practice or theory, at least in Western culture. One stream from which we might draw is the Anabaptist (or Radical Reformation) stream within Protestant Christianity. Against Luther's claim that Christians lived in two kingdoms, guided by two different sets of values, Anabaptists have insisted that a single morality must prevail in every aspect of a Christian's life, specifically, the application of agape to all actions and spheres. This task is not easy, since public institutions and mores tend to a separation, asking always for a choice. Anabaptists answer the challenge by teaching that if it seems impossible to apply truly Christian principles in the public sphere, we must reconceive the polis. It becomes a smaller realm, comprised of direct interactions and accountability. By limiting the number and kind of interactions, Anabaptists argue, it becomes possible to practice their guiding principles, including pacifism and uninterested love. Jesus announced that the reign of God was in our midst, Anabaptist theology contends, which means that Christians must live according to the values of the kingdom here and now, extending agape to every action and every relationship. While insisting on ethical consistency, Anabaptists also acknowledge the difficulties of consistent application, and they institutionalize opportunities for repentance, forgiveness, and renewal within a collective setting. This is easier in small communities with frequent face-to-face contact, another reason that Anabaptists have historically sought to keep their public square as small as the number of people and relationships that can be managed according to the principles of Christian brotherly love. This is especially true for Old Order communities like the Amish and Hutterites.

The Anabaptists challenge the widespread Western suspicion that interpersonal relationships can conflict with or detract from commitments to a larger good, be it God, the church, or a political cause. If we look to non-Western cultures, however, we find other examples of integrative approaches. This is true in part because many Asian, African, and Native American cultures do not share the modern Western notion of religion as a separate sphere, clearly demarcated from the rest of private and public life. This is largely a result, of course, of the constitutional separation of church and state. This legal condition is itself shaped by the kind of Protestant Christianity, with its emphasis on private piety and rectitude, that has been dominant in the United States. In cultures dominated by other religions, be they Catholic, Buddhist, Hindu, or Native American (among others), religion is neither so privatized nor so clearly separated from the rest of life. The separation of church and state, and more broadly of religion from the rest of life, may well make it harder to bring the values of the private sphere into public life. This separation also has many positive results, of course, including legal protections for freedom of religion and tolerance. I am not advocating a theocracy of any sort. However, I do wonder whether the separations we take for granted do not have some negative consequences, including the difficulty of integrating love and politics, values and practices.

Mainstream Western secular philosophy, grounded in the Kantian tradition, has divided private and public just as clearly as Luther divided the kingdoms of God and the world. However, just as the Radical Reformation demonstrates a different possibility within Christianity, some streams of secular political philosophy reject the dualism of most Enlightenment thinking and suggest that a common morality should guide both public and private life. Marx touched on the issue in his discussion of alienation, which entails the separation of people not only from the process and product of labor but also from each other. Under the alienating conditions of capitalism and liberal political systems, people come to believe they need protection from each other, and thus they establish moral and legal systems that, by assuming a false self-sufficiency, intensify the alienation and antagonism between people. As Marx writes in *On the Jewish Question*, "Liberty as a right of man is not founded upon the relations between man and man, but rather upon the separation of man from man. It is the right of such separation. The right of the *circumscribed* individual, withdrawn into himself."[39] The withdrawn and circumscribed individual, like the "suspended self" critiqued in *Habits of the Heart*, is a social construction, not the expression of any biological or otherwise universal human nature. For Marx, humans are social by nature. However, he argues, perverse institutions and economies deny this fact, thereby creating alienation, misery, and exploitation.

According to Marx, modern Western societies, under the influences of capitalism and liberal individualism, encourage each individual to live "separated from the community, withdrawn into himself, wholly preoccupied with his private interest and acting in accord with his private caprice." In such a society, the communal life that is natural to humans appears "as a system which is external to the individual and as a limitation of his original independence. The only bond between men is natural necessity, need, and private interest, the preservation of their property and their egoistic persons."[40] Founding thinkers of liberal, free-market societies, including Adam Smith and John Locke, emphasized a contractual, voluntaristic view of relationships, based on a view of human nature as rational, self-interested, and calculating. In contrast, Marx contends that the separation of people from each other is both unnatural and damaging, psychologically as well as politically. Only in relationship to others can people be fully human, and political liberation necessarily entails social relationships: "Every emancipation is a restoration of the human world and of human relationships to man himself."[41] Liberation, the end of alienation, restores an original good. It brings together things that are by nature united but that have been separated by the distortions of capitalism.

Building on the Marxian insistence that humans are social animals, many leftist thinkers and activists have emphasized solidarity, both political and personal, to counter the structural causes and consequences of alienation. People are meant to live in common life, and the good society is one that is both natural and morally good, as well as personally satisfying. It is not unnatural to live with others, in this view, against the "original state" of isolation conceived by some contract theorists. Insisting that humans are social creatures suggests that a good society is not one in which people are protected from each other, but rather one in which people acknowledge their mutual interdependence as positive and natural, not demeaning or oppressive. Such a society might expand the classic view of friendship to base personal relationships on shared values of justice, equality, and freedom, on common commitment to human improvement, and on mutual loyalty, affection, and enjoyment. Because humans are social by nature, they require each other's company not only for survival but for happiness, meaning, and fulfillment. And because people are capable of, even inclined toward, goodness, their personal relationships contribute to larger social goods.

This understanding of human nature suggests that loving personal relationships such as marriage, friendship, or parenting are not merely private. As love is rethought, politics is also redefined. It becomes impossible, as Gramsci asserted, to separate love for particular people from the desire to build a society more hospitable to all people. Political and personal commitments are not just inseparable but, at least in principle, mutually reinforcing. Both demand attention, empathy, and loyalty, and while they are not identical, neither excludes the other. Undergirding this expansive solidarity is an understanding of human nature according to which the capacity for love has no ceiling. Love is not a zero-sum game. Thus, as Mary Midgley puts it, "compassion does not need to be treated hydraulically . . . as a rare and irreplaceable fluid, usable only for exceptionally impressive cases. It is a habit or power of the mind, which grows and develops with use. Such powers (as is obvious in cases like intelligence) are magic fluids which increase with pouring. Effective users do not economize on them."[42] Love, Midgley emphasizes, is not limited to interhuman relationships any more than it is limited to private life. Love for nonhuman animals does not take away from commitments to humans.

Although the human capacity for empathy and affection may be limitless, time and energy impose limits on how people can act on these feelings. Despite the ideal of mutual reinforcement, in practice personal and public commitments do not always mesh seamlessly. I cannot, in the same evening, eat dinner with my family and also canvass my neighborhood, attend meetings, or volunteer at a soup kitchen. (Nor can I wash dishes, make school lunches, or fold laundry after those activities, at least not if I want to get enough sleep to function the next day.) Further, efforts to live out values often fall short; even people who work tirelessly for public goods such as justice and solidarity may fail to practice these values in their personal relationships.

Critics point to these contradictions as evidence that it is futile to try to apply nonutilitarian values such as love and altruism beyond intimate personal relations. The classic modern expression of this dualism is Christian realism, whose major theorist, Reinhold Niebuhr, argued that unselfish agape love, the highest ideal in personal relationships, cannot be achieved in larger social settings. "Moral man," as he put it, could not extend private values into "immoral society" without suffering disillusionment and perhaps corruption.[43] This idea, reinforced by many other thinkers, has encouraged many people, especially in the United States, to restrict their "highest" values, those not predicated on self-interest and contractual exchange, to close personal relationships. This nurtures the image of the domestic sphere as a "haven in a heartless world," the final refuge for noninstrumental values, unconditional loyalty, and sympathetic nurturing. This isolation of the private sphere has, in turn, reinforced the notion that family life is and should be primarily a means to individual satisfaction, a home for principles and pleasures that cannot survive in the public sphere. Ironically, this dualist view of private and public values may reinforce the entry of instrumental public values into personal life. In emphasizing personal satisfaction, this view defines "family values" as simply enlarged self-interest, based on exchange and voluntarism. The failure to expand noninstrumental values beyond the private sphere, in other words, may weaken these values in their home place. This is related to the discussions of friendship and marriage earlier in this chapter. Are these relationships havens against an impersonal, threatening, and often hostile "outside" world? Or might they be—or become—sites in which we nurture values that we want to see enacted in all aspects of our lives?

Despite these challenges, and despite the grinding daily pressure to survive, many people experience and live by noninstrumental values in some parts of their lives. Close relationships with friends and family can expand our empathetic horizons, stimulate concern for unrelated people, and extend personal concerns into a longer temporal arc. If there is anywhere where we collectively come close to unselfish care for others, it is in these relationships. In them, encounter value comes to the fore, rather than use or exchange value. Such relations underline the social nature of human, our need of each other in order to live a good life. This may be clearest in parenting, where our need for others, both emotionally and physically, is impossible to deny. Like perhaps no other experience in our lives, childrearing forces us to rethink love, politics, and humanness. Such reflections, and the experiences that nudge us toward them, are not always cheerful. Caring for children brings home the realities of conflicting aims, impatience, exhaustion, and loss. However, caring for children also entails interrelatedness, unselfish love, long-term perspectives, connections to others, and deeper commitment to a common good. More than in most aspects of our lives, in parenting we exercise our potential for both selfishness and transcendence. The next chapters explore these possibilities in more detail.

3 / ETHICS, PARENTING, AND CHILDHOOD

In family life we have the opportunity, not always realized, to enact our most important values. Like many people, I find some of my deepest joy and also some of my greatest frustration in everyday encounters with my spouse, children, and other close relatives. They are the people we know the best and care about the most. They share our living spaces and daily routines, and we see each other in unguarded moments, both tender and unlovely. We rarely reflect on the ethical and political significance of our intimate domestic relationships, and when we do, it often seems contradictory and complicated. Part of the problem is figuring out the relationship between domestic life and the "big picture," including questions about what gives meaning and satisfaction to our lives taken as wholes. Family life poses the question, as sociologist Arlie Hochschild puts it, of whether the "smallest acts of care" are "what we get out of the way in order to really live life.... Or are these acts part of what life is all about?"[1] I would answer Hochschild's second question in the affirmative: the small acts of care, daily interactions with their moments of both grudging duty and spontaneous generosity, are indeed what life is all about—and, further, they are crucial to what a progressive political ethic is all about.

The political significance of domestic life, especially parenting, lies in part in the fact that families remain one of the few places in contemporary American life where noninstrumental values hold sway. This is not to say that families are havens of Kantian justice or Christian agape, or even of nondemanding love. Like all relationships, families are made by their members but never in circumstances of their own choosing. Parents almost always love their children, and they usually love them in generous, noninstrumental ways. However, they often do so in settings that make this kind of love difficult. Love faces an uphill battle not only against personal failings but also against cultural, economic, and political forces that make utilitarian and instrumental relationships much easier than other kinds. Thus any consideration of the ethical and political possibilities of parenting must take into account the factors that shape the discourses, values, and practices associated with family life.

U.S. FAMILIES TODAY

In the United States today, both qualitative and quantitative research suggests that families are more fragmented and more isolated than at most times in the past. Like marriage, the institution of parenthood is both fluid and stressed. Parents and children alike encounter regular, sometimes severe, tensions in their relationships with each other and with larger communities, as well as challenges based on changing patterns of work, economic shifts, and consumer culture, among other factors. Recent sociological studies of the family, some done in broad strokes and others with a sharper lens, can help us uncover both the strains and the moments of grace to be found in family life.

While some mothers have always had to work for wages, until fairly recently they mostly did so at or close to home—sharing in farm duties, taking in piecework, or cooking or cleaning for neighbors with their children in tow. One of the most important changes in U.S. society in recent decades has been the increase in the number of women, especially mothers of young children, who work outside the home. Between 1975 and 2000, the percentage of married women working outside the home whose youngest child was between six and eighteen increased from almost 55 to 79 percent, and the percentage with children under the age of three rose from

34 to 61 percent.[2] The fact that most American women with children now work at least part time outside the home has enormous consequences for both private and public spheres. It not only changes the everyday lives of women, men, and children but also transforms the ways women identify themselves; their relationships with spouses and with other relatives; and the time and energy they have for their family, for themselves, and for civic activities. No discussion of politics, social change, or public ethics today ought to ignore these profound developments in American social life.

Women have gone out to work in part because legal, cultural, and educational changes have given many women greater opportunities in many traditionally male fields. However, many women work outside the home now because they need to, as economic shifts, including the decline of well-paid blue-collar work and an increase in lower-paid service jobs for both women and men, have made it harder for a single wage-earner to support a family. These days, as Hochschild points out, "both his salary and hers just about total what a man's salary used to bring in when it was based on union wages in a robust manufacturing sector. In a sense, women's work is a way the family has absorbed the deindustrialization of America and the decline in men's wages."[3] Pointing out that there is an element of necessity in many women's decision to work outside the home is not to suggest either that women should not pursue paid work or that many women who have to work do not also experience satisfaction in their jobs. Nor does it imply that legal and practical barriers to women's equal participation in all careers have been eliminated. Even in fields where women are well represented, including education and health care, differentials exist in salary, promotions, and other rewards.

In any event, the most pressing issue regarding women and work for this book is less ongoing discrimination or the positive results of women's entry into the labor force than it is the conflicts and strains that face women who live in both public and private spheres, the never-ending stress engendered by multiple commitments to family, work, and community. A significant part of the problem is the failure of most fathers to increase their domestic labors. Numerous studies have counted in various ways the hours women and men work at home, concluding in every case that men do not share the burden of housework equally with their female partners.[4] Working women usually come home from their paid jobs to work a second shift of domestic duties. This second shift can be measured in various ways: women work an average of fifteen hours longer each week than men, amounting to an extra month of twenty-four-hour days every year; men and women do different kinds of jobs around the home, with women bearing the burden for more daily tasks and for less pleasant ones—women cook and wash, while men play with the kids; and even when men do jobs, women are in charge of maintaining calendars, making appointments, and reminding other family members what needs to be done.[5]

Both women and men still assume that household maintenance and child care are mainly women's responsibility, even when women work as many hours and earn as much money as their male partner. Men, in general, "think and feel within structures of work which presume they don't do" domestic work, as Hochschild summarizes. This creates problems not just at home but also in the workplace, since "the game is devised for family-free people," who can devote themselves to professional advancement without the pull of domestic duties.[6] (Contrary to some popular images, however, parents put in as many hours at work as do their colleagues without children.) This situation explicitly contradicts the image of home as a "haven in a heartless world," in Christopher Lasch's well-known phrase.[7] For Lasch, the family served historically and perhaps ideally as a means to individual satisfaction, a refuge for principles and pleasures that cannot survive in the public sphere. Increasingly, however, the family and home are places not of refuge but of stress, and workplaces often offer a welcome respite from the demands of home—demands that, ironically, are heightened precisely by women's participation in the workplace.

For many families, as Lillian Rubin points out, "time has become their most precious commodity—time to attend to the necessary tasks of family life; time to nurture the relationships between wife and husband, between parents and children; time for oneself, time for others; time for solitude, time for a social life."[8] Working mothers, in particular, give up sleep and leisure activities, including hobbies and time with friends, in order to get the work done at the job and at home. They sacrifice vacations, they forgo time with their spouses and children, and when they are at home their time is filled not with pleasant activities but rather with household maintenance and, often, with efforts to hurry along other family members. The tensions that women face make them more often "the lightning rods for family aggressions aroused by the speed-up of work and family life," Hochschild writes in *The Second Shift*. "Women are the 'villains' in a process of which they are also the primary victims."[9] This takes place in even the happiest and most stable of families, and it represents one of the many ways in which we experience structural problems in our everyday lives. Both economic institutions and gender attitudes make it hard for couples and families to live according to egalitarian ideals.

Children also suffer as a result of the multiple pulls on working parents' time, physical energy, and emotional reserves. A 1990 *Los Angeles Times* poll showed that 57 percent of fathers and 55 percent of mothers feel guilty that they spend too little time with their children.[10] Other studies from the same period showed that the average parent has just seventeen hours a week of contact with her or his children, the average working couple spends four minutes a day in meaningful conversation with each other, and the average working parent spends around thirty seconds in meaningful conversation with her or his children each week.[11] These trends have only intensified in recent years, and they provide a big picture of experiences that hit close to home for me, as for many women. It is hard to find moments of satisfaction and meaning when we have so few moments together at all, and when that time is full of competing needs and domestic duties, of rushes to get everything done so that we can collapse in exhaustion before starting it over again.

Multiple shifts and time shortages, along with the exhaustion, frustration, and lack of perspective these stresses generate, threaten both families and the larger society. Families lose out most obviously, but there are also negative consequences for neighborhoods, religious congregations, social movements, and the myriad intermediate structures that constitute civil society and help weave noninstrumental values into collective political life. Putnam identifies time shortages as a significant factor in civic disengagement and the weakening of both formal and informal ties. The growth in women's work outside the home is a major factor in this process. In past generations, stay-at-home wives and mothers had more time and energy both to maintain the nuclear family's ties to friends, neighbors, and relatives and to sustain schools, volunteer groups, and other institutions of civil society. Women have been and often still are the most consistent workers in all sorts of volunteer organizations, especially at local levels. The fact that women are less available now has transformed the nature of many charities and social organizations, forcing them to cut back operations or to rely more on paid staff, among other adjustments.

As a result of these various trends, childhood has changed qualitatively in recent decades. One of the most important consequences is that children today spend less time with their families, in nature, and on their own. Their time is more structured and supervised. It is uncommon today for young children to wander through the neighborhood without adult supervision, as most routinely did a few decades ago, when the majority came home from school, yelled a greeting to a stay-at-home mother, and disappeared until dinnertime. It is interesting that children in many stories and comics still live this way. Like the diversified family farm, the free-roaming child is an ideal type that continues to shape our image of what life should be like, even when it is vanishingly rare in real life. Contrary to this image, and to the memories of most people over thirty, few children today have either time or space for unstructured play and exploration. By 1990 the radius around the home where children were allowed to roam on their own had shrunk to one-ninth of what it had been in 1970.[12] My friends with children echo what I experience: our children do not range as widely or as freely as we did at their ages; we see few kids out on the streets in our neighborhoods; our children rarely play with their friends spontaneously but wait for parents to arrange a "play date."

The shrinkage of children's free time and space is due to various factors, including the absence of mothers or other caretakers at home as well as growing parental fears about safety, the shrinking size of average families and the resulting fact that fewer children live in any given neighborhood, and urban and suburban development that have reduced the safe green spaces available for play. The growth of electronic toys also keeps children inside more, as Richard Louv notes: "The choice to play simply and slowly, to grow naturally, is being overwhelmed by an environment defined too much by electronics and speed."[13] Children are also defined by consumer values, as they are increasingly bombarded, even defined, by advertising. The summary consequences of these various trends is that children, like their parents, have less time for noninstrumental pleasures and for encounters with nature, stories, other people, and their own imaginations that are not structured by formal institutions or the market or mediated by electronics.

Ranging freely around the neighborhood is not, of course, a guarantee of a happy childhood. The very concept of a happy childhood, in fact, is class- and context-bound. Lillian Rubin writes that her research with working-class families, like her own experience growing up in a poor area of New York, revealed "very few tales of happy childhoods, some happy memories, some families more loving than others, but not happy childhoods." For such families, Rubin writes, happy times are isolated moments rather than the norm, and dominant memories of childhood "are of pain and deprivation—both material and emotional, for one follows the other almost as certainly as night follows day."[14] Updating her research two decades later, Rubin noted that between the 1970s and the 1990s, the quality of life for all but wealthiest Americans declined, especially for those at the lower end of the class spectrum, regardless of color. Much of this downturn has resulted from the loss of secure, unionized, and relatively well-paying blue-collar jobs, which has made it impossible for many families to survive on one salary, and often difficult even on two.

Experiences in the public sphere, as well as the structures, practices, and institutions that make up that sphere, affect not just what we do at home but also how we feel about and evaluate ourselves, our lives, our values, hopes, and expectations. We expect less for ourselves and our children; we regret but largely accept the fact that our kids lack unstructured, unsupervised playtime or that we have to pay for almost all the pleasures of childhood. Large-scale trends, especially privatization and consumerism, diminish the quality of our lives, and we are largely unable, and perhaps unwilling, to challenge them. These changes in the lives of children and families represent a concrete example of what Habermas means by the colonization of the life-world by the discourse and values of the system. Insofar as "the roles and relationships of the office become benchmarks for those at home," the possibility diminishes that home can serve as a source of alternative values and utopian visions.[15] Some people may even seek out the workplace, as Hochschild suggests, in order to avoid the pressures and disappointments that emerge in the home, thus inverting the image of the family as haven. This reversal, however, does nothing to resolve the larger problem. It is not so much the difficulty of balancing multiple commitments, which is the existential condition of humans and perhaps of all social animals, as it is the deficiencies of a social, economic, and political system that makes it so difficult to maximize the joy and minimize the anxiety engendered by multiplicity.

For all these reasons, loving, mutually pleasing, and constructive relationships between parents and children, as between spouses or friends, are not automatic or even common. Such positive relations demand effort and discipline, a willingness to persevere in the face of exhaustion, distraction, conflict, and sometimes despair. They also require social support and economic security, which are not accessible to many women even in wealthy nations. Many mothers, as Jennifer Nedelsky reflects, "cannot enjoy their children in the ways I have because as a society we have not offered them the necessary support."[16] Delighted absorption in one's parental role, delicious abandonment to the beloved child, is not possible for many parents. Most have to earn a living, and distractions of work and other responsibilities make it impossible to focus on the child for very long. We have to leave our children with others, sometimes strangers, for long periods of time, day after day, in a pattern that would have seemed strange to earlier generations of American women and even today seems odd, perhaps cruel, to people in other cultures. The lives of many American children today are a paradoxical combination of highly supervised and structured pursuits under the eyes of nonparents—a contrast in many ways to previous generations, in which children had less structure and less supervision, but what supervision there was mostly came from parents and other relatives, not from paid caretakers. I do not mean to suggest that children today are harmed by these patterns; a number of the changes in family life in recent decades, especially the increasing involvement of many fathers, are good for children, women, and society as a whole. However, we need to reflect on the ways in which social institutions shape our personal relationships and domestic lives, and what this means for both private and public spheres.

Time pressures and overwhelming commitments keep many women, in particular, from expanding the effective sphere of their maternal concerns. Many parents experience tension between intense affective relations at home and decreased engagement in the world beyond the home. These strains may ease as children grow older; and beyond infancy, children can become less a source of isolation and more an important path into the community and to different sorts of relations, both with other mothers and with the larger society. As a parent, Jennifer Nedelsky recalls, "I felt a kind of empathy with other mothers in the world that seemed new to me. . . . I have felt a kind of urgency about the importance of providing women with what they need to care for and enjoy their children."[17] I think Nedelsky has identified a common, though not universal, phenomenon. After having my first child, I certainly felt new empathy for both children and parents, especially mothers. The death of a child, always terrible in theory, became excruciating to contemplate. I also began thinking about the future in a different way, much like my friend Sam, who noticed that after his daughter was born, "my temporal horizon has totally changed." What happens in our children's or grandchildren's lifetimes becomes immediately, concretely important, no longer of merely abstract concern. This longer time frame can have salutary effects on our thinking about the environment, education, and other issues—and in fact, studies show that people consistently connect ecological issues to children's welfare, as I will discuss later.

Our ability to be the kind of parents we want to be is connected to our ability to make the world a different place; as Arlie Hochschild puts it, our "private strategies" for family life are linked to "public strategies" such as child care and leave policies.[18] In the frustrations of parenthood we encounter not only our own shortcomings but also the failings of social institutions. This is especially true for people who struggle economically. For working-class parents, the deepest expression of love is often just keeping the family together. Frequently this task is so overwhelming that little energy, time, or emotional support is left for children and spouses. For people whose waking hours are largely devoted to alienating and alienated labor, home often functions less as a refuge than as yet another arena of daily struggle, made harder and less pleasant because it is often not humanly possible to leave outside stresses at the front door of home. As Rubin points out, "the parts of human life are interrelated—each interacting with and acting upon the other—so that such a separation [between home and work] is nearly impossible. In fact, any five-year-old child knows when 'daddy has had a bad day' at work. He comes home tired, grumpy, withdrawn, and uncommunicative. He wants to be left alone; wife and children in that moment are small comfort."[19] In such situations, families can reproduce and even intensify negative qualities of the larger culture, becoming sites in which anti-utopian practices such as violence and repression prevail.

Physical and emotional abuse are not the only disvalues that enter the family as a result of outside pressures. Even more subtly, parents may bring their workplace values of utility, efficiency, and results into the home. Our homes are becoming "Taylorized," Hochschild contends, referring to the principles of efficiency, speed, and rationality that govern modern factory production. Often without intending it, the working parents she studied "regularly applied principles of efficiency to their family life. . . . Saving time was becoming the sort of virtue at home it had long been at work." Parents come to focus on results rather than process in their family lives, arguing (or hoping) that they can get the "same result" from one hour with a child as from a whole day. This process, again, illustrates the invasion and transformation of the domestic sphere by the instrumental values of the state and market. This colonization of the private lifeworld by instrumental values comes with a heavy psychic cost, especially to children. It requires what Hochschild calls a "third shift" that parents must undertake after their first shift at the office and second at home. The third shift is less about physical labor than about the "emotional dirty work of adjusting children to the Taylorized home[,] and making up to them for its stresses and strains is the most painful part of a growing third shift at home."[20] Parents' well-intended but often destructive efforts to adapt themselves and their children to the time bind exemplify the dangers of allowing utilitarian, results-oriented models from the market economy to drive personal relationships.

This process, and its emotional and social costs, has important implications for ethics. It sheds light, most importantly, on the relationship between the values that people express and the values by which they actually live. Toward the end of *The Second Shift*, Hochschild reflects that "for all the talk about the importance of children, the cultural climate has become subtly less hospitable to parents who put children first. This is not because parents love children less, but because a 'job culture' has expanded at the expense of a 'private culture.' As motherhood as a 'private enterprise' declines and more mothers rely on the work of lower-paid specialists, the value accorded the work of mothering (not the value of children) has declined for women, making it all the harder for men to take it up."[21] The fact that men and women are spending less time with their children and hiring other women to do most of their domestic work, including child minding, poses again the question of whether small acts of care are something to be avoided,

so we have more time for "real life," or whether these acts themselves give
meaning, value, and joy to our real lives.

Small acts of care are central to the utopian possibilities of domestic life. At their best, parenting enables us to live according to some of the values we most need for collective as well as personal goods. Caring for children can teach and nurture characteristic values that find few other strongholds in contemporary mainstream culture. These alternative values include a relational understanding of selfhood, a noninstrumental approach to social interactions, a recognition of lack of ultimate control, and a decentering of oneself to a more modest place in the universe. These values are crucial not only to caring for children but also to creating a more sustainable, generous, and egalitarian society. As parents, we have a chance to speak a "second language" and find identity as part of a community of memory and hope, however fragile and small in scale. We can see this in how we think and talk about children and parenting, and also in practices that we may not reflect on much. We give up precious things—time, money, peace and quiet—for children without question (though not always without complaint, at least in my own case). We struggle to do the right thing, pondering deliberately about morality, long-term consequences, and the relations between fairness and compassion. We experience, in the flesh, internal relatedness, the concrete ways in which we are constructed and constrained by our relationships—and strangely enough, it doesn't always feel oppressive.

The noninstrumental and relational values that emerge in parenting point to the possibility that families might serve as "schools of love." Families can, like friendship and romantic relationships, exemplify different and better models of social life, and perhaps educate their members to desire these alternative values in the public sphere as well. This may be especially true for families that challenge, by their composition, mainstream images and standards, such as multi-ethnic families created through interracial marriage or adoption. Such families, in fact, are increasingly mainstream: in my college town in the Deep South, my children play and work alongside children from an astonishing range of families. Immigrant families, single parenthood, international adoption, and interracial marriage are all utterly normal to them. My own kids—two the biological products of an interethnic marriage, the third adopted from Latin America—have no need to feel different, the way I did as the child of divorced parents in the early 1970s. I still remember the fourth-grade classmate who asked me, with great curiosity and in all innocence, what it was like not to have a father. I knew one cross-racially adopted child, and the first time I was in a classroom with African American children was seventh grade. The fact that my children know, and know to be normal, such a diverse range of parents and children has to affect the ways they feel about "the family." Their experiences also, I believe, shape the ways they think about humanness and social life more generally.

The question is how these domestic experiences might help us educate desire: how we might uncover the second languages nurtured in experiences of parenting and work for the social changes that will push these languages into the mainstream. These social changes will happen not just because parents and children change but also as a result of structural economic and political transitions. We need to see the structures in everyday life and then analyze and transform them. For example, easing the burdens of the time bind will require social conditions that make possible greater balance between work and family responsibilities. As a step toward this balance, Hochschild calls for "a public debate about how we can properly value relationships with loved ones and ties to communities that defy commodification."[22] Such a debate would go far beyond the nuclear family—it may transform how we think about and experience politics and ethics as well.

CARE ETHICS

This public debate has been initiated by feminist thinkers, especially in relation to an approach known as care ethics. According to care ethics, moral action should be guided not by duty or universal rules but rather by particular feelings for particular people. Nel Noddings articulated this perspective in her influential 1984 book *Caring*. "To act as one-caring," she explains, "is to act with special regard for the particular person in a concrete situation."[23] This challenges dominant ethical models in the West, both secular and religious, for which universality and impartiality are usually paramount. In Noddings's ethical model, "relation will be taken as ontologically basic and the caring relation as ethically basic." This means, she explains, "that we recognize human encounter and affective response as a basic fact of human existence." Most important for Noddings is what she calls "natural caring," defined as "that relation in which we respond as one-caring out of love or natural inclination." In natural caring, which she also calls "caring for," the moral imperative stems directly from the affection between two people. She gives the example of a mother who responds to a crying infant in the night, for whom the action is not a dutiful imperative but one that she *wants* to undertake. The mother–child relationship provides an important reference point for her understanding both of what "caring" entails and of the ethic that it grounds. Taking care of one's own child, she writes, is not "moral" as most people define it but rather grows naturally out of love.[24]

For Noddings, caring and care ethics ought to replace the rule-based ethics that dominates philosophical arguments and also everyday thinking. Other feminist philosophers argue that caring should complement and not simply replace the values of justice and fairness that tend to take center stage in rule-based ethics. Carol Gilligan, for example, advocates an ethic that values both care and justice, as a more integrated view of morality for both sexes.[25] Gilligan's contributions to ethics emerge from her work on moral development in young people. In her groundbreaking 1982 book, *In a Different Voice*, Gilligan found that adolescent girls tended to understand and decide moral dilemmas in very different terms than boys, often putting relationships and people's feelings before clear-cut moral rules. Ethics based on abstract concepts such as "fairness" or other rules was favored more by boys and, not coincidentally, defined as the "highest" stages of ethics in scholarly understandings of moral development. Gilligan argues, however, that for women "the moral problem arises from conflicting responsibilities rather than from competing rights and requires for its resolution a mode of thinking that is contextual and narrative rather than formal and abstract." In this view, moral development centers on understanding of responsibility and relationships, while a conception of morality as fairness ties moral development to understanding of rights and rules. Women tend to see ethical dilemmas in the context of a "narrative of relationships that extends over time," she notes, while men, in contrast, more often frame the problem in more abstract terms, separated from interpersonal relationships. Thus women often consider it acceptable to change or ignore rules in order to preserve relationships and feelings, while men are more likely to dismiss emotional and relational consequences as irrelevant to ethical decisions.[26]

The mother–child relationship serves as an ideal type and also a starting point for care ethics. Nel Noddings, for example, contends that the moral imperative to care (or to natural caring) arises most clearly in the relations between mothers and children, in the mother's natural response to the child's needs and demands. Most intimate situations of caring are natural, not ethical. Taking care of one's own child is an innate response.[27] The demands of children and maternal responsiveness can contribute to a passionate, often overwhelming engagement with young children that can make parenting a utopian experience, a haven for alternative values of noninstrumental love and generosity.

There are dangers, however, in the primacy of caring familial relationships. Intense personal commitments can lead to complacency and even to hostility against outsiders, to what Sara Ruddick calls "the parochialism of maternity, of passionate loyalties to one's children, kin, and people."[28] Racism, tribalism, and many other forms of political exclusion can be grounded in the ideas, practices, and emotions learned at home. There are no guarantees that interpersonal attachments lead to constructive political engagement. Even Ruddick, an advocate of "maternal ethics," admits that "I see mothering, at its best, as a *struggle* toward nonviolence, a *struggle* not to hurt what is strange, not to let other children be abused out of fear or loyalty to one's own."[29] This is a danger of other relationship-based politics, whether the relationship is to a nation, a faith, or a place.

Hostility to or withdrawal from the outside world may be due not just to positive experiences at home but also to negative situations in the larger society. People who are politically or economically marginalized might take refuge in the family and cling to the familiar sights, sounds, and activities of a safe home place. Not only members of disprivileged groups feel alienated, as Putnam and other students of civic disengagement have demonstrated. This alienation can push people toward the haven of home and hearth. As sociologist Arlene Skolnick writes, "The more complex, impersonal, and large-scale the public world, the more intense the need for a small-scale, intimate, private small world rich in the very qualities lacking in the world at large—love, concern, tenderness, nurturance."[30] Increasingly families must do their "emotion work" without significant support from larger social groups and institutions.[31] As formal and informal bonds of support weaken and shrink, people turn to a few close relationships to serve all their emotional and social needs, to signify the warmth and care that are missing from the world beyond.

The danger is that familial love may be the heart of a heartless world, an opiate that generates not so much provincialism as passivity toward the outside world. Given how difficult the world outside can be, and how frustrating and disheartening it can be to try changing that world, it is indeed tempting to live, as Raymond Williams puts it, as if "you and your relatives, your lovers, your friends, your children—this small-unit entity is the only really significant social entity." This willful withdrawal into a comfortable private space has a price, however: the deterioration of the very conditions that allowed it.[32] Neither the pleasures nor the challenges of everyday life can be separated from large economic, political, and ideological structures. If the connection between these structures and everyday life is not made explicit, personal life serves as a home for our best practices and values but does not connect these values to the world outside. Love and generosity halt at the edge of the familial inner circle. Care ethics, then, may be "used as an excuse to narrow the scope of our moral activity to be concerned only with those immediately around us," worries Joan Tronto. Caring only for people with whom we are in direct relationship "ignores the ways in which we are responsible for the construction of our narrow sphere." Helping a stranger at the door but refusing to help starving children in Africa, Tronto argues, "ignores the ways in which the modern world is intertwined and the ways in which hundreds of prior public and private decisions affect where we find ourselves and which strangers show up at our door."[33] Proximity to persons is shaped by our collective social decisions; we can choose to isolate ourselves from others and thus reduce our moral burden of caring. If moral life is understood in narrow terms of interpersonal caring, then we are absolved from broader responsibilities. Social institutions and structures determine who we come into contact with regularly enough to establish relationships of care.

Thus even when people do think about and live out alternative values in the course of caring for young children, they may not act in similar ways beyond their household. As Nedelsky reflects, "The irony is that while my affective relation to the world increased in intensity when my children were little, I also felt a strong inward turning, away from active involvement in things outside my home. . . . I felt the need for changes in the world more keenly and did less to promote them than ever before."[34] I can relate to Nedelsky's experience vividly. With a baby, everything seems to matter more, and at the same time everything seems much more difficult, especially when it involves getting out of the house (literally or mentally). There is a life-cycle pattern here, as Nedelsky also notes. As children grow more independent, mothers can turn their gaze away and may reenter the wider world, sometimes even bringing the children along, thus encouraging children's education as citizens and potential activists. I have taken my kids to participate in ecological restoration and cleanup projects, to volunteer at animal rescue groups, and even to canvass the neighborhood for political campaigns. We also socialize our children in public goods in subtle ways. By commuting on bicycle, for example, not just to work but on family outings to the market, library, or ice-cream store, I hope to teach my children not to assume that private automobiles are the default way of getting somewhere. We vacation in a national park every summer, hoping our children will not only appreciate wild nature but also think of hiking and camping as especially desirable leisure activities. (Our decision not to have cable television is the flip side of this, a denial that we hope will also become internalized.) Some of these activities are possible when children are small—mine have been on a bike seat since late infancy—but many others become feasible, or at least pleasant, only when children move beyond toddlerhood. Just as I try to connect my growing children to larger communities, they help connect me, in multiple ways—not only in my increased concern about some issues but also in my willingness and ability to engage different kinds of people and communities. Because I have children, I am involved with people from religious, economic, and cultural backgrounds that I might otherwise never meet. At the park, in grocery stores, at school events, we find common ground with people we might otherwise never have talked to. The social capital thus generated has political potential, if we can learn how to mobilize it.

MATERNAL POLITICS

Perhaps the best-known activist against the U.S. war in Iraq is Cindy Sheehan, whose son Casey was killed in Iraq in April 2004, at age twenty-four. Sheehan rose to national prominence after she spent three weeks near

President George Bush's ranch in Crawford, Texas, waiting in vain for him to speak with her during his 2005 summer vacation. Sheehan attributes her activism to her maternal role, a combination of regret for her inability to protect her son, anger at the men she holds responsible for his death, and a desire to prevent similar tragedies from shattering other families. In August 2005, in the middle of her stay in Crawford, she summarized her mission concisely: "I'm a mother out here who has a broken heart that doesn't want any other mothers to have a broken heart."[35] In an April 2006 interview, she repeated her point, adding a new condition: "I buried my son, and I don't want anyone else burying their son for lies."[36] She is angry not just because her son died but because he died in vain, for untruths and an ignoble cause. While the Central American activists I discussed earlier felt compelled to continue struggling for the just cause in which their loved ones sacrificed, Sheehan fights against the cause for which her son died, or rather, against the government that sent him to die for that cause.

Sheehan's struggle echoes social movements that emerged in Argentina, Chile, and other parts of Latin America during the 1970s and 1980s, as mothers organized against the torture, assassinations, and abductions committed by right-wing governments. Most famously, the Madres (Mothers) of the Plaza de Mayo in Argentina performed daring acts of public protest at the presidential palace in Buenos Aires, demanding the return of their children, mostly young people who had been "disappeared." They protested every week for years, a growing line of mostly middle-aged women, dressed in black, pictures of their missing children hanging from their neck. The Madres became major political players in Argentina and inspired human rights groups elsewhere in Latin America, all anchored by relatives, usually mothers, of victims. These movements demonstrated how the fierce love and protectiveness that parents feel toward children could be expanded outward, to encompass "other people's children" and larger communities.

In the United States, similar motivations inspired the environmental justice struggle of Lois Gibbs, who helped expose the dangers of hazardous wastes. Like the Madres of the Plaza de Mayo (and around the same time), Gibbs began her activism out of concern about the well-being and safety of her own family. Gibbs believed that hazardous wastes buried in the neighborhood were causing the constant illnesses suffered by her young son. When school and local officials failed to respond to her requests for assistance, she launched a door-to-door campaign that uncovered a host of health problems, including cancer and miscarriages, that were eventually attributed to the buried waste. Her activism led, in the short term, to the closure of her son's school and the evacuation of the neighborhood, and in the long term to the creation of the national Superfund program to clean up hazardous waste sites. Members of other environmental justice organizations in the United States and elsewhere have followed Gibbs's example, insisting that their parental responsibilities include providing safe homes, schools, and communities in which to raise their children.

A major study of American environmental values in the 1990s found that one of the most important justifications for environmental protection was concern for future generations. The researchers report that their initial set of questions did not address children, but 85 percent of respondents volunteered issues of children or future generations as a reason for their ecological concerns. This high proportion is unusual for an open-ended question, the researchers note, and "in fact, concern for the future of children and descendants emerged as one of the strongest values in the interviews."[37] Similarly, a study commissioned by the Merck Family Fund found that children and future generations are the most important route to engage adults in environmental issues.[38] For many, their own children gave this value a personal and emotional reference point, but even people without their own children emphasized their commitment to future generations as an important factor in their ecological values. The link between the environment and parenthood reflects a redefinition of parental responsibility beyond traditional areas, to include protection of nonhuman nature.[39] People's temporal scale lengthens dramatically when they have children. Their horizons no longer end with their own life span but extend into the lives of children and even grandchildren, prompting concern and perhaps action over ecological destruction as well as social and economic problems. In this respect, again, parenting and care for children can nurture the kinds of values that our society needs throughout public life.

The struggles of Cindy Sheehan, the Madres of the Plaza de Mayo, and Lois Gibbs represent concrete examples of the sorts of political action that might build on and be inspired by the values embodied in mothering. They exemplify what Sara Ruddick calls maternal politics, "mother-identified movements in the United States and around the world that deploy the symbols and passions of mothering in struggles against war, local violence, racism, ruthless employment practices, environmental destruction and institutionalized neglect."[40] In these movements, maternal care becomes both an inspiration to political struggle and an example of what a society ought to provide for its people. If mothers ought to care for and protect their children, meet their basic material and emotional needs, keep them safe and not put them at risk for dubious reasons, then so ought a whole society to support and value its members. At the core of maternal politics is an expansion of a parent's loving care and protectiveness. "The mother's battle for her child—with sickness, with poverty, with war, with all the forces of exploitation and callousness that cheapen human life . . . [becomes] a common human battle, waged in love and in the passion for survival."[41] In our most intimate relationships, we encounter big ideas and big structures—hopes and goods, constraints and obstacles.

THE MICROETHICS OF EVERYDAY LIFE

Maternal politics is one way that the values nurtured in intimate personal relationships can ground a political ethic. Jeffrey Goldfarb describes another version in Eastern Europe during the 1970s and 1980s. Resistance to repressive governments, Goldfarb contends, was nurtured around the kitchen table, a "free zone" where people could speak their minds "without concern about the interaction between the official and the unofficial. . . . Here personal and collective memories were told and retold in opposition to the official history. This was the private place that was most remote from official mandates and controls."[42] In these private places, even under a repressive regime, it was possible, as Adam Michnik put it, to "act as if one lived in a free society." This idea of acting out values that are not present in the public sphere constituted the central organizing principle of the Polish opposition during the 1980s. Michnik argued "that if people acted as if they lived in a free society, they would, in the process, constitute free public space."[43] What developed in the private spaces of family and friends, then, led to momentous political changes. This process takes Melucci's understanding of new social movements even deeper: not just the movement is the message, but the micropolitics of everyday life is also the message, the embodiment of a different vision of how to organize the public sphere.

This happened, according to Goldfarb, because personal interactions gave birth to, and nurtured, an "embedded autonomy" that came to ground a democratic political agenda in Eastern Europe in the 1980s.[44] This "embedded autonomy" emphasizes individual freedom to act and demand respect. When people could not exercise it publicly, they could do so privately, and eventually, according to Goldfarb, they began to expand it to the polis, with historic results. Like Goldfarb, I want to explore "the theoretical implications of what was developing in the private spaces of family and friends." Instead of the individual autonomy that was crucial in pre-1989 Eastern Europe, in the United States today we need to emphasize other values, underrepresented or underappreciated in the public sphere but potentially nurtured in private life. As social ethicist Warren Copeland notes, different values reflect various dimensions of human experience, and to do justice to human complexity, social ethics needs to find balance and compensation. A society that overemphasizes individual liberty, such as the contemporary United States, needs cultural values and policies that can highlight equally necessary values of equality and solidarity. In concrete political terms, Copeland says, this means we should advocate for whatever is missing. "The basic ethical warrant is to serve the fullest expression of what it means to be human."[45]

Following Copeland's principles of balance and compensation, I argue that rather than autonomy, we should seek in our personal lives the grounds of an embedded relationality. The ways we interact with friends, spouses, and children, for example, can provide models of nonutilitarian relationships that might challenge the instrumental values of the market. From the mutuality, vulnerability, and internal relatedness we experience in personal interactions and relationships, we can uncover and strengthen an awareness of ourselves as social, interdependent beings. This awareness, and the willingness to act on it, begins at home. To be politically effective, it must expand outward to other children, other families, other neighborhoods, and ultimately the larger communities and institutions on which children, families, and neighborhoods depend. This suggests the possibility that a political and social ethic can develop as parents expand their understandings of what is required for their children to thrive. If their children cannot be safe, healthy, and happy in the world as it now exists, then parents must undertake an "effort of world protection and world transformation."[46]

The promise of generalizing maternal care and nurture to all the needy of the world is appealing, but we need to understand more explicitly what makes this expansion possible. One link, according to Noddings, is found in the relationship between caring about and caring for. Caring about is a less valuable and less costly form of care, but it can serve as an important training ground and also field of application for the harder, more fulfilling, and morally significant practices of caring for. Caring about resembles what Aelred of Rievaulx called charity, a virtue and an emotion that is directed toward those in need regardless of individual preferences or the promise of mutuality. Charity, according to Aelred, can and should be extended to all people in need, even those who do not respond virtuously. Friendship, however, must involve mutual care and affection and exists only as a reciprocal relationship between persons who are both good. Like caring about, charity can connect care for those in our inner circle and positive work (for justice and structural change) in the public sphere. When practices of care are understood, appreciated, and deliberately expanded, they can help build what Noddings calls "a world in which 'it is possible to be good'—one in which carers are enabled to care without sacrificing their own lives and in which caring goes beyond politically correct rhetoric."[47]

This extension took place in the lives of Central American activists who undertook great risks in order to continue the struggles of people they loved. In their interpersonal relationships, including those within the movement, they experienced—and learned to desire—qualities that they wanted to expand into the world; loyalty, generosity, unselfishness. These qualities characterized the experiences that brought them joy and pleasure in private life, and which they learned to value as crucial aspects of a good society, a society in which it is indeed possible both to be good and to experience deep and enduring love, solidarity, and joy. In these cases, personal ties served as schools for love. This education of desire is possible only in certain conditions, especially when people connect their everyday lives to larger political structures.

Despite our best efforts, the outside intrudes in countless and often destructive ways. Violence, pollution, suffering, and uncertainties enter the family circle and change it. However, this boundary crossing never goes in only direction. The qualities that make parenting and family life so valued—patient and unselfish care, noninstrumental appreciation for another's uniqueness, tireless nurturing and encouragement—may be taken into the outside world as well. What parenting can give us, or what we can salvage from it, as Adrienne Rich writes, includes "tenderness, the passion, the trust in our instincts, the evocation of a courage we did not know we owned, the detailed apprehension of another human existence, the full realization of the cost and precariousness of life."[48] These values may not enter the public sphere as often as negative qualities from outside encroach upon private life, but when they do, possibilities arise that might transform our societies.

I do not imagine that the right social system could somehow eliminate human frailties, conflicts, and suffering. I know, however, that we can do much better. We see this possibility in our best relationships and experiences. These experiences are crucial resources for the necessary search for alternatives to dominant cultural attitudes and political structures. The intensely personal practices, or "disciplines," of mothering, friendship, and marriage can and must be extended to broader spheres if we are to develop a more relational, responsible ethic and the sorts of institutions, laws, and cultural norms that can reinforce it.

A PRACTICE-BASED ETHIC FOR PARENTS AND CHILDREN?

Amidst the multiple, interrelated, and ever-changing experiences of parenting and family life, certain values and practices are especially important seeds for an alternative ethic. I focus here on four qualities that people often experience and appreciate in parenting, but which receive little support in mainstream culture.

THE RELATIONAL SELF

Becoming a parent transforms people's relationships and challenges their established identities and priorities. It can even shake deeply rooted assumptions about what it means to be human and to be a good person. In particular, it can change, sometimes unnoticed, people's acceptance of voluntaristic, atomistic views of human nature, the assumption that "people who are by nature free and independent agree to form societies in order to secure their fundamental rights and to establish mutually advantageous cooperative arrangements."[49] This perspective has roots in Enlightenment political philosophy, especially contract theory. The individualistic and rationalist view of human nature implicit in this model helps legitimize a widely shared, though often implicit, conviction that relationships are authentic and morally acceptable only when they are freely and mutually chosen, benefit both parties, and can be ended if and when the benefits cease. In this light, obligations are incurred, and privileges gained, only when chosen. Applied to social ethics generally, this model assumes an ideal of human relationships as voluntary, symmetrical agreements between rational and equal participants.

Feminists and other critics have pointed out that this makes nonsense of many close interpersonal relationships. Parenting, in particular, is never wholly voluntary or wholly symmetrical, and the participants are never entirely rational or entirely equal. This does not make it immoral but rather challenges mainstream Western definitions of both morality and human nature. In parenting, a "different account of the self"[50] emerges, not so voluntaristic and autonomous. As parents, Ruddick argues, "We *think* differently about what it *means* and what it takes to be . . . a person, to be real."[51] In their relations with each other, parents and children are fundamentally social beings, and their experiences can nourish an ethical perspective that acknowledges interdependence and takes relationships and relationality as central for human flourishing.[52] This is the "embodied relationality" I mentioned earlier; concrete experience of what it means to live and relate to others as a social animal.

In this model, relationships become constitutive of one's own identity: internal relations, in contrast to the external relations that are added, so to speak, onto an already-complete individual. This more relational view of human nature was evident in earlier streams in Western philosophy, including both classical Greek and medieval Christian perspectives. There are many versions as well in Asian traditions of thought, most notably, perhaps, in Buddhism. In Buddhism, there is no "self" prior to relationships. Persons cannot be separated or extracted from supporting webs of relationships and experiences. The image of "Indra's net," an influential Buddhist story, embodies the Buddhist understanding of humans, and all of being, as relational "all the way down." Confucian, Daoist, and Hindu traditions, as well as many indigenous cultures, similarly offer deeply contextual, relational views of humanness that contrast sharply with Western assumptions of the self-sufficient, preformed individual.

Similarly relational experiences of personal identity are perhaps possible, even inevitable, in parenthood. Peta Bowden speaks of maternal experience as "an extension of self that is not yet self; a sense of being in two places, or being two persons, at the same time, or of not knowing whether one is mother or child."[53] This is not a loss of individuality but rather a "less individualist version of individuality," in which individuality "becomes defined by responses to dependency and to patterns of interconnexion, both chosen and unchosen. It is not something a person *has*, and which she then chooses relationships to suit, but something that develops out of a series of dependencies and interdependencies, and responses to them."[54] This echoes Buddhist understandings of relationality, although Bowden does not have non-Western philosophies in mind. The fact that something like this occurs in a Western context underlines both the point that all views of humanness are socially constructed and the possibility that different models of selfhood make sense or "work" in different contexts.

Sometimes the change is momentous, as revealed in Anne Lamott's reflections on her son's birth: "I am fucked unto the Lord. Now there is something that could happen that I could not survive: I could lose Sam. I look down into his staggeringly lovely little face, and I can hardly breathe sometimes. He is all I have ever wanted, and my heart is so huge with love that I feel like it is about to go off. At the same time, I feel that he has completely ruined my life, because I just didn't use to care all that much."[55] Caring that much makes possible new extremes of both sorrow and joy. It makes true the cliché that only when we feel deeply enough—are deeply involved enough—to be hurt badly are we also able to experience happiness with a particular intensity. This intensity stems from the fact that as parents we are no longer islands unto ourselves. Someone else's fate becomes intertwined with our own so deeply that it changes who we are. We live the internal relatedness about which philosophers debate. Relationality is embedded and embodied in our very selves.

The relational self is less created than revealed in parenthood—and parenting is not the only practice that reveals it. Parenting is one of the most common, and perhaps the most obvious, ways that we live as relational beings. Humans are always social beings, mutually dependent on other humans (and nonhumans) for our physical and emotional health. Our relatedness is always internal to us, in other words, but it can be easy to ignore until a particular relationship brings it to the surface. This is one of the chief political contributions that parenting can make: it shows in concrete and inescapable ways that we are in fact social beings, needy in relation to others and also needed by them. A political ethic demands that we move from admitting our mutual dependencies toward letting them be constitutive of our public identities, loves, and joys.

The relational understandings of selfhood shaped by parenting are born in new ways of living. Rather than new ideas changing behavior, here new practices lead to new ideas—about parenting, personal identity, and the world. In turn, new understandings help transform behavior. This "hermeneutic circle" of continuous mutual transformation represents a very different way of conceiving the relationship between theory and practice than is common in either philosophical or everyday understandings in the United States. Such an alternative conception is necessary if we are not only to uncover the values embedded in everyday practices but also to systematize and expand them.

NONINSTRUMENTAL RELATIONS

Parenting diverges from not only the individualistic but also from the utilitarian assumptions of mainstream culture. Parenting and family life, like religion, may be among the few spheres in which we speak a second language, in which people regularly consider and talk about values, commitments, and relationships in terms other than those of utility and economics. "In an increasingly commercialized world," as Viviana Zelizer notes, "children [are] reserved a separate noncommercial place."[56] This is one of the deep and often unexpected joys of parenting, as Jennifer Nedelsky explains: "part of the wonder of having a baby is that when one falls in love like that, one experiences a kind of relationship whose possibility is subtly but relentlessly denied by the pervasive market mentality of negotiated self-interest as the foundation of human affairs."[57] Voluntaristic, self-interested, utilitarian calculation does not rule in parental relationships. Parenting may in fact mark the final frontier of Habermas's lifeworld, the last realm of human practice and interaction not to be overwhelmed by concerns about exchange-value and associated voluntaristic, contractual approaches to interpersonal relationships. This refuge, however, is not immune from attack. Many aspects of childhood and of parenting have felt the influence of the commercial discourse and utilitarian values that dominate not only the market economy but most aspects of everyday life.[58]

Still, parental love remains unusually and distinctively nonutilitarian. Most of the time, at least, parental care is not based on means–ends calculations or expectations of utilitarian benefit. The relationship itself and the well-being of the loved one are their own reward. The rejection of instrumental and utilitarian value is behind the stereotype of unconditional parental love, crystallized in the notion of "a face only a mother could love"—the ability to find beauty and loveableness where others cannot. This unconditional quality of parental love is captured by Molina's description of his mother's affection in *Kiss of the Spider Woman*. She "takes me for what I am," he explains, "and loves me just that way, plain and simply." Parents love their children wholly, as they are, quirks, weaknesses, warts, and all.

This total, transformative, and noninstrumental parental love is an ideal. Like any ideal, it is not always fulfilled in practice. The love between parents and children, like that between friends or spouses, is not always, maybe not usually, as good as it can be or should be. Many gay men and lesbians, for example, do not receive the unconditional acceptance that the fictional Molina describes. Parents can be violent or indifferent, and even loving parents may exert control in destructive ways or fail to accept their children for who they are. In short, parenting experiences are far from utopian all or even most of the time. Real families of parents and children, like real friendships and real marriages, exist in an inescapable context of human frailty and conflict. What is utopian in parenting, at its best, is not what parents receive or even what they do, but who they are in the context of their all-important relationships to their children. Parents—good parents—are not just better persons in their parental role but a better *kind* of person.

They are less calculating, less self-absorbed, more generous, braver, more willing to admit dependency and vulnerability. These best moments are not transitory deviations from who we really are but rather define our best selves. In them we learn not only about ourselves but about what we desire, for our children, for ourselves, for the world. They point to our hope of creating a world in which it is indeed possible to be good, and moreover, to be good in this particular way. For these reasons, parenting contains seeds of an alternative ethic, glimpses of a different telos for human life.

RELINQUISHMENT OF CONTROL

In part because parenting reveals us as interdependent, relational beings, it brings home our lack of control over other people and the world in general. "With the birth of her first child," as Ruddick writes, "a mother learns that her power in respect to her children is limited. Children are born with a distinctive physical constitution and soon display a host of traits and moods that appear inborn. To deny that there is much in the character of an infant that is innate turns a relation that is to some extent determined and 'natural' into one entirely subject to management and therefore subject to blame and guilt."[59] As much as parents love their children, as much as their relationships shape the identities of all involved, parents cannot control their children—who they are, who they will become, how the world will treat them. Like any parent, I experience this daily with my children. From earliest infancy on, they have demonstrated preferences and desires that are undeniably their own. One simple example that sticks in my mind was the first time I took my oldest son, then about ten months old, along a relatively busy street in the bike seat on the back of my bicycle. He showed what he thought about my quiet, carbon-neutral transportation choice by jumping up and down and shouting "bus!" in ecstasy at the top of his lungs every time we passed an especially loud, smelly vehicle. All the politically correct intentions in the world could not make that little boy find diesel engines any less fascinating.

Over the years I have had countless similar experiences, reminding me again and again that my offspring are their own persons, following trajectories that often diverge from paths I would have them choose. Without underestimating the influence parents have on children's attitudes, values, and actions, we certainly do not have anything approaching complete control over our children's attitudes about gender roles, food, entertainment, and other people. I have sensibly dressing lesbian friends whose daughters beg them to wear high heels, egalitarian coparenting friends whose sons (like my own) rejected all the tenderly offered baby dolls, and nerdy academic friends whose sons and daughters turn out to be both motivated and gifted athletically. One of my favorite encounters with gender-neutral play was with the son of friends, scientists who share parenting with remarkable equity. One day, when he was three or four, he asked if I would like to see his dolly. "Of course," I replied, delighted at his nurturing instincts. He ran out of the room and returned with a baby doll. "Know what my dolly can do? She can THROW UP!" He tossed the doll in the air and ran off, laughing wildly. Clearly many of our children's preferences are influenced by mainstream culture (like the high heels), but much more is going on as well: the dimly understood social life of the playground, the mysterious alchemy of nature and nurture, of relationships and responses, that creates the unique persons we raise and then send off into the world.

The fact that children have their own perspectives and moral agency is remarkably neglected in writing on mothering and the family. A massive scholarly literature exists on motherhood, and another on childhood, but very little research exists that "simultaneously takes into account both mothers' and children's needs, desires, and perspectives concerning their relationships." To understand parenting and its ethical and political implications, we need to know more about both parents' and children's lived experiences together.[60] How do they transform each other's ideas and practices? As the experiences and conceptions of parents, especially mothers, and those of children have developed together historically, transformed ideas about parenthood and motherhood ought to be accompanied by changes in thinking about children, and especially by attention to the agency and distinctive interests of both parents and children.[61]

What might recognizing children's agency mean for social ethics? This parallels a move made by some environmental philosophers with regard to the agency of nonhuman animals and even nature itself. Such arguments rest on scientific research about nonhuman capacities and characteristics as well as on diverse intellectual streams. The suggestion that nature has agency raises radical possibilities, overturning the common assumption that only humans are intellectual, emotional, and moral actors. Similarly, asking about the implications of children's agency is both radical and potentially troubling, politically and personally. At the minimum, it creates hard choices for parents who must confront both their children's agency and their own lack of control. In 1988 I met Raquel, a Salvadoran woman from Santa Tecla, near San Salvador. Raquel and her husband had two daughters and one son. During the 1970s they all participated in progressive Catholic movements and were close to both their parish priest, Rafael Palacios, who was murdered in June 1979, and Archbishop Oscar Romero, who was assassinated in March 1980. These deaths had a great impact on Raquel's son, who had greatly admired both Palacios and Romero. In late 1980, when he was fifteen, the boy told his mother that he wanted to join the guerrillas of the Farabundo Martí Front for National Liberation (FMLN) in order to participate in a planned general offensive. Raquel and her husband tried to persuade him that there were other ways he could contribute. She told him he could work through education, for example. She also said he was too young to be a combatant. Her son responded: "You gave me wings, and now you want to cut my wings." She had no answer to this. He joined up, and he was killed a few months later, during a major guerrilla offensive in January 1981.[62]

Most recognitions of children's autonomy do not, fortunately, prove so dramatic. However, the stakes are high emotionally even when it is not a matter of literal life or death. The inevitable process of growing up calls on us to relinquish control, to respect our children's own choices, again and again. This is obvious and is dealt with in different ways by different cultures, but what it means politically and ethically here and now is far from self-evident. How do we balance our desire and duty to protect children with the responsibility to respect their own moral perspectives? How do we evaluate appropriate responses for different ages and situations? Answers to these question vary, of course, across cultures, as well as among families in the same neighborhood. Until recently, and still in many non-Western societies, children begin acting responsibly for their family and community at a very young age. Their jobs have included caring for younger children, housework and farm work, labor in factories and mines, political participation, and even military combat. These experiences show even quite young children as caring, responsible moral agents. Such experiences muddy the distinctions not only between adulthood and childhood but also between the individual and the community.

A good example of this is the experience of Brazilian street children documented by anthropologist Tobias Hecht. These children live outside the "right" place for children, which is the parental home, and care for themselves and each other, sometimes badly but often with remarkable competence. Challenging images of street children as simply victims, Hecht argues that they are also moral and intellectual actors, who interpret and act upon their world. The agency of street children is embodied in Brazil's National Movement of Street Children, founded by children themselves on the belief that "children and adolescents are agents with the potential to effect change, actors in the creation of their own history."[63] The same message comes through in accounts of children and teenagers who fought with revolutionary political movements in El Salvador and Nicaragua.[64] Seeing children as political activists suggests a possibility that rarely, if ever, arises in discussions of childhood, parenting, or ethics in the United States: children might have political as well as intellectual and moral agency, and their values and commitments might legitimately be connected to participation in the public square. They educate their own desires, developing their own utopian and dystopian images in and through the experiences of caring and being cared for, acting and being acted upon.

DECENTERING

When we accept our lack of control, we acknowledge our relative rather than absolute significance. This acknowledgment is ethical, insofar as "all morality begins in and is an elaboration of the discovery that something other than ourselves is real—whether it is nature, another person, or God— and the moral life is the ongoing attempt to understand, deepen, and apply that discovery."[65] As Bill McKibben notes, raising children is one of the most effective ways to displace tendencies toward "living as if you were the most important thing on earth." While there are countless ways to widen one's moral and political perspective beyond narrow self-interest, "the most time-honored way to become mature is to be a parent many times over, and a good one."[66] If encounters make beings real, as Donna Haraway contends, then the repeated, intimate, passionate, and mundane encounters between

parents and children make us unbearably real to each other. Other people's
needs, interests, pains, and pleasures may seem abstract in other circumstances, but not when our children are at stake.

This reality facilitates moral discovery and growth, an expanded sense of
self and of self-interest as well as concern for the conditions in which growth
is possible not only for ourselves. Parenthood encourages moral development
not only because it is hard but also, McKibben adds, "because it's so joyful,
because it shows you that real transcendent pleasure comes from putting
someone else first. It teaches you how dull self-absorption can be." Paradoxically, McKibben cites the political and ethical benefits of parenthood in a
book arguing for smaller families. While parenting can and should be both
joyful and ethically productive, the environmental pressures of overpopula-
tion and overconsumption demand that "we need to find ways to be adults,
grown-ups, *people who focus on others*, without being parents of large families." What this requires is "some substitute discipline for repeatedly ranking
someone or something else at the center of their lives."[67]

The decentering generated by parenting coincides with recognition that
one is part of larger processes, histories, and communities; tied to these are
values that extend beyond personal pleasure and utility, commitments to
others in one's own circle and beyond. Just as parenting decenters us, so can
encounters with the "more than human" world of nature. Our concrete practices in nature—living out relationships with diverse places and creatures
with distinctive histories, characters, trajectories, and interests—offer both
a unique source of utopian encounters and a vital resource for rethinking
social ethics.

4
ENCOUNTERING NATURE

DESIRING NATURE

One of the greatest joys of parenting is permission to play, especially outdoors: to run in the waves, fly a kite, follow butterflies, even jump in a lake. When people play, they inhabit time and space differently. They worry less about consequences, payoffs, measurable benefits, or even other people's opinions. There may be no going back to childhood's perspective, and many habits of childhood are not desirable for adults, but spending time with children on their terms can help adults see and act in unaccustomed ways. They help us learn and speak a second language, in which reciprocity, emotional intimacy, and aesthetic pleasure can take precedence over use-value, profit, time management, and efficiency.

These alternative values also come to the fore when humans encounter nonhuman nature—when we spend time in places that are not structured primarily by human priorities and in interactions with nonhuman animals, who experience the world in distinctive ways, without the same goals, priorities, or assumptions as humans. Interactions with the "more than human" world, found in natural places and with nonhuman animals, facilitate moments of grace for adults and children alike. Wilderness, as Gary Paul Nabhan puts it, "is where you go to play."[1] For many people, noncultivated areas—from urban parks to remote wildernesses—facilitate special sorts of behavior and interactions, set aside from ordinary duties and burdens. Work does not happen in the mountains or at the beach, on a trail or in a river, or even in the vacant lot on the corner. Playing in natural places helps both children and adults perceive, experience, and cultivate appreciation for nature's intrinsic value, as well as imagination, cooperation, and a host of other qualities.[2] These practices contain utopian moments that can serve as critical grounds for evaluating and perhaps transforming the rest of our lives. By experiencing and learning about what we love, we educate our desire.

Attraction to nature and desire to learn about it are well documented in virtually every human culture and literature. In the West, some of the best-known examples are the nineteenth-century romantics. Reacting against the ascendance of reason in the philosophical Enlightenment, writers like Johann Wolfgang von Goethe, William Wordsworth, William Blake, and Walt Whitman stressed emotion, imagination, and awe, especially in relation to nonhuman nature. While romanticism encompasses a wide range of themes and styles, many romantic writers looked to nature as both a refuge from the ugliness and materialism of industrial society and a source of artistic inspiration, a site where people could find and express their best and truest qualities. Thus Wordsworth found "In nature and the language of the sense, / The anchor of my purest thoughts, the nurse, / The guide, the guardian of my heart, and soul / Of all my moral being." Further, he added famously, nature leads "from joy to joy" and "never did betray / the heart that loved her."[3] The most popular romantic literature, including Wordsworth's, influenced conceptions of nature toward a more positive and holistic, albeit ultimately unrealistic, model.[4]

American transcendentalism constituted another nineteenth-century expression of a desire for nature, also in reaction against mechanistic worldviews. The best-known transcendentalists, Henry David Thoreau and Ralph Waldo Emerson, had a powerful influence on modern U.S. environmentalism. Thoreau, in particular, shared the romantic notion that only away from "civilization" could people live happily and morally. He advocated "simplicity" and sought it out most famously during his two-year stay at Walden Pond. Thoreau explained his purpose in moving to Walden thus: "I went to the woods because I wished to live deliberately, to front only the essential facts of life, and see if I could not learn what it had to teach, and not, when I came to die, discover that I had not lived."[5] In nature, away from the complications and illusions of city life, Thoreau contended, people could learn what really mattered and experience true joy and meaning.

For Thoreau, as for many other transcendentalists and romantics, nature was not only a source of joy but also a way to connect to the sacred. Ultimate goods are to be found as far as possible from human society and as close as possible to "wild" nature. John Muir, a founding figure in American environmentalism, was strongly influenced by Thoreau and Emerson, and he shared with them a sense that nonhuman nature was not only valuable but divine. Muir described his first sight of Yosemite Valley thus: "Never before had I seen so glorious a landscape, so boundless an affluence of sublime mountain beauty. The most extravagant description I might give of this view to anyone who has not seen similar landscapes with his own eyes would not so much as hint at its grandeur and the spiritual glow that covered it. I shouted and gesticulated in a wild burst of ecstasy."[6] Yosemite was a sacrament for Muir, a visible and outward sign of an invisible, transcendental grace.

If Yosemite was Muir's cathedral, a host of other sites have served the same purpose for others, offering special access to the divine, a sense of connection to larger values and forces. Frequently the sites of worship are mountains, as for Muir, but they also encompass deserts, trout streams, southern swamps, and virtually every other ecosystem. Henry Beston has celebrated Cape Cod, Barry Lopez the Arctic, Edward Abbey the desert, and Wendell Berry the Kentucky hill country. People have found the divine (and written about it) in African rain forests, the Australian outback, English country lanes, and every ocean. No natural place, it seems, lacks the capacity to inspire reverence, to reveal the holy that appears, as Tillich put it, not in "every reality," but "only in special places, in special contexts."[7] In such places people experience places, creatures, and forces that we cannot control but to which we belong, in some sense—what Beston called "elemental things," citing our need "for fire before the hands, for water welling from the earth, for air, for the dear earth itself underfoot."[8]

The sense of the divine found in nature is expressed in a wide range of forms, including solitary bursts of ecstasy such as Muir's and collective rituals such as the "councils of all beings" held by deep ecologists.[9] All of these express what Beston termed the "sense that the creation is still going on, that the creative forces are as great and as active to-day as they have ever been, and that to-morrow's morning will be as heroic as any of the world. *Creation is here and now*."[10] This widely shared and variously expressed sense of spiritual connection has been the topic of a host of contemporary scholarly explorations, which have greatly expanded both the seriousness with which "nature spirituality" is treated and understandings of how it relates both to more traditional religions and to activism. It has become relatively common to think of nature in spiritual terms, for mainstream religious organizations, including the National Council of Churches and the U.S. Catholic Conference, as well as for smaller groups such as Wiccans. Even secular environmental groups, ranging from the Sierra Club to Earth First!, have framed the value of nature in spiritual terms. These diverse expressions share beliefs that natural places express qualities and powers of the divine and that people can experience and come to know the sacred in and through nature.

SOCIAL NATURE

Not only natural but also social goods may be prefigured in wild places. Nonhuman creatures and natural places may embody values that humans desire for their own society, such as harmony, diversity, and renewal. For Chilean poet Pablo Neruda, the abundance, exuberance, and beauty of wild places, and especially the ocean, served as metaphors for what human life might and should be: "The inextinguishable sky, the new air / of each day, the invisible shine within, / that gift of a wide and vast springtime."[11] Neruda found in nature opportunities for quieter reflections than those manifest in his explicitly political poetry, though still guided by a larger vision of social justice. Just as glimpses of a good human society might come in and through visions of an abundant and healthy nature, visions of proper interhuman relationships might be found in interspecies bonds. In one poem, he celebrated his dog who "never stooped to becoming my servant. / He offered me the friendship of a sea urchin / who always kept his sovereignty."

His relationship to his dog even points him to the possibility of transcendence: "I, a materialist who does not believe / in the starry heaven promised to a human being, / for this dog and for every dog / I believe in heaven, yes, I believe in a heaven / that I will never enter, but he waits for me / wagging his big fan of a tail / so I, soon to arrive, will feel welcomed."[12] Neruda offers a tantalizing glimpse of a secular kingdom of god: a heaven that he will never enter but where he is soon to arrive.

As he aged, Neruda's attention to the connections between human and natural cycles intensified. He often placed the events of human history and of his own life into a context of longer biological time lines. "This is the hour," he wrote in a poem published posthumously, "of fallen leaves, their dust / scattered over the earth, when / they return to the depths of being and not being / and abandon the gold and the greenery, / until they are roots again, / and again, torn down and being born, / they rise up to know the spring."[13] Close to the end of his life, physically ill and deeply troubled by political events in Chile, Neruda sought to understand human lives and accomplishments in light of larger natural cycles. This sort of attraction to nature is not antihumanistic. It embraces a vision of people as both natural and social beings, capable of joy when they recognize their connections to nature, just as joy can come in experiences of solidarity and love among people. Nonhuman creatures and places help make us who we are, as individuals and as a species. Love of nature is part of what makes us human, not something opposed to our social nature. "Experience of animals is not essentially a substitute for experience with people, but a supplement to it—something more which is needed for a fully human life," as Mary Midgley contends.[14]

Midgley expresses something that seems obvious to most people with children, companion animals, or more than one friend: there are different kinds of love, not mutually exclusive even though they might be quite distinctive. Caroline Knapp makes this point in regard to her relationship with her dog, Lucille: "People have very powerful relationships with their dogs and that doesn't mean they're crazy, or that they're substituting dogs for humans, or that they're somehow incapable of forming intimate attachments with people. It's a different *kind* of relationship, but it's no less valid."[15] Given how basic are our relationships with nonhuman animals, especially dogs (domesticated for over ten thousand years), it is worth asking why so many people trivialize, even pathologize, intense relationships with animals like dogs or with wild places. Passionate attachments to non-human animals might be acceptable for children, but not for adults. Many dog-lovers, for example, have had experiences similar to the ones that Knapp describes, such as her friend Lisa's comment, after hearing her talk about Lucille: "You're scaring me." And even the "scary" things she said, Knapp recalls, did not scrape the surface of her feelings about the dog. "I didn't talk about what a central force in my life Lucille has become. . . . I didn't use words like 'joy' or 'love' or 'affection,' although it's safe to say that Lucille has given me direct and vivid access to all those feelings. Nor did I tell Lisa how much I *need* the dog, which might have been the most honest thing to say."[16] Perhaps it is this need that is scary, the fact that we are emotionally, socially, perhaps even neurologically constituted so as to require other species in order to live full and happy lives, or at least good and honest ones. "Our cultural history as well as our evolutionary history is thoroughly shared with other animals," as philosopher Anthony Weston summarizes: "Our minds, our lives, are permeated by animal forms."[17]

Relating to nature can reinforce the best of our human values and perhaps help guard against some of our excesses. Wendell Berry writes that even peripheral natural places—"lanes, streamsides, wooded fencerows, and the like—are always freeholds of wildness, where limits are set on human intention." These uncultivated places, host to diverse inhabitants and activities, provide models for an appropriate kind of human society: "This is the landscape of harmony, safer by far for life of all kinds than the landscape of monoculture. And we should not neglect to notice that, whereas the monocultural landscape is totalitarian in tendency, the landscape of harmony is democratic and free."[18] This natural landscape is indeed a model of what human society should be, in contrast to the monotonous and joyless human-made landscapes of commercial agriculture, strip malls, and subdivisions.

The notion that humans need nonhuman nature to live fully is central to the concept of biophilia, a term coined by Edward O. Wilson to describe "the innate tendency to focus on life and lifelike processes." The biologically based human affinity for and curiosity about nonhuman life is the ground for wanting to know nature, to experience wild places and communicate with nonhuman creatures. The inclination "to explore and affiliate with life," according to Wilson and other scholars, grounds much of human psychological, social, and intellectual development. This tendency, Wilson summarizes, is deep, complex, and undervalued: "our existence depends on this propensity, our spirit is woven from it, hope rises on its currents."[19] A connection with other living things is literally, biologically part of what it means to be human.

This hypothesis has powerful implications for childhood development. Children often identify strongly with nonhuman animals, from family pets to wild animals seen from a distance (or only in pictures). Like human children, further, the young of other species also slip "under the fence of the species barrier," as Mary Midgley puts it, much more frequently and comfortably than adults of any species.[20] The desire for nature may be crucial for children's intellectual and psychological development, insofar as biophilia is not only affective but also "cognitive." In other words, symbols and images of nature facilitate human intellectual development. The natural world is the most information-rich environment people encounter and also the most appropriate and productive one for human development.[21] As Wilson explains, "For more than 99 percent of human history people have lived in hunter-gatherer bands intimately involved with other organisms. During this period of deep history, and still farther back, into paleohominid times, they depended on an exact learned knowledge of crucial aspects of natural history. . . . As language and culture expanded, humans also used living organisms of diverse kinds as a principal source of metaphor and myth. In short, the brain evolved in a biocentric world, not a machine-regulated one."[22] It is more natural and fitting to understand ourselves as one among many interrelated species, dependent upon the same natural processes, than it is to see ourselves as separate from and above all these other life forms. The task is less to seek out connections to nonhuman animals and ecosystems than to acknowledge and embrace the connections that are already part of us. More broadly, we need to recognize that "Earth is our home in the full, genetic sense."[23]

Humans have evolved, in sum, to be curious about the places, plants, and nonhuman animals with which we have coexisted throughout all of our shared history. The contemporary decline of direct experiences in nature contributes to a host of problems, neatly captured in Richard Louv's concept of a "nature deficit." Children lose out on a uniquely information-rich environment, perhaps the best setting for nurturing and perfecting skills in observation, imagination, and social cooperation. Louv also cites studies showing that unstructured time in natural places is therapeutic for children with attention deficit disorder, among other problems. Other research shows that time in natural settings helps children deal with stressful events and increases overall well-being. Nature is restorative for children and adults alike, Louv suggests, because it often entails involuntary attention, or what William James called "fascination," rather than the directed attention that is demanded in most school and work tasks. While too much directed attention can generate fatigue, restlessness, irritation, and a lack of concentration, involuntary attention is restful and restorative. As environmental psychologist Stephen Kaplan explains, "If you can find an environment where the attention is automatic, you allow directed attention to rest. And that means an environment that's strong on fascination."[24] Fascination points to the intrinsic value of nature; time spent in nature is an end in itself, not a means to any other goal.

Despite the benefits of experiences in nature for humans of all ages, contemporary U.S. culture discourages them, directly and indirectly. Realization of our ties to nature is made difficult or impossible by living, studying, working, and playing places that separate people from nature, and also by production, distribution, and consumption patterns that distance people from the environmental consequences of their behavior. We rarely realize the ways that our everyday attitudes, institutions, and habits distance us from the nonhuman world, through educational institutions, urban design and planning, and laws as well as cultural attitudes that associate nature with danger and dissociate it from pleasures.[25] Many people associate attraction to nature with youth and naïveté, as seen in the common dismissal of "animal lovers" and "tree huggers" as not to be taken seriously. Identifying with nature is something people "grow out of," and if they do not, they are seen as somehow immature or unbalanced, even pathological. Only children and perhaps "primitive" people take animals seriously and see themselves as connected to animals, in this perspective; with maturity comes indifference to animals and an end to attempts to communicate with them.[26] Children can express deep affection for nonhuman companions like dogs, and so in some cases can old or sick adults, but, as Knapp puts it, "the rest of us are supposed to keep our feelings contained and compartmentalized, in the box labeled 'Just a Dog.'"[27] This disdain may mask fear, generated by our need for relationships that cross species boundaries and so transcend our ability to control.

Whatever its sources, cultural contempt for deeply felt connections to nonhuman animals and nature is a powerful, and powerfully destructive, force. It can make us censor ourselves, as Knapp points out, hiding and even ignoring some of our deepest and most positive feelings and attachments. It may even keep us from acting as good citizens, insofar as deliberate efforts to distance ourselves from the more-than-human world prevent us from protecting that world. Ideas and practices regarding nonhuman nature surely reinforce each other. If negative attitudes toward nonhuman nature lead us to physically and socially distance ourselves from it, the lack of interaction will only make our attitudes more negative and even fearful. Conversely, if we give free rein to our desire for encounters across the species line, we may increase both understanding and appreciation for nonhuman worlds.

EDUCATING NATURAL DESIRE

Because valuing nature seems so closely tied to getting out in it, many educators and environmentalists stress the importance of encounters with the nonhuman world for the development of ecological conscience, especially in children. Reaffirming the importance of youthful experiences for later attitudes, many environmentalists and naturalists recall special places that helped them appreciate nature, not only by learning about ecological processes but also by feeling connected. Such encounters need not happen in grand, remote wildernesses but can happen in ordinary places, close to home. E. O. Wilson remembers his walks in the piney woods and swamps of his native Alabama as formative to both his scientific interest in ants and his environmental commitment.[28] With much less remarkable outcomes than Wilson (who has won Pulitzer prizes for both his work on social insects and his calls to ecological action), I have vivid childhood memories of weekend hikes in the small redwood forests of Marin County, in northern California. My husband recalls, similarly, outings to the volcanic mountains of El Salvador, where he grew up. Like countless other adults who count themselves as "nature lovers," we are formed by the colors, sounds, smells, and flavors of the places where we first encountered the more-than-human world. Our children will be shaped by their own home place in northern Florida, with its palmettos, live oaks, Spanish moss, alligators, possums, and overabundant insects of all biting, flying, and crawling kinds, even the smell of summer's humid, buzzing air—not so lovely to parents who grew up in arid, hilly regions but meat and drink to our children who are native to this place.

Like most kids, our children seek out and remember mainly the small, humble parts of nature, rather than grand vistas. Gary Paul Nabhan recalls taking his young children backpacking in the Colorado Plateau, where they would "scour the ground for bones, pine cones, sparkly sandstone, feathers, or wildflowers," while the adults were busy "trying to count how many ridgelines there were between us and the far horizon." Nabhan came to realize that "a few intimate places mean more to my children, and to others, than all the glorious panoramas I could ever show them." When children wish to gain a sense of wildness, they choose "not the large, but the small."[29]

This echoes our family's recent experience in Glacier National Park, where what the children loved best was catching grasshoppers in the grass, finding signs of a beaver pond, and chasing frogs in the shallows of a lake. The fact that all these activities happened in the shadow of the Continental Divide meant little to them. They were struck by and still remember their close-up encounters with other species, even ordinary ones like frogs and grasshoppers, and the sense of freedom and possibility engendered by runs in meadows and ponds. We experience similar feelings on urban nature paths close to home; at our friends' farm, full of horses, dogs, cats, and chickens as well as armadillos, hawks, and bald eagles; and even in our own yard, where we have had close encounters with barred owls and raccoons. My four-year-old calls our backyard "the forest." It has a few big trees and a lot of little ones, and to someone who is three feet tall, it feels mysterious and wild. In homely settings such as these, many children learn to discover, interact with, and love the more-than-human world. This does not mean we do not need scenic vistas, but it does mean that we should not limit our definition of or appreciation for nature to vast wildernesses. Large tracts of uncultivated wild lands are necessary for other species and for our own, but appreciation of big places may emerge on narrow and well-traveled paths around the neighborhood.

Play in nature and with nonhuman animals, especially in childhood, can stimulate lives of interest in and care for the natural world. Even with these experiences, people may suffer from what environmental psychologist Peter Kahn calls "environmental generational amnesia." As Kahn explains, "we all take the natural environment we encounter during childhood as the norm against which we measure environmental degradation later in our lives. With each ensuing generation, the amount of environmental degradation increases, but each generation in its youth takes that degraded condition as the nondegraded condition—as the normal experience."[30] Although the nature we experience may never be pristine, if people do not come to know and care about particular places in childhood, they will not work to save those places as adults. This connection between local attachment and environmental concern has become increasingly important to environmental philosophy, education, and advocacy. Local experiences can help people, at any age, to educate our desires through hands-on experiences in nature, so that we come to know and see the more-than-human world as fascinating, intrinsically valuable, even animated with its own agency and selfhood. Such experiences can help us educate, or reeducate, our desire for a nature that is not simply a source of utilitarian resources for humans.

Any education of our desire for nature must include awareness of the risks of loving nature too much or badly. We cannot trust our love for nature in any unqualified way. Desire, for animals, places, other people, or objects, often leads to destruction. Simply being in relationship with nature—like being in relationship with other people—does not guarantee that the relationship is constructive for all parties. More specifically, recognition that our evolutionary histories and ecological realities connect us to other animals does not answer all the questions about the kinds of relationship we can and should have with other creatures, trees, even places. There are countless ways of being "in relationship," and many are unhealthy for one or all parties. This is true for interhuman relationships, certainly, and also true for human encounters with nature and nonhuman animals.

Attitudes toward nature are almost always ambivalent, and emphases upon feelings of connection and reverence can obscure the very real, and widespread, damage that humans have done and continue to do. This damage is often committed not in the absence of but in spite of expressed love and appreciation for nature. Many cultures dominated by worldviews that seem to value nature have poor records of protecting nonhuman animals and places. In other words, environmental damage occurs even when dominant value systems do not legitimize it. Even Native American cultures, often praised as the greenest of all, have experienced overhunting and other abuses of nature. For example, anthropologist Shepard Krech has attacked the image of the "ecological Indian" in North America, arguing that the historical record is mixed in regard to Native American treatment of animals and the land.[31] Asian belief systems such as Hinduism, Taoism, and Buddhism are also frequently held up as examples of environmentally friendly systems of thought because they emphasize the interdependence of humans and the natural world, the intrinsic value of nonhuman nature, and the value of avoiding gratuitous harm to other beings. However, many Asian societies have well-documented histories of deforestation, water contamination, unsustainable agriculture, cruelty to nonhuman animals, and so forth. In an international comparison of practical attitudes toward nature, Stephen Kellert concluded that although concepts of nature in Japan emphasize harmony and compassion, they are highly abstract and rarely include ecological knowledge. Kellert found little explicit support for nature conservation in Japan, other than an "indiscriminate" covenant not to cause suffering and to be compassionate. While criticizing Western mechanistic conceptions of nature as well, Kellert cautions against romanticizing any particular culture.[32]

My purpose here is not to rank cultural worldviews in order of greenness rather to underline the fact that ecologically aware or concerned worldviews do not prevent the destruction of nonhuman nature.[33] More specifically, if we admit an innate attraction to nature, questions remain about the practical consequences of this affinity. Many positive portrayals idealize and reify nonhuman nature in an unrealistic and uncritical way, from the Japanese attitudes that Kellert describes to European and American romantic literature. In these visions of the world beyond human civilization, the lion lies down with the lamb, predation ends, and harmony reigns. Such views of the natural world are so far from realistic that they might constitute a mirror image of the flawed rationalist notion that human society and the natural world are separate and opposed. The romantics who are drawn to nature in a quest for joy and meaning apart from human society are just as mistaken as the Enlightenment rationalists for whom the nonhuman is nothing but inert matter.

Related to this critique is the charge that the nonhuman world is far less benevolent than romantics believe, perhaps even "red in tooth and claw," as Tennyson famously suggested.[34] Those who, like Wordsworth, look to nature as an unalloyed source of harmony and joy will inevitably be disappointed by the pain and destruction that permeate natural cycles, relations, and places. In *The Origin of Species*, Charles Darwin put it well: "Nor ought we to marvel if all the contrivances in nature be not, as far as we can judge, absolutely perfect; and if some of them be abhorrent to our ideas of fitness."[35] He gave the example of the *Ichneumonidae* wasps, which paralyze caterpillars and then lay their eggs on their bodies; the growing wasp larvae later eat the immobilized but still living caterpillars. As a contemporary Darwinian, Richard Dawkins, points out, nature "is neither kind nor unkind. She is neither against suffering nor for it. Nature is not interested one way or the other in suffering, unless it affects the survival of DNA." The consequence, as Dawkins summarizes, is that "the total amount of suffering per year in the natural world is beyond all decent contemplation."[36] In light of the pain that accompanies evolutionary processes and everyday life for most creatures, it might be hard to maintain a positive attitude toward nature. If nature is indeed the site of predation, of continual struggle and competition, it seems paradoxical to claim that it can also be an expression and link to ultimate good, a site of the deepest joy and meaning.

All these critiques are valid and necessary. Our response to them, however, should entail not a rejection of nature as a source of value but rather an acknowledgment of complexity and ambiguity. It is true that the social and the natural are continuously interacting in multiple and complex ways, in every person as well as in social life. It is also true that nature, like human society, contains pain and loss. However, this does not mean that all efforts to find meaning, joy, and inspiration in the nonhuman world are mistaken, any more than are efforts to find meaning and joy in family life. What we find in nature might not always be pleasant but is nonetheless morally good, argues environmental philosopher Holmes Rolston. In nature, "Pain and pleasure are subsumed under a bigger picture." We should seek ethical insight in this bigger picture, rather than "the maximum happiness of particular sentient animals." Nature, writes Rolston, "is not a moral agent; we do not imitate nature for interhuman conduct. But nature is a place of satisfactory fitness, and we take that as a criterion for some moral judgments. We endorse a painful good."[37] Rolston's conclusions resemble the Christian theocentric ethics of James Gustafson, who insists that the diversity God created is good, though "not *necessarily* good for humans and for all aspects of nature."[38]

Darwin himself made a similar evaluation, even though he shuddered at some of the cruelties of the struggle for life. "When we reflect on this struggle," he wrote in *The Origin of Species*, "we may console ourselves with the full belief, that this war of nature is not incessant."[39] Cooperation and nurture, he believed, are as necessary for evolutionary history as are competition and predation. Building on this point, Mary Midgley notes acts of generosity and care that counterbalance suffering and conflict in nature. Many animals act in ways that do not directly benefit themselves, defending and babysitting others' young, bringing food for sick or injured adults, and rescuing companions from difficulties. Many also take risks by mobbing predators, giving warning cries, and searching out new food or homes.[40] While nature often entails struggle and suffering, then, it also contain moments of grace, expressions of protective care, non-self-interested giving, and mutual pleasure that can help humans educate our desires, both for nature and for ourselves. As Henry Beston summarized:

> It is true that there are grim arrangements. Beware of judging them by whatever human values are in style. As well expect Nature to answer to your human values as to come into your house and sit in a chair. The economy of nature, its checks and balances, its measurements of competing life—all this is its great marvel and has an ethics of its own. Live in Nature, and you will soon see that for all its nonhuman rhythm, it is no cave of pain. As I write, I think of my beloved birds of the great beach, and of their beauty and their zest of living. And if there are fears, know also that Nature has its unexpected and unappreciated mercies.[41]

Appreciating these mercies requires recognizing the agency of nonhuman creatures, processes, and places and the mystery and otherness of even domestic animals. Failure to recognize this autonomy is common, often coexisting with the best intentions. Many deep ecologists, for example, view nature, and especially wilderness, as extensions of themselves. A well-known example is Australian activist John Seed's statement that to claim "I am protecting the rain forest" means that "I am part of the rain forest protecting myself. I am that part of the rain forest recently emerged into thinking."[42] For Seed, and for other deep ecologists such as the Norwegian philosopher Arne Naess and the American Buddhist Joanna Macy, the key to environmental protection lies in a sense of identification with the natural world. Naess insists that we need "an expanded sense of self, one in which acting on behalf of others and the ecosphere is ultimately acting in terms of 'enlightened self-interest' and not out of some sense of moral obligation or duty, or even the rights of others perceived as separate from our own interests."[43] In other words, the key to protecting nature lies in eliminating the sense of separation between humans and nonhuman nature. Ecofeminist philosopher Val Plumwood points out that while this identification with nonhuman nature may be well intentioned, it collapses differences and denies the autonomy of nonhuman creatures and places. Extensionism can become an expanded egoism, in which widened interest is obtained at the expense of failing to recognize the difference and independence of the other.[44]

An ecologically healthy alternative to this expanded self might entail recognition of both relationality and difference. In a well-known passage from *The Outermost House*, Beston proposed that "the animal shall not be measured by man. In a world older and more complete than ours they move finished and complete, gifted with extensions of the senses we have lost or never attained, living by voices we shall never hear. They are not brethren, they are not underlings; they are other nations, caught with ourselves in the net of life and time, fellow prisoners in the splendour and travail of the earth."[45] The sovereignty of nonhuman creatures and worlds takes center stage here. They are not to be judged by human values and standards, or even interpreted in human terms, perhaps, since the other nations have their own, other languages. Nonhuman creatures, like humans, should not be treated only a means to the ends of others. This means not that relationship is impossible, only that any relationship must entail respect for nonhuman ends, a nonutilitarian appreciation like that to be cultivated in true friendship, as Aristotle and Aelred both argued.

The multiplicity of languages and worlds, in nature as in human society, need not make communication impossible. We share so much with other creatures, from our nervous systems to our signals for play and affection, that it is no surprise that we can relate to them and want to try (even if we often get it wrong). We can and should stretch across species boundaries, just as we reach toward other humans, who are also mysterious and other to us in countless ways. The self, as Rolston reminds us, "has a semipermeable membrane." Skin is not a solid wall.[46] However, communication must begin with respect for difference, and for the fact that other creatures' ways of being and knowing always surpass human capacities for understanding. Modern ecological science, in this light, reinforces worldviews that encounter the divine in nature, insofar as the sacred is that which surpasses human knowledge and control, a power that both supports and constrains human life.

Balancing the recognition of difference and otherness, equality and interdependence, is difficult and rarely achieved. It might become less daunting, suggests Mary Midgley, if we "get rid of the language of means and ends, and use instead that of part and whole. Man needs to form part of a whole much greater than himself, one in which other members excel him in innumerable ways. He is adapted to live in one. Without it, he feels imprisoned; the lid of the ego presses down on him."[47] This echoes a point made by E. O. Wilson and others: we cannot decide whether or not to be connected to other animals and ecosystems. Our relations to nonhuman nature are internal, part of our identities as individuals and as a species. Our choice is not about whether to be connected but about what to do with those connections, how to acknowledge and interpret them. Nonetheless, many people deny that they are part of a larger whole and that the other members of our whole, other creatures, are also agents, with their own ways of seeing and being in the world that are not, and never can be, wholly determined by humans—no matter how hard we try, as in the case of many domestic animals. The objectification and instrumentalization of many nonhuman animals in the service of human food, labor, and entertainment are moral, ecological, and political problems about which thousands of pages have been written. Deep ethical and psychological, as well as ecological, contradictions reside in the huge divide we have perpetuated between the care for nonhuman animals and nature that most people profess, on the one hand, and the way these same people mostly treat the nature they encounter everyday, often without even recognizing it as such.

Nonhuman animals, especially domestic species, serve as links between people and wildness and as facilitators of care for nonhuman world. Pets and domestic animals, like children, help connect adult social worlds and wild worlds. The key is to respect the otherness of other animals—their sovereignty, as Neruda put it—while also finding doors between our different worlds that make positive relationships possible. In these relationships, communication takes the form of a "second language" based on the other species' distinctive ways of experiencing the world and of relating to others.

Illuminating examples can be found in approaches to training nonhuman animals that emphasize an understanding of the animals' evolutionary history and species nature. For example, horse trainer Pat Parelli explains: "It is important to understand that the horse is a prey animal . . . the human is the horse's biological enemy; in other words, a predator. Most people get upset when their horses act like prey animals instead of partners. And most horses get upset when their humans act like predators instead of partners." Understanding equine nature provides a foundation for successful communication and relationships between horses and people: "Most people are inadequate when it comes to horses because they think like people. My goal is to get people to think like horses." The best way to do that, he adds, "is to play with horses on the ground,"[48] underlining the need to ground theory in practice. Knowledge about horses' evolutionary history is necessary but not adequate; information and theory cannot replace direct encounters and shared experiences that build and maintain any relationship. Donna Haraway makes a similar point in writing about dog training. Good trainers, she contends, share a "focused attention to what the dogs are telling them, and so demanding of them. . . . These thinkers attend to the dogs, in all these canines' situated complexity and particularity, as the unconditional demand of their relational practice." For the right sort of training, according to Haraway, "'method' is not what matters most among companion species; communication across irreducible difference is what matters."[49]

Both Haraway and Parelli emphasize the agency of nonhuman animals. As Parelli explains, "Communication is two or more individuals sharing and understanding an idea. If I pat my leg and the dog comes, we've communicated. But I can talk to a post until I'm blue in the face, and I'm just talking. Communication is a mutual affair between two or more individuals."[50] This exemplifies Midgley's argument that people who do well in training animals do so by interacting socially with them and coming to understand things from their point of view. Nonhuman animals, she adds, do have a "point of view" because it means something to be a bat or a horse, in a way that is not true of machines.[51] She reinforces a point central to the approach of Parelli and other trainers: to work successfully with nonhuman animals requires respect for the distinctive characteristics of each species and each individual, on the one hand, and willingness to find common ground, on the other.

Communication across difference opens doors into a world in which mutual respect, appreciation of otherness, reciprocity, and the fulfillment of possibility are higher values than individual achievement or material self-interest. Nonhuman animals challenge our timetables, our cost-benefit analyses, and our predictions for the future. They form part of what theologian Stephen Webb calls the "anti-economy" of giving, generosity, and grace, opposed to the dominant economy of use-value and profiteering.[52] Although there is no guarantee that anti-economic values will actually be lived out in a given relationship, they can be cultivated in particular kinds of relationships, especially with children, as noted earlier, and with nonhuman animals. While training animals, for example, can be dominating and abusive, it can also be an ethical enterprise, the coconstitution of a joint morality by trainer and animal.[53] It can be a practice of value creation, as Bill Jordan claims for ecological restoration.

Certain kinds of relationships between humans and nonhumans embody a different way of living and relating. In them we speak a second, often nonverbal, language, which can open a door to a different way of being. For Caroline Knapp, this door was opened by her relationship with Lucille, who led her "into a world that is qualitatively different from the world of people, a place that can transform us. Fall in love with a dog, and in many ways you enter a new orbit, a universe that features not just new colors but new rituals, new rules, a new way of experiencing attachment." Knapp recalls that she "once heard a woman who'd lost her dog say she felt as though a color were suddenly missing from her world: The dog had introduced to her field of vision some previously unavailable hue, and without the dog, that color was gone. That seemed to capture the experience of loving a dog with eminent simplicity. I'd amend it only slightly and say that if we are open to what they have to give us, dogs can introduce us to several colors, with names like *wildness* and *nurturance* and *trust* and *joy*."[54] Wildness, nurturance, trust, and joy can be experienced with people as well, but many aspects of human society can make them harder to find, or at least to recognize. Encountered with nonhuman animals or in wild places, they can help teach us dissatisfaction with the norm and a desire for more of these utopian moments.

COMMUNITIES: MIXED, LOCAL, AND NATURAL

Trainers like Parelli and Haraway understand their work with animals as the construction of relationships, in which both human and nonhuman participants develop rights and obligations, as well as bonds of affection and loyalty. The animals in these relationships have "face," as Haraway puts it.[55] Such relationships constitute part of what Mary Midgley calls "the mixed community" between humans and other animals. People live and always have lived, Midgley writes, in communities of multiple species, with some diverging and some common interests.[56] At their best, a mixed community can be a "genuinely co-inhabited world," as Anthony Weston puts it, with real bonds across species boundaries. Such communities can thrive in "intermediate spaces" located between the extremes of a wilderness without people and a civilization without the wild. Backyards, city parks, forest paths, farms, lakeshores, and riverbanks are examples of intermediate spaces that are both human and more than human.[57] In these spaces that straddle and connect different worlds, humans and other "boundary creatures" can thrive.[58]

A combined focus on social and natural relationships suggests a distinctive direction for ecological thinking and action. Environmentalism, in this framework, focuses less on preserving distant wildernesses and more on learning about and taking care of our own home places. This bioregional or watershed-based environmentalism begins with "the idea that the majority of solutions to both global and local problems must take place at the level of the expanded tribe, what civilization calls community," as Wes Jackson summarizes. "In effect, we will be *required* to become native to our little *places* if we are to become native to this *place*, this continent."[59] This notion of "becoming native" has been proposed by Jackson, Wendell Berry, and other bioregionalist thinkers as a necessary antidote to the "pioneer mentality" that has destroyed land and communities, then moved on to the next frontier. Berry's influential book *The Unsettling of America* (1977) argued that in contrast to Native Americans, European settlers did not "look upon the land as a homeland."[60] Thus they never felt the need to care for and protect the places where they resided; they could exploit local human and natural resources, then move on when these were exhausted. Bioregionalists advocate a reversal of this process as the best chance for creating environmentally and socially sustainable societies, for making, as Scott Russell Sanders writes, "a durable home for ourselves, our fellow creatures, and our descendants."[61]

Visions of homes that serve people and our fellow creatures contrast sharply with dominant images of environmentalism as a form of misanthropy, interested only in pristine wilderness and not in places where human beings live and make their livings. This image has been grounds for criticism of the mainstream environmental movement, embodied by groups like the Sierra Club and Wilderness Society, as elitist and out of touch with the everyday concerns of ordinary people, especially those who are poor, who are minorities, and who live in despoiled urban or rural places. Advocates of environmental justice have articulated this critique with passion and power and have influenced many environmental groups (the Sierra Club now has a major focus on environmental justice, for example). Many social justice activists, nonetheless, still dismiss environmentalists as unable to make common ground with people whose primary concern is human welfare. This critique is often valid, and its influence on environmentalism has been positive in many respects.

Environmental justice concerns, however, should not eliminate the radical extension of value and concern to nature for itself. To attend only to environmental issues that are explicitly tied to human welfare limits not only our ability to protect nonhuman creatures and habitats but also our understanding of what constitutes humanness and what makes a human life good. Acknowledgment of the intrinsic value of nonhuman nature, apart from usefulness to humans, poses a challenge to the systemic values and first language of utilitarian individualism. We need these challenges and the expanded vision that an appreciation of nature in and for itself can bring.

In fact, the stereotype of "mainstream" environmentalism as focused on pristine wilderness and grand vistas is not entirely accurate. Many influential naturalists, including Henry David Thoreau, John Muir, Henry Beston, Rachel Carson, and Aldo Leopold, celebrated the small and "unspectacular" too. In one of the most important American nature studies, *My First Summer in the Sierra*, Muir described his first sight of Yosemite Valley in the familiar terms of grandeur and amazement, quoted above ("Never before had I seen so glorious a landscape . . ."). However, Muir also devotes attention to more homely delights, such as his favorite Yosemite animals, to whom he declares "Good-night, friends three—brown bear, rugged boulder of energy in groves and gardens fair as Eden; restless, fussy fly with gauzy wings stirring the air around all the world; and grasshopper, crisp, electric spark of joy enlivening the massy sublimity of the mountains like the laugh of a child. Thank you, thank you all three for your quickening company. Heaven guide every wing and leg. Good-night friends three, good-night."[62] Muir expresses not just appreciation but a sense of relationship with small and homely creatures as well as with charismatic megafauna such as bears. The nonhuman world with which he communes is expansive and diverse, and it is in fact the links among different kinds and levels that make it so appealing.

Life in such a community challenges traditional approaches to ethics, according to which moral decisions entail choosing among clearly ranked priorities. In the usual view, moral claims can be seen as concentric circles arranged with most important values at the center and less urgent ones at the periphery. In a mixed community, however, diverse social and natural relationships give rise to complex, often overlapping sources of value and moral demands. To think about ethics in such a setting, Mary Midgley proposes replacing the concentric-circle model with an overlapping web of "flower petals." Each petal represents a moral claim or value, all of which are important for different reasons. These values are not necessarily opposed to each other and not necessarily in hierarchical relationship to each other, and some overlap while others seem to have no connection with each other. These connections vary over time. Sometimes we do have to choose among competing moral claims, Midgley admits, but often we can respond to more than one, and sometimes the same feelings or values will be involved in different sorts of claims. Many early advocates of animal welfare, for example, also campaigned for human rights, historical evidence that concern for humans and nonhumans need not preclude each other.

In this expansive vision, compassion for humans and compassion for nonhumans can coexist and reinforce each other. This often occurs in practice, but it has been undertheorized. Historical evidence, contradictory and partial as it is, points to the need for a larger ethical and political framework in which diverse concerns for ecosystems, for human communities, for individual people and individual animals, can make sense even if they are not all experienced as equally compelling. One example of such a framework is Midgley's mixed community, a concept that has influenced environmental philosophers writing about the relations among humans and animals and, more broadly, about human life in a biologically diverse world. However, the notion of a mixed community has not been elaborated in relation to cultural, social, and political realities. We do not have any systematic reflection, in other words, about how we might make mixed communities both desirable and practicable.

Bioregionalism can help start this reflection. The political promise of bioregionalism has been noted by a number of environmental philosophers of varying persuasions, including the land ethicist Baird Callicott, the evolutionary critic Lisa Sideris, and many ecofeminists. However, none of these has filled in the details of bioregionalism's potential as a practicable environmental ethic. At its best, bioregionalism can help environmentalists overcome the false dichotomies between "nature lovers" and "people lovers" and revise moral relations into overlapping petals rather than stark hierarchies. This starting point is vital if we are to build an everyday ethics out of ongoing encounters, intimate relationships, and mundane experiences.

Our most common and momentous encounters with nature occur not in distant wildernesses, nor even in neighborhood parks, but in the kitchen. The most common way most people in industrialized world encounter nonhuman nature is as food. Few people interact frequently with wild places and creatures, and many do not even spend much time with domestic animals and semiwild places, but all consume nature regularly. In eating, and in consumption more generally, we enact our values, consciously or not. Most often our actions are not conscious, which means that we end up contributing to problems such as environmental degradation, exploitation of workers, destruction of rural economies, or inhumane treatment of animals, even though we may oppose all these things. Every one of us participates in many different relationships—politically, economically, and ecologically—most of which we fail to recognize.[63] Our consumption of natural and social resources offers prime examples of ways we are in generally unacknowledged relationships with other people, places, and creatures.

Eating puts us in relationship with animals, farmers, watersheds, and countless other people and places, most of them far from our home places. Most of the food eaten in the United States has traveled over a thousand miles from origin to table, which entails a huge investment of fossil fuel for transportation, on top of an already enormous energy investment in production by conventional (nonorganic) methods (about ten fossil fuel calories expended for every food calorie produced). Not only do mainstream food production and distribution systems use huge amounts of fossil fuels, they have other detrimental effects on both human communities and natural environments. Worst of all, perhaps, they sever the ties between producers and consumers.[64]

Reflecting on consumption, especially of food, opens up new ways of thinking not only about relations to nature but also about relations between values and practices. Despite (or perhaps because of) its scope and significance, consumption has received relatively little attention from environmental philosophers or activists, with the notable exception of *Confronting Consumption*, edited by Thomas Princen, Michael Maniates, and Ken Conca. Another promising angle of approach comes from studies of overconsumption as a characteristic problem of American culture. Economist Juliet Schor has written several books on the issue, including *The Over-Spent American: Why We Want What We Don't Need*, a study of "the new consumerism," and *Born to Buy*, about marketing to and consumption by children.[65] Schor discusses environmental destruction as one among many problems generated by overconsumption, with a particular interest in the connections between production and consumption.

Schor is rare in highlighting this connection. More often, economists separate production and consumption processes, even though both entail consumption of natural resources. Consuming occurs all along the chain of production and distribution, not only at the final "downstream" site of consumer demand. Raw material extraction and manufacturing, for example, represent not only production and value added but also consumption and value subtracted. As the editors of *Confronting Consumption* note, "Producers are consumers; production is consumption," even though "what is being consumed at each node is not obvious."[66] Making the often hidden processes and consequences of consumption explicit is an urgent task for environmental activists. This requires, in particular, reducing the "distancing" that occurs when end-point consumers are far removed from the origins and processing of what they buy and use. Distancing, accomplished through a series of "middlemen," breaks the direct links of accountability between producers and consumers and also eliminates the feedback necessary to restrain resource use. When distance is excessive, as is the norm in modern industrial societies, it is not clear who has responsibility for the use and abuse of "natural resources."[67] This lack of clarity is one reason that abuse is rarely checked.

Perhaps the most important ethical issue raised by contemporary studies of consumption is who is responsible for the negative environmental and social consequences of overconsumption or malconsumption. Many mainstream environmental organizations target governments and corporations, largely because they shape policies and consumption practices at large scales. Focusing on individual consumers, in their perspective, simply cannot generate changes on the scale needed. Thus the Sierra Club, for example, works more to raise national fuel efficiency standards than to encourage ordinary people to drive less. As the first chair of the club's national sustainable consumption committee, I repeatedly heard arguments against focusing on the actions of individuals. Our response was that both large- and small-scale changes were needed, not only to reach the critical mass required to avert ecological catastrophe, but also to transform people's ways of living in and thinking about nature. It is vital to legislate on issues such as greater fuel efficiency, better urban planning, clean air and water, and protection of wilderness areas. However, legislation alone seems inadequate to transform people's everyday practices and attitudes. Changes in individual habits would help create political support for policy changes, just as better policies would make it easier for people to change their own practices. Our committee ran up against a host of challenges, from within and outside the club, including sincere activists who believed that new technologies would enable us to solve environmental problems without significant behavioral changes, and equally sincere activists who believed that people were so selfish and lazy that only legislative decrees would change their behavior. From the other side, we faced activists who believed that individual changes were sufficient and rejected any attempt to think structurally or legislatively. And then there were the true believers for whom a single change—becoming vegetarian, or giving up a car, or going solar— was the road to ecological salvation. To me the "both-and" approach still seems obviously right: we need small and large changes; we need to eat, travel, and live differently; and we need different people in government and maybe a different kind of government. These changes are so inextricably connected that we cannot start with a chicken or an egg but must plunge in wherever we see the possibility of doing something better.

One of the best places to start is food. Eating is perhaps our most ecologically significant and underanalyzed activity, and certainly our most frequent and mundane. Understanding the real environmental and social costs of what we eat helps us to see the structural in the everyday, to connect our individual choices to big ideas and big results. With this in mind, the sustainable consumption committee's first major national campaign was called "The True Cost of Food."[68] The campaign advocated three major changes: eating more plant-based food (lower on the food chain), eating more locally grown food, and eating more organically produced food. Routes to achieving these goals include community-supported agriculture and farmers' markets, which connect production and consumption by facilitating direct feedback between producer and consumer and minimize the wastefulness inherent in commercial agriculture and food distribution.

Such practices, as bioregionalist Robert Thayer explains, can help consumers "become more involved in decisions about how their food is grown, how their local ecosystems can be protected, and how the entire food delivery system can be made more regenerative or sustainable."[69]

Most notably, the desire for this kind of change has given rise to the local food or "locavore" movement, which advocates eating locally produced food for both ecological and social reasons. Community-supported agriculture and farmers' markets, along with other local food mechanisms, bring consumers and producers into relation with each other and with their local places. When people purchase their food from the producer, as Frederick Kirschenmann notes, they are buying a relationship as much as a food product.[70] They become part of their local "foodshed," more able to influence the ways food is grown and sold, how local places and communities can be protected, and how food production, distribution, and consumption affect local and larger ecosystems.[71] An emphasis on eating regionally and seasonally contrasts with modern food production and distribution systems, which have damaged or eliminated the links between producers and consumers, resulting in harm to both human communities (urban and rural) and the natural environment.

Eating locally, developing relationships with farmers, and caring for local foodsheds have become important themes for environmental philosophy and activism. Three prominent writers, Barbara Kingsolver, Gary Paul Nabhan, and Bill McKibben, have recently taken on the challenges of eating only locally produced food: Kingsolver at her farm in Virginia, Nabhan in Arizona's Sonora desert, and McKibben in Vermont. Both Nabhan and McKibben touch on the political and economic, as well as environmental and spiritual, dimensions of eating. One of the great pleasures of eating locally, McKibben explains, is "that everything came with a story attached to it. Every night when we sat down to dinner, we knew who and how and why our food had come to us . . . the good taste eating locally leaves in your mouth is not just the food, but the strong sense of community; the food really means something." Sometimes locally grown food costs more or is less convenient to purchase, he admits, but that is the "price that comes with community," and a price worth paying.[72]

My family has similar experiences with our local farmers' market and community-supported agriculture (CSA) participation. Because we receive a weekly bag of produce through our CSA, we eat seasonally, appreciating strawberries and tomatoes all the more because we have them for only a short time. We know who picked the greens, and we have been to the farm to take bugs off of them ourselves. We know a host of local producers by name, and we know their products personally: Charlie's honey, Bubba's milk. We see them weekly at the downtown farmers' market, where we also run into work colleagues, school friends, and neighbors. This feels like community, networks of people we interact with in more than one setting. These overlapping networks reinforce our ties to each other and to the places we share. We also grow some of our own food, which adds a whole new dimension: the peaches that we enjoy for a too-brief season, the berries and figs for which we compete with squirrels, the way sun and rain determine what we might get to eat.

Such experiences reinforce Norman Wirzba's claim that eating locally and home-grown food encourages people "to become aware of the gifts and limits of place . . . and the costliness of those gifts, since the processes of life are always intertwined with processes of death." As people become actively involved in food production, he suggests, "we will come to see our own lives as enveloped in a much larger drama that is life-giving but also vulnerable to exhaustion and destruction. The responsible, sacramental sense that we must care for this natural drama, see that it is maintained and not destroyed or compromised, will be a natural outgrowth of our sustained engagement and work with it."[73] Our desire is educated here, as we learn to want something different. What we want is moral and perhaps even spiritual, as well as edible: it entails a felt connection to other people and to natural processes, satisfying social and biophiliac needs and not just physical ones.

Like other spiritual practices, gardening and eating locally offer utopian moments, encounters with nature and with other people that embody positive alternatives to life as usual. They can help to reeducate our desires for more sustainable, humane, mutual relations to nature. At the same time, consumption and food issues underline the gap between what we say we care about and how we act. In no other sphere of life, perhaps, do people contradict their own values so regularly: animal lovers eat factory-farmed meat, conservationists consume thousands of fossil fuel calories in a single January tomato, wilderness advocates purchase soy grown on clear-cut rainforests. This pushes the problem further, or turns it around, or gives it a different spin—not only do we have implicit values that we live out without formalizing them, and not only do these values often differ from, or even contradict, the public values of the larger society, but we also have disvalues that we enact even though we may publicly reject them, such as cruelty to nonhuman animals or destruction of native forests. I explore these dilemmas further in the next chapter.

This leads back to the question of experience in nature as the grounds for environmental commitment and practice. While it is true, as many teachers and activists believe, that people learn to care about nonhuman creatures and untamed places through direct experiences, this process is far from straightforward. The links among experiencing nature, learning about it, caring for it, and finally acting on that concern are not simple, direct, or unidirectional. The connections are made even more complex by the fact that powerful economic, political, and physical structures discourage us from perceiving, valuing, and deepening our connections to nature. Direct experiences in nature can provide glimpses of alternative values and practices, of a second language regarding the nonhuman world, but these must be expanded and deepened into different ways of living in nature.

5

IDEAS AND PRACTICES: MINDING THE GAP

I can will what is right, but I cannot do it. For I do not do the good I want, but the evil I do not want is what I do.

—ROMANS 7:18–20

ENVIRONMENTAL VALUES AND PRACTICES

Good intentions do not always lead to good actions.[1] For countless reasons, people do things they know are not good for their own health or for the health of their families, their communities, or the planet. Almost all of us engage in behaviors that undermine what we value, as Saint Paul pointed out nearly two thousand years ago. The question of whether we can learn to enact the goods we want, then, is ancient and open-ended. Without pretending to answer it here, I want to reflect on the ways we might educate our desire in order to close, or at least narrow, the gap between the good we love and the evil we do.

The disjuncture between values and practices has received remarkably little attention in Western philosophy, especially the secular varieties. It has been a concern mostly of religious thinkers, including Paul and, notably, the Buddha, whose teachings addressed the problem of desiring what is bad for us. Philosophers have avoided the gap between values and practice in part, I suspect, because it appears so intractable. They have also defined their job so as not to include the problem: their task is to think of good ideas, not to worry about their realization in practical terms. Foregrounding the relationship between values and practices suggests a fairly radical redefinition of ethics, away from central assumptions of mainstream Western philosophy. In this chapter and the next, I make a start on this redefinition, in the process of considering the connections among values, practices, and the utopian moments of everyday life.

Disparities between values and practices exist in so many parts of our lives that the choices for a case study to illustrate the dilemma seem almost limitless. I focus on attitudes and relations to the nonhuman world, which for several reasons provide a particularly illuminating example. Attitudes toward the environment have been well-documented for at least the past couple of decades. A series of national surveys show that environmentalism has become mainstream in U.S. culture, with around 80 percent of Americans considering themselves environmentalists or expressing strong concern for the natural world. "Most Americans share a common set of environmental beliefs and values," as a study done by scholars at MIT summarizes: "Patterns of agreement in surveys show . . . a single cultural consensus."[2] This consensus encompasses a number of different forms of environmentalism, some more Earth-centered or biocentric and others more human-centered or anthropocentric. The variations exist, however, on a continuum of widespread agreement that the natural world is valuable and deserves protection.

This consensus on the value of the environment has not generated environmentally sustainable behavior on a comparably broad scale. While as many as four out of five Americans identify themselves as environmentalists, fewer than one in five regularly participates in environmentally responsible activities such as recycling, reducing personal consumption, supporting green businesses, eliminating waste and pollution, or engaging in environmental activism. Many "green" practices have in fact stagnated or even declined since the onset of the mass environmental movement in the 1970s. Significant declines in resource consumption have occurred only in the wake of crises, such as the 2001 energy shortages in California or the 2008 rise in gasoline prices.[3] In these situations, conservation seems much less an expression of environmental concern than a response to individual or collective economic factors—rules and subsidies encouraging conservation, in the California case, and sharp increases in cost, in 2008. The high price of gasoline presently is encouraging conservation but may also be generating antienvironmental values, as more people appear to support oil drilling in Alaska and off the Gulf coast as an alternative to energy conservation.[4] In all these cases, environmentally responsible practices such as energy conservation have little if any connection to the ecological values that people express.

In voting and other political behavior, similarly, expressed environmental concern rarely leads to effective practical action. More than 70 percent of U.S. survey respondents say they have never voted for or against a political candidate based on his or her environmental views or record. An October 2005 poll conducted by Duke University, for example, found that while 79 percent of respondents favored "stronger national standards to protect our land, air and water," only 22 percent said environmental concerns have played a major role in determining whom they voted for in recent federal, state, or local elections.[5] Candidates' personal qualities and their positions on "moral" issues such as abortion, gay rights, and gun control appear more important to voters. Environmentalists have called for a "reframing" of ecological issues as matters of "values," although the success of these efforts remains to be seen.

The failure to translate environmental concern into effective action has dire consequences. Consumption of natural resources, in the United States and elsewhere, has grown ever more rapidly in recent years. Consumption of energy—the largest component of our ecological impact, accounting for more than 60 percent of U.S. use of natural resources—grew by 21 percent between 1992 and 2002.[6] This is much higher than the U.S. population growth rate, so even as population growth slows, our consumption of natural resources continues to rise. Further, the failure to make environmental concerns central to political behavior has led to a loss of legal protection for many endangered species. The desire for large amounts of personal space creates more sprawl, and our attachment to single-user, fossil-fueled transportation contributes to global warming. Our culture's love of meat and of highly processed and out-of-season food exacerbates many of these environmental problems, including not just global warming but also biodiversity loss and desertification of land and ocean habitats. Our daily activities, in sum, undermine the nonhuman creatures and places we tell pollsters, and ourselves, that we value. We cannot build a more sustainable—or more humane or just—society without transforming the relationship between values and practices. The transformation of this relationship, further, cannot begin at the level of theory. To change the way we understand the ways values connect to practices, we have to begin with the latter, or at least address the two simultaneously and with an eye to their continuous, mutually transformative interactions.

Environmentally responsible practices are as varied as definitions of what it means to be an environmentalist. There is no single way to protect the natural world. Some people may work for structural change by volunteering for environmental organizations, donating money to good causes and candidates, affecting local community planning, land use, and transportation decisions, and so on. Environmentalists often try to help nature directly, through projects such as restoration of native species, removal of harmful exotic species, reforestation, or river cleanups. Other activists focus on environmental education at various levels, from small children to graduate school, and working through religious communities to educate and enlighten. Still others emphasize personal consumption practices, including recycling; using alternative transportation; buying efficient appliances, compact fluorescent bulbs, and hybrid cars; buying products that are recycled or otherwise "green"; and eating in ways that reduce our negative environmental impact.

Despite differing priorities and emphases, most environmentally educated people know that all of these activities reduce our negative impact on the Earth and thus reflect the value we place on nonhuman nature. Many people make conscious decisions that lead to personal inconvenience or higher costs because it is better environmentally and we desire to walk our ecological talk. However, no one can walk the talk all the time. Because of differing talents, life situations, home places, jobs, and incomes, we can all fight different battles, but none of us can fight them all. I have young children, which limits my time for meetings, but I live in a town and climate in which I can bike to work, dry my clothes on the line, and eat local produce most of the year. People who live in different places, in different circumstances, have other choices available to them. All of us will choose at times, consciously or not, to save time, money, or our own energy instead of the planet: to skip a meeting, to drive rather than walk, or to buy out-of-season produce. I often feel a pang of conscience or regret when I make choices that I know are not best for the Earth. These pangs are both a healthy prod to push myself further and a poignant reminder that I will never, despite my best efforts, do all that is necessary. Only collectively will we manage that, and there is no guarantee even then.

EXPLAINING THE GAP

If environmental and social ethics are to contribute to the goal of building a more sustainable society, we need to reconceive our task as not simply developing more good ideas but rather understanding how people can live according to the good ideas we already have.[7] We need to educate our desire so what we want is in line with our values, our wish to create a more sustainable and just world. This requires, as a first step, identifying some of the reasons for the current gap between our expressed values and our actual behavior in relation to nonhuman nature. These reasons are related, in many cases, to similar dilemmas in other areas of our lives, where we also, for equally complex reasons, fail to do the good that we desire.

There is no single reason that we fail, in environmental behavior or in other areas of our lives. Scholars of environmental behavior have suggested many reasons, ranging from individual laziness to structural obstacles, and almost everything in between. For every individual and for groups, multiple factors prevent environmentally responsible behavior, and multiple solutions will be required to move us toward more sustainable practices. Amidst the complexity, we need to uncover the most important obstacles and understand them better, so that our practical efforts to expand sustainable behavior will have an impact. I started trying to identify obstacles, on a very small scale, with a couple of surveys that I conducted in classes during the fall of 2007. The answers revealed some interesting answers to the question of why people do or do not engage in environmentally responsible behavior. While these results are highly anecdotal, they largely coincide with, and in some cases shed light on, more systematic research done by scholars of environmentally responsible behavior.

I gave students a list of about twenty-five practices that are good for the environment, divided into the four categories of eating, transportation, household resource use, and political behavior.[8] The choices included items like eating local food, being vegetarian, driving a very fuel-efficient car, riding a bicycle or walking to work, insulating one's home, voting, going to local planning meetings, and so forth. Respondents were asked to rate their participation in these practices with a Likert scale of 1 to 5, with 1 meaning "I do this every time I can" and 5 meaning "I never do this." After they circled their numbers, I divided the group in half. One half was asked to look at all the practices they engaged in frequently (1 and 2 answers) and explain the reasons they do them. The other half was asked to look at all the practices they rarely or never did (4 and 5 answers) and explain why they did not do these.

The answers of the latter group point to some of the most important obstacles to environmentally responsible behavior. Their reasons for not doing things they thought they should do mostly fell into three broad categories: too little information, too little time, and too little money. There were a few other kinds of responses, primarily personal preference ("I like hamburgers too much" or "I'm too lazy to walk to work"), fear ("I'm afraid I'll be run over if I ride my bike"), and a sense of helplessness ("One vote doesn't matter"). While this is far from a scientific survey, the responses complement existing literature and suggest some new directions.

Lack of information, for example, is an obstacle that scholars of environmentally responsible behavior often cite. Many believe that better environmental education is a central factor in efforts to improve environmental behavior. Lack of information, or ecological illiteracy, comes in various forms. One is a lack of knowledge of the right kind of behavior. Sometimes this is very significant, as for people who do not realize the ecological harm done by meat production. In such cases, getting accurate information to well-intentioned people can effect a major change in behavior. Sometimes, however, simply providing information is not enough. People may learn that a behavior is destructive but remain so attached to the behavior that they are not willing to stop ("I like hamburgers too much"). In such cases, being concerned and having correct information is not enough. In fact, sometimes people feel that they have too much information, or at least too much to deal with in a given situation. It is not hard to feel overwhelmed by the complexity of environmental problems, even to the point of paralysis. Since it is impossible to do everything, we end up doing nothing. Furthermore, because the issues are so complicated, people are often not sure whose information to trust, since we receive many contradictory messages. It is not that scientifically sound information is unimportant, but simply "getting the information out there" is only a first step. The knowledge that matters is knowledge presented accessibly and in ways that highlight and positively encourage ways for people to act with real impact: information that is "relevant, practical, and easily available."[9] The MIT study cited earlier suggests, further, that even faulty information can lead to environmentally responsible behavior, demonstrating that there is not necessarily a direct link between ecological literacy and environmental action.[10] The primary challenge for environmentally concerned people today may be not to accumulate more knowledge but rather to persuade people to act on knowledge already received. We fool ourselves if we think that overcoming the information deficit will, all by itself, transform values into action.

Effective ecological knowledge, further, must not only be about general issues but connect specific actions to concrete environmental consequences. The notion of "distancing" highlights the increasingly isolated character of consumption choices as individual decision makers are cut off from contextualized understanding of the ramifications of their choices.[11] As Tom Princen explains, "When critical resource decisions are made by those who will not or can not incur the costs of their decisions, accountability will be low and what gets counted is likely to be financial capital, not social and natural capital. Decision authority must shift from those who, directly or indirectly, knowingly or unknowingly, overexploit the resource to those who receive negative ecological feedback and who have the capacity and incentives to act on that feedback."[12] Because most of us do not have such feedback about most of our actions, environmental problems remain largely abstract. Few affluent people in the contemporary West, in particular, experience the consequences of our unsustainable actions in direct, painful ways. Insulated from most of the relevant impacts of our actions, many of us understand crucial dimensions of the moral situations in which we reason and act in abstract terms, if at all. All too often we fail, in other words, to see connections among our expressed values and the practical consequences of our actions.

In part because we define environmental concerns (and other moral values) in abstract terms, narrowly defined self-interest often drives environmental behavior. This is especially true in relation to economic considerations. Expense is a major, often defining, obstacle to environmentally responsible behavior in a wide range of circumstances. Even middle-class consumers may feel unable to afford organic food, hybrid cars, or high-efficiency appliances, which are usually much more expensive than the less sustainable alternatives. Here relative, not just absolute, expense is important: it's not just that the organic potatoes cost six dollars for five pounds, but that the conventionally grown ones cost less than three dollars. For more significant items, such as appliances and cars, absolute price is a real obstacle: the premium of up to ten thousand dollars that one pays for a hybrid Prius rather than a similarly sized nonhybrid car is substantial for all but the most affluent consumers.

The economic constraints experienced by individuals often point to collective failings. For example, the fact that my husband and I, reasonably well-paid professionals, cannot afford to install solar photovoltaic panels on our house is due to structural factors: a consistent lack of public investment in solar energy, combined with perverse subsidies that make "conventional" energy sources such as coal artificially inexpensive. It is relatively inexpensive to drive big cars, to eat beef, and to develop rural lands because of government policies, from local to national levels. At the same time, other policies make it expensive to buy energy-efficient cars and appliances, to install solar panels, and to eat organic food. The list goes on: public transportation is slow and cumbersome and bicycle commuting is risky because city planning is oriented to automobile traffic. In countless concrete, practical ways, our society makes it hard, expensive, and even dangerous to do the right thing. In this light, it seems unreasonable to ask people to make the sometimes significant sacrifices necessary to act sustainably. And it seems even more daunting to build the political will that will be required to achieve major structural changes.

Even though our culture teaches us to look first and foremost to individual causes and solutions, we cannot solve all our ecological problems at the individual level. Different people have different options available to them. Some may be able to walk to work, others to install solar water heaters, others to buy organic food. Few people, however, can live truly green lives on their own. For this reason, I am skeptical of "green consumerism," or at least of many of the claims made for it, especially the notion that purchasing "ecologically friendly" items is a silver bullet solution to large environmental problems. The possibility of consuming our way to sustainability is tempting, however, and more than thirty-five million Americans regularly buy products that claim to be ecologically sound, including organic cosmetics, clothing made from hemp and recycled plastic, hybrid automobiles, and ecotourism.[13] This hunger for easy environmentalism has given rise to books with titles like *It's Easy Being Green* and *Green Living for Dummies*, as well as countless titles for children who want to save the Earth in a few easy steps. Advocates of green consumerism suggest that individuals can reduce their negative environmental impact without depriving themselves of necessary or desired goods. The problem is that a focus on consuming "green" products can distract our attention from more important tasks. For Paul Hawken, "green consumerism is an oxymoronic phrase," while another activist calls it "eco-narcissism." Most environmental scholars, including natural scientists as well as policy analysts, agree that we cannot build more sustainable societies or avert large-scale ecological catastrophes simply by making "slightly different shopping decisions."[14]

The tendency to focus on "shopping decisions" is understandable, given the complexity of information about environmental problems and their often overwhelming nature. Further, purchasing more ecologically friendly items can indeed constitute a significant step toward reducing resource use and shifting toward a more sustainable lifestyle. For green consumerism to have these positive results, care is required both in linking consumption to larger environmental concerns and in choosing products. Because not all consumption carries the same environmental weight, some behavioral shifts matter more than others. If people want to reduce their ecological impact substantially, as Warren Leon and Michael Brower argue, they need to focus on the most environmentally damaging aspects of their consumption.[15] Leon and Brower highlight transportation, food, and home energy use as the most important areas in which individuals and households should make changes. People seeking to reduce their environmental impact should choose alternative transportation (bicycling, walking, riding the bus) whenever possible and use fuel-efficient cars when driving is necessary; they should make their living spaces energy efficient; and they should adopt a more sustainable diet, meaning one that is plant-based, locally grown, and organic. Such actions make a much greater difference than purchases of organic cosmetics or recycled fleece. They also, however, often involve significantly greater effort and expense.

In addition to savings on energy or reduced use of pesticides, green consumerism may, in certain circumstances, provide an "entryway activity" that leads people from small-scale actions to larger ones. "Skeptical environmentalist" Michael Shellenberger makes this argument based on a series of focus groups in April 2007 for the environmental group Earthjustice (the legal arm of the Sierra Club). Shellenberger found surprising results: "We didn't find that people felt that their consumption gave them a pass, so to speak. They knew what they were doing wasn't going to deal with the problems, and these little consumer things won't add up. But they do it as a practice of mindfulness. They didn't see it as antithetical to political action. Folks who were engaged in these green practices were actually becoming more committed to more transformative political action on global warming."[16] Shellenberger's findings, while anecdotal, are provocative: they suggest that people who begin with small steps do not necessarily stop with changes in individual consumption choices but may experience a progressive expansion of both concern and action.

This expansion will not occur by itself, however. We will have to connect our individual actions explicitly and rigorously to the structural factors that ultimately make the most significant difference in our consumption of natural resources. Sustainable structures and institutions will also make it easier for more individuals to live sustainably in their own everyday lives, so changes at small and large levels reinforce each other. This is necessary because small changes are inadequate to the scale of problems that we face. These are "hard facts," as Michael Maniates underlines: "If we sum up the easy, cost-effective, eco-efficiency measures we should all embrace, the best we get is a slowing of the growth of environmental damage. That's hardly enough: Avoiding the worst risks of climate change, for instance, may require reducing U.S. carbon emissions by 80 percent in the next 30 years while invoking the moral authority such reductions would confer to persuade China, India and other booming nations to embrace similar restraint." The task is daunting, and, as Maniates continues, "obsessing over recycling and installing a few special light bulbs won't cut it. We need to be looking at fundamental change in our energy, transportation and agricultural systems rather than technological tweaking on the margins."[17]

We need more than technological tweaking or good shopping decisions. We need public support, including good science that tells us about
the ecological consequences of particular behaviors, about what ecosystems need, about how we can harm or restore them, and so forth. We do
need technology that helps us use existing resources, especially energy,
more efficiently, but this technology must be accessible to people in a wide
ranging of places, living conditions, and income groups. We need ecologically sound infrastructure, including transportation systems, food production and distribution systems, and housing. To achieve all of these, we
need responsive political institutions that will facilitate the creation and
expansion of good science, technology, and infrastructure. These structural,
political changes are the necessary context for any discussion of small-scale
actions.

Structural and individual practices are linked every step of the way.
Transformed structures will help remove another significant obstacle to
many sustainable practices at the individual level: their relative inconvenience. It often takes more time and more physical or mental effort to act in
environmentally responsible ways. This is one reason that green consumerism is so appealing: just buy the organic carrots rather than the conventional ones, without spending any more time at the grocery store. Glenda
Wall, a scholar of environmental behavior, argues that most people tend
toward laziness or at least will minimize efforts that seem less than necessary, and that environmental advocates must take this element of human
nature into account in efforts to encourage more sustainable practices. She
suggests that in order to increase participation in conservation programs,
environmentalists should aim to make structures and procedures easy and
convenient.[18]

Convenience, of course, is a relative term, and perceptions of convenience depend on social factors such as peer pressure or support, as well as
individual histories and life circumstances. When I conducted my class exercise, respondents often framed convenience in terms of time constraints.
They felt they had too little time to bicycle, walk, or take the bus to work
or school; to hang laundry on a clothesline; to go to a county commission
meeting; to seek out local food and prepare it; or to learn about environmental issues so that they know what is the right action to take. Lack of
time can point to structural factors: if buses were more efficient, if we had

trains, bike lanes, and so forth, it would not be necessary to carve out so much time to do the right thing. However, sometimes "lack of time" really means an unwillingness to rearrange time. This is related to personal preference: "I really like the taste of meat," or "I really don't want to get to work all sweaty."

I am sympathetic to concerns about convenience and, especially, time. I am as busy as anyone I know, with three children, a spouse, a full-time job, and various volunteer commitments, not to mention multiple dogs, horses, and chickens. However, I ride my bicycle to get my three children to three different schools every day, to get myself to work, and often to get groceries, go to the library, and run other errands. I do so not because I am an environmental saint or Wonder Woman, but because bicycling is so much a part of my life that I take it for granted. To bike the kids to school, I get up earlier, which means I go to bed earlier, which means I don't do some things I would like to do. We deliberately chose a neighborhood that was within bicycle commuting distance of work, and we have chosen schools with this in mind as well. I have commuted by bicycle virtually all of my adult life, in many different places—in rain and snow, up and down hills, in cities and small towns. (I have not gone as far as my friend Whitney Sanford, who constructed snow tires for her mountain bike in order to commute in Ames, Iowa.) Like many other sustainable habits, bicycle transportation can become part of our lives, as taken for granted as the "natural caring" that we do for children. Nonsustainable habits can also become ingrained in this way, often more easily, since they tend to require less physical effort. To inculcate sustainable practices, we need a healthy dose of determination and self-discipline.

We also have to confront and resist powerful cultural norms that reinforce nonsustainable habits and preferences. These norms are revealed in the funny looks you get if you bring your own canvas bags to the grocery store or the not so kindhearted jokes you hear if you serve tofurky at Thanksgiving. People who buck the tide are often made to feel eccentric or just plain weird (not unlike the experiences of people who admit to loving their dogs too much, as Caroline Knapp discovered). Activists are often told that they are immature and naïve and will "grow out" of their ecological "phase." In the face of this pressure, from coworkers, neighbors, relatives, and the culture as a whole, it can come as a relief to stop trying.

Despite the obstacles, sometimes people do act on their environmental values. The next piece of the puzzle is to ask what helps them do so—what factors facilitate the adoption and maintenance of environmentally responsible behavior? Again, my class exercises, while far from definitive, highlight some important points. One is that while reasons for failures to act in ecologically sound ways may be fairly consistent, the reasons for success are much more diverse. Among my students, the half asked to explain their positive answers by listing reasons they started and persisted in ecologically sound actions gave a wider variety of reasons than those asked to explain why they did not do certain actions. There was no clear-cut consensus akin to the clustering of too little information, money, or time. However, there were some common threads in their answers.

One is social support and peer pressure. When people felt supported and even coerced to engage in certain behaviors, they were much more likely to do so. For example, one student said if she did not vote, her mother would kill her. Another pointed out that all his friends rode their bike to school, and he would feel self-conscious driving. Eating habits were similarly shaped by peer group habits. This reinforces a point that scholars of environmentally responsible behavior have often made: community support is crucial for sustainable practices.[19] People get pleasure from activities like recycling and ecological restoration projects. They not only enjoy the activities themselves but also build friendships and find satisfaction in being active members of a larger community. Thus sustainable practices build social capital, which involves trust and accountability in interpersonal relationships, and which is an important part of democratic politics at local and larger levels. However, this relationship is mutually reinforcing: environmentally responsible behavior builds social capital, and social capital makes environmentally responsible behavior more likely. When people trust their neighbors and leaders, they feel engaged and invested in a community and are more likely to participate in activities that contribute to the long-term health of the community. This mutual reinforcement is heartening, on the one hand, since it suggests that good things, like social trust, lead to more good things, like sustainable practices. On the other hand, in a society short on both these things, it is hard to know where to start.

Another frequently cited factor might be called identity. "I see myself as the kind of person who. . . ." To act otherwise would feel contradictory, not only morally but also psychologically and emotionally. This is often tied to habits instilled in childhood, which points to the importance of environmental education not just in providing information but especially in inculcating attitudes and practices that carry over into adulthood. On this point, again, my small-scale research reflects a theme that is important in more systematic studies of sustainable behavior. Students remembered environmental issues and campaigns from their childhood very vividly and remarked upon the continuing impact of these early images and feelings. Experiences in childhood make a difference on people's long-term environmental attitudes and practices. Sometimes these formative early experiences are shaped by mass media, as my students pointed out, from ecologically concerned movies to public service ad campaigns such as Smokey the Bear or the Crying Indian. However, environmental attitudes are also shaped by formal environmental education efforts in elementary and secondary schools, and by informal experiences such as family excursions to national parks, hiking, fishing, and so forth. Through activities like these, children develop an attachment to nature in general and also to specific places, which they may later work to protect through hands-on restoration activities or political actions.

Another significant reason for starting or continuing sustainable practices is pleasure. While acting in environmentally responsible ways often requires more work, many people also find it deeply satisfying. This satisfaction takes diverse forms, including a sense of community ("I know my neighbors better since I started shopping at the farmers market"), physical well-being ("I lost twenty pounds since I started biking to work"), and emotional gratification ("I feel better knowing I am doing everything I can to make the world better for my children"). Once again, the anecdotal evidence points to a larger issue, present in the literature on environmentally responsible behavior. The point is fairly self-evident, at least at first glance: people are unlikely to adopt sustainable practices that seem to subtract from their quality of life. Ecologically sound activities need to be described and experienced as pleasurable, challenging our deep and pervasive equation of pleasure with consumption.

Changes in personal behavior are also necessary, before, during, and after structural changes take place. People may have to give up certain pleasures, such as sleeping late, for others, such as a brisk walk to work. Reconceiving pleasure so that it encompasses environmentally responsible behavior is a vital part of the struggle to create a more just and sustainable society. Sometimes the change will entail not the substitution of pleasures for pleasure but rather the sacrifice of pleasure and convenience for a less comfortable but more sustainable alternative. Bicycle commuting in Florida, for example, is a pleasure in November but a sweaty burden in August. The pleasures and the sacrifices will vary, as different people have different options available to them. All of us, however, can make connections between our personal and local practices and larger structures and work for necessary changes in the latter.

While structural changes are not sufficient to alter all of people's everyday practices, they are a necessary condition. We need institutions and infrastructures that make environmentally responsible choices easier and more desirable—different forms of transportation, of farming, of housing, and of energy production, to name a few. Creating such structures is a formidable challenge, since many institutions in the United States are organized to maximize rather than minimize our negative impact on the natural world. For example, many ecologically destructive agricultural products and processes receive government subsidies, while more sustainable farmers struggle. Environmentally harmful patterns are similarly supported by many regional planning, transportation, and energy policies. In many areas, people lack reasonably convenient and affordable alternatives to high-impact ways of eating, traveling, and living. The rising cost of oil and a related increase in political support for conservation and alternative energy have begun to change these patterns, as seen in rebates at local, state and federal levels for purchasing solar water heaters, energy-efficient appliances and windows, and hybrid cars. The individual actions supported by such subsidies mitigate but do not overcome the impact of these structural factors. For example, people who live in states where most electricity is produced by burning coal have a much higher per-capital impact on global warming than do residents of states where electricity comes from other sources. While individuals and households can certainly conserve energy, they cannot change the way it is produced through their consumption practices. Only political action on a large scale can accomplish that transformation.

Not only structural and material factors but also cultural and ideological ones make it hard to live up to our deepest values. *Habits of the Heart* describes a linguistic and moral impoverishment stemming from the hegemony of our culture's "first language" of utilitarian individualism. Because this first language so powerfully shapes the way we think, even nonindividualistic actions are filtered through the lens of individualism. I witnessed a striking example of this when I asked students in an environmental ethics class if they could think of something they had done for reasons other than self-interest. None of the thirty-five students, many of whom were volunteers and activists, listed a non-self-interested reason for doing good. A number of the students were deeply religious, but none mentioned even the notion that God commanded something as an unselfish motivation for doing good deeds. They described their altruistic practices as motivated by their interests in, for example, self-esteem or good company. "It makes me feel good," they often explained, without connecting that feeling to deeply held, noninstrumental values.

We may be so deeply influenced by the first language of human exceptionalism that we see even our ecocentric inclinations as grounded in some sort of human centeredness. In a society so permeated by assumptions of human exceptionalism and radical individualism, it is very hard to act according to any other values. On those occasions when we do act in nonanthropocentric ways, it is hard to describe our behavior in those terms. This failure to recognize and name actions in terms outside the dominant frameworks of utilitarian individualism and exceptionalism or anthropocentrism shapes our inability to think and act in heterodox ways. This is intimately tied not only to the relations among values, practices, and structures but also to the problem of desire: our culture and institutions educate us to desire ways of living that contradict our efforts to live out moral principles.

Reeducating that desire, like reconceiving pleasure, is crucial. This theme emerged again and again in a gathering of environmental thinkers that Les Thiele and I organized in April 2007. Participants repeatedly pointed to the need to make sustainability seem an essential part not just of the responsible life but also of the "good life." The goal, as philosopher Nathaniel Barrett puts it, is to develop the tastes (as opposed to the will-power) for environmental action. In other words, we might have to reeducate ourselves to desire the pleasures possible in a sustainable way of life. Simply denying ourselves will not work, in the long haul. Some environmental organizations are taking up this challenge explicitly. The Center for a New American Dream (CNAD), for example, proposes the slogan "More fun, less stuff!" CNAD, along with many advocates of "voluntary simplicity," emphasizes what people gain from reducing consumption, rather than what they give up. This notion has been put into practice by the "Compact" in San Francisco, a group of professionals who decided to give up new purchases for an entire year. While the project began with an image of environmental activism as "penitential fasting," as Barrett puts it, the reality for the participants seems to have been quite different. The group's dependence on social networking has greatly enriched their sense of community, and perhaps their quality of life. Having developed a taste for their new lifestyle, some members of the Compact are carrying on for another year.[20]

On a smaller scale, and in my own experience, walking or bicycling to work or shopping at a local farmers' market generates pleasure (and friends and better health) in addition to civic and environmental benefits. These examples suggest that the reeducation of desire along more sustainable lines is in fact possible, and they indicate some possible paths toward the larger cultural, political, and economic transformations that will be necessary. To live in accord with the values we express, we will have to recognize different sorts of pleasure, literally reeducating our desires. Rather than seeing environmentally responsible behavior as a series of sacrifices, a painful altruism, it might better be conceived as part of a satisfying way of life. Ecological practice might mean not the relinquishment of all pleasures but rather the fulfillment of certain underlooked but nonetheless real and profound desires. This suggests that ecological problems will be resolved not by inhibiting immediate gratification, as in the deliberate suppression of self-interest that Kant, Niebuhr, and others define as morality. Rather, we will begin to fix our world by making sustainable practices satisfying, pleasant, and feasible, and at the same time making unsustainable behavior difficult, costly, and unpleasant.

Part of the difficulty of acting on our values, paradoxically, stems from our assumptions about what ethics involve. Sometimes, as Sharon Welch has argued, the root of certain problems lies in "what counts as goodness."[21] People often assume that ethical behavior is separate from ordinary behavior: acting on principle is a relatively rare, usually obvious, change of track in which we set aside our usual priorities and habits in order to act according to an idea or cluster of ideas. Mainstream models of ethics assume that ideas come first. We must know what the good is before we can undertake a good action or seek a good goal. This means that the primary task of ethics is to develop better theoretical models, and that the primary task of ordinary people seeking to live moral lives is to learn about the appropriate values. This idealist logic defines a good action as one done with the right understanding or intentionality, and this understanding must be in place before action is taken. This understanding, further, is abstract and general: love of a universal God or good, not homegrown knowledge rooted in everyday life. We see these assumptions in the fathers of the Western moral tradition. Plato elevated abstract ideals—the essences or forms—above all concrete embodiments. Saint Augustine believed that the will, or what one loves most, determines the city to which one belongs. Steeped in the Augustinian tradition, Martin Luther insisted that belief or faith must precede action, so that justification or salvation can never come through works. With Luther, many other mainstream Protestants insisted that right intentionality and will must be achieved before works can be meaningful or valuable, at least in any ultimate sense. Most notably, the father of modern secular philosophical ethics, Immanuel Kant, took up the same logic. For Kant, intention is what makes a decision ethical or not; and an action done for the wrong reasons cannot be ethical, regardless of its consequences. While Kant removes religious faith from the equation, then, he reiterates the idealist methodology of Augustine and Luther.

Despite their differing foundational assumptions, sources of legitimacy, and social aims, there is agreement among these different approaches that the idea comes prior to the act, chronologically, symbolically, and perhaps ontologically. Thus moral systems need not, and in fact should not, change as a result of their application to any given situation. In many idealist models, including secular ethics emphasizing rights and rules as well as religious moralities based on divine revelation, good moral principles are by definition abstract, unchanging, and universal. Thus, for example, if it is wrong to lie (or take a life, or use drugs, etc.) in any circumstance, then it must be wrong to do so in all circumstances. The fact that few people live up to these rigid standards has led many ethicists to argue that people are morally weak. Reinhold Niebuhr, for example, was scathing about this hope that reason, knowledge, and education could create a moral society. "Even the most rational men," he wrote, "are never quite rational when their own interests are at stake."[22] Niebuhr assumed that (perceived) self-interest would nearly always trump moral behavior. This assumption is grounded on an unexamined opposition between good ideas and everyday life. Ethics is about ideas that have little if anything to do with ordinary behavior, which is largely determined by self-interest, habit, and structural constraint. Morality, in this perspective, is a top-down affair, in which people decide what values they should hold and then try to "apply" them in concrete situations. The fact that this procedure rarely works very well has led many ethicists to assume, like Niebuhr, that people are generally "immoral." It should have led them to question their own definitions of morality and of everyday life. Perhaps, for example, people do not find or create moral values in a vacuum, once and for all.

The idealist logic of these great Western philosophers and theologians has a folk version: "It's the thought that counts." This notion is deeply ingrained in our culture, part of what Gramsci called "common sense" philosophy, the ways that ordinary people make sense of their world and establish concepts of right and wrong that enable them to judge and act.[23] Beyond "it's the thought that counts," we have a host of catch phrases that affirm the moral relevance of intentionality: "I meant well," "Don't look a gift horse in the mouth," and so forth. The equation of good intentions with morality is so deeply ingrained, in fact, that it is hard to bring to the surface, let alone to question.

If we do reflect on these nuggets of everyday philosophy, however, it is not long before a host of everyday examples, large and small, reveal times when "the thought" was not the most important factor. This is true not because our beliefs, intentions, and feelings are unimportant but because they do not lead in any straightforward way to actions that reflect them. As environmental educator David Orr has pointed out, the relationship among ideas, feelings, and actions—"I know," "I care," and "I do"—is not nearly as straightforward as we have assumed.[24] The surveys cited earlier make it clear that concern or care for the environment does not guarantee action on its behalf. Nor does having good information or knowledge, or even good stories. All too often we fail to act on what we know to be right or necessary, or to embody our deepest feelings in appropriate actions.

This poses obvious practical problems, but it also raises a philosophical challenge: Are there other ways of thinking about the relationship between values and practices that can help us out of our current mess? I want to propose a model that upends the usual relationship between values or ideas and practices. In this approach, sometimes practice matters even without right intention, belief, or knowledge behind it. The idea of starting with action, regardless of intention or understanding, has been roundly condemned by mainstream Western ethicists, in both Lutheran and Kantian traditions, as works righteousness, empty ritualism, and the like. The folk version of this approach is captured in the not always approving phrase "fake it 'til you make it."

However, starting with practice has some powerful precedents, including both Marxist dialectical materialism and American pragmatist philosophy, as well as a range of religious traditions. In Christian scriptures, we can look at the letter of James, which proclaimed that "faith without works is dead." (Luther hated that letter.) Roman Catholic theology has elaborated this concept in its emphasis on acts of charity and discipline that might precede proper understanding and faith, and which might contribute to righteousness regardless. This Catholic insight has been elaborated in Latin American liberation theology, according to which theology is a "second step" after engaged practice.[25] As practice changes us and the world, we reflect upon these new experiences, in an ongoing "hermeneutic circle."[26] Real-life experiences and practices constitute the starting point, not the repository, of theory. We do not "apply" already perfected ideas, in this model, but rather we work out ideas in and through work in the world, and practice and ideas mutually critique and transform each other. Another inversion of the theory–practice relationship comes in Buddhism, which suggests that through discipline and practice, for example, meditation, as well as vegetarianism and less "religious" activities, you can develop correct consciousness. In other words, sometimes the right thing to do is the right thing even if you do not fully understand, or appreciate, its rightness. Thus Buddhist novices are enjoined to take up their begging bowls, to sweep paths, to meditate, to act upon wisdom they do not fully understand. Spiritual practices need not be undertaken only after full knowledge is achieved. Enlightenment is, rather, approached precisely in and through such practices. Such religious perspectives offer a helpful counterpoint to the Protestant-influenced idealism that is so pervasive in the West, especially in the United States.

Among Western secular philosophies, one of the most notable exceptions to this idealist logic is pragmatism. As developed by Charles S. Peirce, John Dewey, and other nineteenth- and twentieth-century thinkers, pragmatism rejects the formalism and abstraction of other philosophical models, and particularly the assumption of fixed, prior, absolute, and unchanging moral criteria as the basis for ethics. It also rejects "foundationalist" epistemology, the notion that humans have access to some prior truths, be these moral or intellectual.[27] Pragmatic ethics and epistemologies are interested primarily in the effects of ideas. Philosophical reflection begins with practice, actual human behavior. People's effective values do not stem from abstract principles but rather are habits of a sort, shaped by our social and individual histories and practices. The goal of pragmatist ethics, then, is not to build totalizing theories but rather to develop workable, flexible, yet not completely relativist models of moral action that can guide people in particular situations. Since there is no single, unchanging foundation for knowledge, ethical principles are always partial and subject to change. Thus no given morality can be correct for all, and people with differing moral convictions might work together to achieve shared practical objectives. Pragmatism has been an especially valuable resource for environmental philosophers, among others, who fear that a focus on theoretical purity detracts from collective efforts to address concrete environmental problems.

I share with pragmatists a conviction that theorizing and practice must be considered together, that theorizing should start with actual practices rather than with an ethical framework that is later worked out in particular situations. Also like pragmatists, I am interested in the practical effects of philosophical reflection. However, my goal is not the pragmatist aim of a workable morality that can guide moral behavior. This strikes me, in most cases, as still an effort to apply values to concrete situations (although pragmatists themselves disagree on this issue). I find a more sustained and comprehensive challenge to ethical idealism in philosophical Marxism. This challenge is grounded in Marx's radical rethinking of the relationship between ideas and practice. Ideas are forged and transformed, he argues, in and through human practice, in constant interaction with material conditions. Further, as he added in his eighth thesis on Feuerbach, all theoretical mysteries find resolution in practice.[28] These alternatives challenge the unilinear model of idealism, according to which good ideas precede and give rise to good behavior.

I do not propose to substitute for idealism its mirror image, a simplistic materialism that sees ideas, including moral claims, as emerging from material life. Such an approach cannot account for human (let alone nonhuman) agency. Marx himself roundly rejected crude materialism. His third thesis on Feuerbach insists that even though changed circumstances make changed men, "it is men who change circumstances."[29] The agency and will of concrete individuals is vital to praxis of any sort. As Marx famously asserted in the "Eighteenth Brumaire," people are always making their own history, even though "they do not make it just as they please; they do not make it under circumstances chosen by themselves, but under circumstances directly found, given and transmitted from the past."[30] Values and practices, desires and structures, are always interacting with and transforming each other; to single out one as the dominant or sole factor in any social process reflects a deep failure of understanding.

Research in India conducted by political scientist Arun Agrawal sheds some light on the mutual shaping of environmental values and practices, and especially the way that the latter can help generate the former. In the villages he studied, Agrawal found that gender and caste did not predict much about attitudes to environmental protection. The more important variable was participation in environmental projects: "Ultimately, it is those who are involved in the activities of their forest councils, contributing materially to environmental enforcement, or directly involved in monitoring and enforcement who are more likely to agree with the need to protect forests, to say that forests need to be protected for environmental rather than economic reasons, and to accept some reduction in their own use so as to ensure forest protection." These findings lead Agrawal to challenge "the common presumption that actions follow from beliefs." Instead, he argues, "people often first come to act in response to what they may see as compulsion or as their short-term interest and only then develop beliefs that defend short-term-oriented actions on other grounds as well."[31]

In other words, attitudes and values may follow even practices that have been undertaken without full willingness. Another example of this is school desegregation in the United States, which began with the Supreme Court decision in *Brown v. Board of Education of Topeka* in 1954. The Court's decision that schools could not, in fact, be "separate but equal" sparked massive opposition from many white people and their place-based communities. Military intervention was required to enforce the decision. Had the Court waited until most white southerners approved of integrated schools, my children might attend segregated schools today. As it stands, while school desegregation certainly did not end racism, it has had a significant effect on the lives and values of both white and black southerners. White southerners had to act as though black people were equal, even though most of them did not believe this in their hearts or minds in 1954. They were not acting morally, by Kantian or Lutheran standards. Nonetheless, they acted out better values than they would have without the Supreme Court decision, and their children's attitudes changed. *Brown* generated major shifts in values that probably would not have occurred had institutions and practices not changed first.

Perhaps an environmental *Brown v. Board of Education* could help bring our practices into accord with our expressed values. Less dramatically, local laws and regulations combine with peer pressure and other cultural processes to motivate environmental practices even without "right intention" or full enlightenment. These actions may well generate environmental values as well as positive practical results. A first step might be to seek out more and better encounters with the nonhuman world, to live a life in which not all sources of value, interest, creativity, danger, and affection come from humans. The previous chapter suggested that encounters with nonhuman creatures and places can be transformative, for children and adults alike. As anyone who has lived in another culture or raised a child knows, living differently changes how the world looks and what we value in it. So does meeting another species face to face and confronting the agency of nonhuman others. Different practices lead, in such cases, to different attitudes and values. The influencing is not unidirectional, of course. People's ideas, perspectives, and moral principles do affect their actions, in varying ways and to varying extents, depending on context, actors, and other factors. Beginning to make sense of the mutually transformative interactions between ideas and practices is key to understanding the possibility of changing either.

We cannot understand either moral values or the practices they shape and are shaped by if we oppose ethics to everyday behavior. Rather, we have to uncover and analyze the values present, explicitly or implicitly, in mundane as well as extraordinary practices. This entails a challenge to the common academic and popular assumption that acting morally is both difficult and rare. According to this view, people enact moral values only when consciously acting "on principle," most often when deliberately curbing desire or sacrificing self-interest. In this perspective, a moral action is something like giving someone else the larger piece of pie, voting to raise our own taxes, or risking personal safety for another. People act morally when they consider, as Reinhold Niebuhr puts it, "interests other than their own in determining problems of conduct." Such self-transcendence, Niebuhr believed, was possible only on rare occasions, usually in "personal, intimate, and organic contacts." Ethical attitudes, then, depend upon direct relationships, which become increasingly rare and difficult in modern society due to declines in face-to-face contact and mutual responsibilities—trends that Niebuhr saw already in 1931, when he wrote *Moral Man and Immoral Society*.[32]

I think Niebuhr is right that ethics rest on, or at least are intimately tied to, interpersonal connections and knowledge of others, but not always. This claim raises questions, however, about his assertion that moral behavior requires deliberately setting aside self-interest. If moral commitments are rooted in interpersonal relationships, and if truly ethical behavior occurs most easily and frequently in the context of such relationships, then perhaps moral values do not require conscious self-abnegation but rather emerge spontaneously from interpersonal relationships and encounters. As Niebuhr himself acknowledged, "The failure of even the wisest type of social pedagogy to prompt benevolences as generous as those which a more intimate community naturally evolves, suggests that ethical attitudes are more dependent upon personal, intimate, and organic contacts than social technicians are inclined to assume."[33] This makes sense in light of family life, for example, where people routinely sacrifice their apparent self-interest for those they love.

The fact that people regularly act morally in this sense, and moreover that they do so willingly and spontaneously, even happily, suggests that such behavior does not always feel difficult or onerous. Few people experience care for children or protection of beloved places as sacrifices or even as deliberate choices. Rather, such actions feel natural, even necessary, since they emerge from core aspects of our personal histories and identities. Everyday experiences and relationships engender commitments and loyalties that translate into ethical values: commitments to something larger than our own self-interest.

If values come, at least in part, from good experiences, then in order to have better ethics, we need to have better experiences, or at least to recognize and expand the good experiences that we already have. This reverses the usual ordering of ideas and practices. The first step is not knowledge but action. We act in the world, engage and change it, at the same time as, or even before, we create ethical theories. As environmental philosopher Anthony Weston proposes, "We need to deanthropocentrize the world rather than, first and foremost, to develop and systematize non-anthropocentrism—for world and thought co-evolve. We can only create an appropriate non-anthropocentrism as we begin to build a progressively less anthropocentric world."[34] In such a world, humans are decentered. Humility, fragility, weakness, and dependence constitute not just ecological realities but also social ones. They are the conditions of life for all beings. It is only our illusion of human exceptionalism that makes us think we are entitled to a pass on the hard and painful parts. Further, this sense of entitlement belongs to a small, extraordinarily privileged and protected portion of humanity, historically and culturally. Most people do not labor under the illusion that they are exempt from the ordinary hardships and humilities of life as biological beings. Their lives do not allow for this sort of naïveté or arrogance. Unfortunately, the relatively small collection of people who feel exceptional in this sense have disproportionate power over the natural world as well as over other human beings.

Even privileged people are not all equally privileged. Life experiences, including those shaped by gender, class, race, health, and other factors, have taught and will teach many of us that we are in fact subject to the slings and arrows of nature, other people, and perhaps an indifferent universe. Still, most well-off North Americans and Europeans are comfortable and protected, at least most of the time. The material fact of this privilege undergirds our moral and psychological feeling of being exceptional. We think we are exceptional, and we generalize this illusion to all or most humans, because our own lives are largely exempt from the vulnerabilities that are the common lot of other people, other creatures, plants, and places.

This is true both of our experiences in the natural world and of our social relations. In the latter, in particular, there are traumatic ways to experience fragility and oppressive ways of experiencing dependence. These are parts of the existential and also political conditions of our lives, and some of these politically traumatic and oppressive elements can and should be changed. However, we cannot, and should not, eliminate all dependence, weakness, and vulnerability. We should not because our material privilege and our feelings of exceptionalness have a cost in human and nonhuman terms. The truth of ecological and social interdependence is that our actions affect others, regardless of whether we realize or admit it. The fact that we often do not feel these effects reinforces our illusion of independence and exceptionalism. Again, we distance ourselves by living far away from the effects of our actions and also from the sources of our lives. We do not know where our water comes from or where our garbage goes. We do not know who sews the clothes we wear or picks the lettuce we eat. And we do not know how our actions affect other people, places, and creatures. We believe we are separate because we live as though we were.

It is not that we are really self-sufficient, but rather that we think we are and act on this false assumption. This points to the importance of distinguishing among different kinds and understandings of relationship. "Being in relationship" with another person means many different things, as some feminist critics have pointed out, and some relationships are destructive to one or all parties. Getting married or having children is no guarantee of a happy ending (or beginning or middle). The same is true for "being in nature." Simply getting out in the woods or on the water may not generate a commitment to a particular place or to environmental protection more generally. Robert Thayer raises this question indirectly when he describes a hillside littered with beer cans after a local event.[35] He shrugs off the trash as part of the bioregional subculture of the people who frequent the hills. He is wrong to suggest, however unintentionally, that all "lifeplace cultures" or locally rooted habits are equally admirable. Locally rooted and engaged cultures have been not only ecologically devastating but also racist, violent, and xenophobic. Love of place, like parental love, can help justify negative practices as well as positive ones. This perverse bioregionalism is not helpful for environmentalists or anyone.

On the one hand, time spent in natural settings can nurture ecological awareness and concern, since exposure to green places and nonhuman animals often creates affinities and desire for nature. On the other hand, people often separate such experiences from environmental values, especially in explicitly political form. Many people who engage in outdoor recreation, for example, do not extend their love for a particular place or activity to a broader environmental commitment. Sam Snyder's study of the conflict over the Rodman Dam in north central Florida sheds light on this issue. The dam was built across the Ocklawaha River in 1968 as part of an envisioned cross-Florida barge canal. At the time of construction and since, environmentalists argued strongly against damming the river, which had negative ecological consequences including disruptions to fish and other species. The barge canal project was deauthorized in 1971, and for the decades since then Rodman Dam was set to be decommissioned. However, some local residents, especially those engaged in bass fishing on the reservoir, have argued strongly, and so far successfully, against removing the dam. In the face of powerful ecological arguments in favor of "freeing the Ocklawaha," a strong local subculture wants to retain the dam.

On both sides of the debate, there is strong local participation, as well as education, but this has not yet led to the resolution of tensions and cooperation in place. This poses the question, as Snyder puts it, of how bioregionalists, and environmentalists more generally, should "deal with a situation where two local parties believe they are doing the best for the community."

The only long-term solution, he suggests, must entailing healing "the community and the ecosystem at the same time." To achieve both the necessary social healing and required ecological restoration, Snyder proposes that deepening people's relationship to the river—not the reservoir—might be crucial. Time on the reservoir, in sum, does not lead to the same kind of environmental commitment as time on the river. [36]

In the right context, some forms of participation in nature can help generate moral frameworks. One good example is ecological restoration. Restoration, argues Bill Jordan, does not just reflect or express already-held values but in fact is a work of value creation.[37] This is a collective, not a private, process. In restoration we participate in and create community both among humans and between humans and nonhuman nature. For Jordan, ecological restoration is a ritual process, through which we clarify meanings and articulate and sometimes resolve conflicts. In and through the practice of ecological restoration we redefine the value of nonhuman nature and clarify our own role in it.[38] If we want to experience communion we have to create it in and through our practices. We need not to identify more credible and constructive understandings of human nature but to create conditions in which we experience the interdependence, fragility, and humility taught by evolution and ecology and by green religions and ecocentric philosophies. This can be done not in theory but only in and through practice, by opening ourselves to the nonhuman world. In and through those encounters, we may learn to desire something that is better for both people and the planet.

6

TOWARD AN IMMANENTLY UTOPIAN POLITICAL ETHIC

NOT YET

"Life is hard" asserts the title of Roger Lancaster's ethnography of every-day life in Nicaragua during the 1980s. He takes the phrase from a letter that a Nicaraguan man living in the United States has written, after six years of silence, to the family he abandoned. Life is hard in particular ways for the absent father and husband, perhaps harder still for the loved ones he left behind, and hard in other particular ways for other people. Life is also existentially hard for every person, maybe every living creature, at least in certain moments and circumstances. It is more difficult still for people without goods such as health, material resources, supportive com-munities, or political power. In part because of this, Lancaster writes, to assert that "life is hard" represents "the simplest possible strategy for link-ing the particular to the general, the personal to the social."[1] It makes manifest the connections between our personal challenges and structural problems.

We also link the particular and the general, the personal and the social, when we assert that "life is good." Our private joys, no less than our private miseries, are connected to larger groups, structures, and patterns. I think this is what Tillich meant when he wrote that "the Kingdom of God does not come in one dramatic event sometime in the future. It is coming here and now in every act of love, in every manifestation of truth, in every moment of joy, in every experience of the holy. . . . The hope of mankind lies in the here and now whenever the eternal appears in time and history."[2] The problem is how to recognize the eternal in history, knowing what is true and holy. If we fail to recognize the manifestations of truth in our midst we may miss the subtle signs of an immanent utopia. We may risk even more, however, if we act in absolutist or totalitarian fashion on the basis of glimpsing (we think) something true or eternal.

We might aim to recognize not truth or eternity but rather moments of joy and acts of love—a task that can be just as difficult but perhaps not quite so dangerous. It is made harder by the fact that joy and love unfold in circumstances not of our own choosing, taking forms we do not control and may not even recognize. What Habermas calls "systemic pressures" shape the ways that people relate to their friends and families and to nonhuman nature. Many potential sources of joy and love in everyday life are distorted in both reality and presentation. Experiences and perceptions of family life, for example, are shaped by economic processes and metaphors. Arlie Hochschild found many workers do not take advantage of "family-friendly" policies or fight when work encroaches on personal time, at least in part because of the devaluation of family life. "The more women and men do what they do in exchange for money and the more their work in the public realm is valued or honored, the more, almost by definition, private life is devalued and its boundaries shrink," she writes. As a result, "the valued realm of work is registering its gains in part by incorporating the best aspects of home. The devalued realm, the home, is meanwhile taking on what were once considered the most alienating attributes of work."[3] Home is not a haven, in these circumstances, because it is alienating, demanding, rushed, its burdens far outweighing the obvious benefits.

I am easily persuaded by Hochschild's description of family life—it resembles my own all too often, with harried mornings and exhausting evenings, and relatively little "quality time" in between to savor pleasant activities with people I love. I admit that my job intrudes into my home, as when I need to finish grading exams and my children want to take a walk or play a game after dinner. Even more, perhaps, my family life is affected by a host of structural factors over which I have little control, including the public school system, local planning decisions made decades ago, even national and international food systems. Aware of these factors, I try to resist whenever possible. For example, by living close to work and schools, my husband and I spend less time commuting. By shopping at the farmers' market and establishing relationships with local growers, we make the necessary task of getting groceries more enjoyable and meaningful. However, our resistance is limited if we do not address the underlying structural factors themselves.

I am less persuaded by Hochschild's argument that work has taken on the "best aspects" of home life. She points out that some workplaces now have social events, recreational activities, gyms and beauty salons on site, and so forth. However, I wonder if these innovations really replace the relationships and experiences that suffer because of the way work (and our whole economy) is structured. It is more likely, I think, that the substitutes are lacking, but that our desires are educated to accept them. Just as lifestyle enclaves replace real communities, according to the authors of *Habits of the Heart*, voluntaristic, contractual connections may come to replace more demanding, noninstrumental relationships. And we suffer a social amnesia that parallels "environmental amnesia" by dulling our collective recollection of nonutilitarian relationships and communities.

The colonization of the home and other lifeworlds intensifies the disjuncture between what people say they value (friends, family, time in nature, self-realization in creative pursuits), on the one hand, and what people actually do with their time (earn money, usually in unsatisfying jobs, and spend it on well-advertised consumer items), on the other. For example, Americans regularly say their families are their most important priorities, according to national polls in which belief in "the family" is second only to belief in God. Echoing this trend, the working parents that Hochschild interviewed insisted that their families are their top priorities and lament the shortage of time together. Very few of them, however, organize their lives in ways that really put families first, even when this is economically feasible and when their employers offer programs that would facilitate more flexible work schedules. As Hochschild notes, practices embodying parents' expressed commitment to family, "such as sharing breakfast and dinner," continue to decline.[4] She describes parents, especially fathers, who owned leisure-time equipment such as boats, cameras, skis, tents, and guitars that they "bought with wages that took time to earn" but had no time to use. Such tools, she writes, "seemed to hold out the promise of another self, a self he would be 'if only I had time.' . . . a magical substitute for time, a talisman."[5] She describes these families as in a sense two households: the rushed family they actually are and the relaxed family they imagine they could be, if only they had time.

This duality in particular households reflects deep cultural contradictions. "The goods extolled by society," as British theorists Martin Ryle and Kate Soper point out, "are not those by which it is ruled. It teaches altruism, but depends on egoism, approves social responsibility but rewards financial self-interest, advances goals of critical autonomy and all-round personal development while endorsing the system that condemns the majority to long hours of dull and undemanding labour."[6] The gap between what people say they value and the practical choices they make about how to spend their time, energy, and money can be explained in part by the structural obstacles to "walking the talk." For parents, these include the demands for long work hours, absence of family-leave policies, and lack of affordable housing close to jobs; for environmentalists, the ways that regional planning and many social institutions, along with advertising, reinforce excessive consumption and waste. Many people experience the paradox that Marx described: "The less you are, the more you have."[7] Our peculiar kind of dystopia may be to live in a society that undermines and even destroys what we say we most value.

Our hope of escaping this dystopian reality may lie in the possibility of expanding or reproducing the occasions when we do live what we value. First we have to find these values and understand what makes them possible and also what blocks them. Then we have to try to apply them in wider frames of reference. All this requires that we learn to educate our desires in politically effective ways. We need to learn how to use the values embodied in our most mundane and intimate practices to serve as resources for constructing a more just, sustainable, and humane society. This task points not only toward a social ethic with a specific content but also toward a theory about how moral systems are developed and applied—a metaethic. The new content and new methodology for ethics are linked. Rather than a new content addressed by means of established theoretical frameworks, new themes and conclusions emerge as a consequence of a different way of seeing and being in the world. The idealist logic that is common to mainstream ethics, as discussed in the previous chapter, assumes a top-down methodology. It starts with a theory of the good and assumes that getting the theory right will lead to right behavior.

In contrast, my goal is to uncover and reflect upon the values embodied in particular practices. I seek, as Mennonite theologian John Howard Yoder puts it, not "a beautiful vision to impose from above," but rather "critical resources to apply from below."[8] What happens to the content of ethics—its claims about what is good and what people should do—if we start with everyday life? What moral priorities and assumptions actually shape the ways people understand and act in the world? Uncovering the effective, albeit often unrecognized, ethical values embedded in mundane activities and social structures is the first step for a practice-based ethic, the "seeing" that must precede moral judgment and political action.

The values we uncover may not be the values we ultimately affirm. Many implicit ethics are destructive, contradictory to human and natural well-being and often to the values we say we hold dearest. There is truth in Hume's critique of the naturalistic fallacy, insofar as naturalism derives "ought" from "is" in a simple, linear way, as though whatever is, is good. It would be equally false, however, to assume that "ought" should and can be completely divorced from "is." Without necessarily validating all of our operative moralities, we have to perceive and acknowledge them before any further analysis or action can take place. The practice-based ethic that I aim to develop is not purely naturalistic, although it takes up certain naturalistic assumptions, especially the notion that we can learn about important goods by understanding what is really happening. To avoid simply sanctifying the status quo, a naturalistic ethic must have a standard outside the status quo by which it can judge. Some environmental ethicists find this standard in ecological and evolutionary processes. Holmes Rolston contends that "what *is* in nature is taken as a criterion for what *ought to be* when culture overtakes nature."[9] Along similar lines, Wes Jackson and Wendell Berry direct us to ask "what does nature allow us to do here?" as a basic moral question. We must first understand, quite literally, the lay of the land, the history and characters that precede our appearance on the scene, before we can hope to identify ethically correct ways of acting in any given situation.

A more socially oriented naturalism turns not to nonhuman nature but to humanness itself as the standard for moral and political judgment. Marx's concept of alienation, for example, assumes an understanding of human nature in some nonalienated form, sometimes described in relation to the "species being" from which people are estranged in the course of labor in a capitalist system.[10] Pushing Marx further, Tillich insists that "every valid ethical commandment is an expression of man's essential relation to himself, to others, and to the universe."[11] Humans and the larger world have a nature that points toward an ethical standard. Just as the good is related to something intrinsic to human nature, so evil is a distortion of natural relations, as when humans create social structures that deny essential aspects of human nature. The various forms of alienation produced in and through the organization of labor under capitalism provide the best example, especially in the tension that capitalism creates between "the meaning of life and the meaning of work."[12]

Tillich reads Marx's concept of alienation theologically, equating alienation and sin, which he defines as the separation of things that should be united. "To be in the state of sin is to be in the state of separation," in three senses: This separation is threefold: separation among individuals, of individual from self, and of all people from ground of being. "We know we are estranged from something to which we really belong, and with which we *should* be united."[13] The effort to reunite what has been separated is ethical, for Tillich. It entails love, which is the drive to reunion, and justice, which "is the form in which and through which love performs its work."[14] Justice is never an abstract principle standing over human existence but always takes concrete forms in that existence: "*this* justice for *this* time and in *this* social situation."[15] Thus moral concepts such as justice, or even love, are never abstract or timeless; they are always embodied in concrete, unavoidably political realities. Ethics starts, then, with "the theological insight . . . that man lives on earth and not in heaven."[16] We cannot understand good or evil without starting on Earth as well.

When we start on Earth we find, as Marx famously asserted, that "men make their own history, but they do not make it just as they please; they do not make it under circumstances chosen by themselves, but under circumstances directly found, given and transmitted from the past."[17] People have infinite potential for creativity, joy, and love, among other things, but this potential can be realized only in concrete conditions affected by historical forces large and small. This points to the need for a social ethic that begins with everyday life as a source of goods and goals. It does not end here, but it must start with concrete relationships and practices. Along these lines, feminist philosopher Sara Ruddick proposes a "practicalist" ethic that aims to bring the ethical possibilities of family life into explicit moral and political debate. Exploring what actually happens in mother–child relationships, she argues, helps to identify the kinds of reasoning—including moral reasoning—associated with maternal practice or discipline. This is an example of her more general practicalist conception of reason as a specific kind of thinking that arises out of distinctive practices, be these scientific, religious, or maternal.[18] Ruddick identifies key goals of mothering, and the values associated with them, as the basis for a political ethic of mothering—one that, she contends, favors nurture over conflict. Beyond the specifics of her maternal ethic, Ruddick hints at a larger model for political ethics, one that begins with intimate relationships and daily practice.

There are some obvious dangers in attempting to extend moral assumptions and demands from private life into the public sphere. Some principles are right for one kind of activity or relationship, while other principles work in other spheres. Just as we cannot expect everyone else to follow our religion, we cannot expect that the same principles and values will hold at work and at home, or in the neighborhood and also in national politics. I can avoid eating certain foods or reading certain books, and I can even keep these from my children (up to a point), but I cannot impose the same strictures on my colleagues at work. A practice-based ethic cannot ask individuals to live by a single morality in all activities nor can it impose one person's or group's morality on all others. What a practice-based ethic can do is call into question our common and generally unreflective assumption that some of our best values must be limited to a very few, apparently shrinking, practices and realms of our lives. We are unselfish with our children, cutthroat in the office; we listen carefully to our friends' stories and explanations but tune out political debates; we take time to clean and beautify our own living spaces but despoil the world outside; and so forth. These separations often have the effect of relegating our better values and selves to close personal relations, while public lives—work, politics, the market—are run on the basis of compromise and utility. I ask here whether our relations and actions in our personal lives adhere, at least sometimes, to values that might also be good and worth striving for in political and public life.

This is a charged question, with no clear answers even for those most interested in the moral dimensions of private relationships. Even feminist care ethicists are ambivalent about the possibilities of extension into the public sphere. "We cannot love everyone," as Nel Noddings points out. "We cannot even care for everyone, and we do not need to love in order to care for." What is left, as an extension of care from private to public, is what Noddings terms "caring about," which she dismisses as "too easy."[19] Caring about is too easy because it does not entail the mutual commitment of direct personal relationships ("caring for"). Caring about thus strikes Noddings as a morally suspect sort of benign neglect, along the lines of donating money to help starving children without taking on the more demanding and important task of caring for those with whom we are in direct relationship. Expanding the private value of care into the public sphere, in this perspective, cheapens caring for. The kind of caring we practice in close personal relationships cannot be extended to larger and more distant relationships without suffering fatal changes. We face a dilemma, as Paul Ginsborg describes: "We would like to connect our everyday lives and our individual actions to making the world a better place to live in—even a possible place to live in—but we do not know how."[20]

We know that our everyday lives are connected to the larger world, but this connection is complex, twisting, often confusing and obscure. We have to look for and analyze multistranded ways to connect the caring practiced in personal relationships to public concerns. Concern for others' well-being in the absence of reciprocal personal relationships might not always be a substitute for or avoidance of more personal kinds of care. Caring about and caring for may not be mutually exclusive, in other words, but rather complementary and sometimes overlapping: more like Midgley's flower petals than a set of hierarchical, all-or-nothing choices. Caring about may thus provide, as Noddings has recently proposed, a link "between caring and justice," a way to bring the noninstrumental concern that is realized most fully, but not only, in close interpersonal relationships to social groups and institutions. Although care "starts at home," in other words, it may not be permanently stuck there.[21] In revising her narrower understanding of caring, Noddings points to the possibility of moving beyond a Niebuhrian dichotomy between the ethics of personal life and the ethics of the public sphere. Perhaps the reality of "moral man" has something, after all, to do with our hope for a more moral society.

I find this possibility extremely promising—it lies at the heart of this book. It raises, however, a host of urgent and difficult questions. Most important is the issue of the specific mechanisms, relationships, and practices that link the values of home to the public sphere. In very specific terms, how might our deepest attachments shape our political actions? It is true, as Raymond Williams asserts, that "we begin to think where we live."[22] From this starting point, however, a thousand possible paths depart. The ones we choose, in circumstances never wholly of our own choosing, will determine how we continue to think and to act, even if we never leave our home places entirely behind.

Not all the relationships, values, and ways of thinking nurtured at home are healthy for the people directly involved or for the larger society. Domestic life is not always a school for love—it can be a school for intolerance, selfishness, and hatred as well. Deep personal bonds exclude more than they include, which is one reason they are not easily translated to larger realms. We have to turn a critical eye on the negative as well as positive features of caring for. We need to see the commitments of home—what Williams calls "militant particularisms"—in relation to the concerns of other people, creatures, and places.[23] Only then can we identify the patterns that connect our joys and hardships to those of other people and other places. These larger patterns are the key to an effective political ethic. They help us avoid the pitfalls of a movement that Williams describes: "because it had begun as local and affirmative, assuming an unproblematic extension from its own local and community experience to a much more general movement, it was always insufficiently aware of the quite systematic obstacles which stood in the way."[24] Only if we identify larger patterns, including economic and political structures as well as patterns of feeling and value, can we recognize and begin to shift the obstacles to social change.

Similarly, beginning with actual practice cannot mean just identifying and then legitimizing whatever people are actually doing, whatever values are currently operative. If we simply meet people where they are, as Wes Jackson points out, we will meet them "at Wal-Mart, where things are cheap and don't last."[25] The education of desire should not stop with the identification of people's desires but must also stir people up "not to be contented with a little," in the words of nineteenth-century English socialist utopian William Morris. The task that Morris proposed is "to help people to find out their wants, to encourage them to want more, to challenge them to want differently, and to envisage a society of the future in which people, freed at last of necessity, might choose between different wants."[26]

In the kind of society that Morris envisioned, people need to be able to envision better alternatives and have access to better choices. This lies at the heart of the education of desire: it requires that we identify something better and also that we try to expand this good. At issue is not just the connection between the personal and the political or between small and large scales, but also about the connections between ethical ideas and practices and how they mutually shape and depend on each other, and how values guide and are embedded in actions at all levels. We need to pull these out, understand them, clarify them, and make them explicit. We must explore how to build on personal and local experiences of a positive "already" in order to transform them into structural and collective dimensions to build different kinds of societies. If our experiences of relationality, in other words, give us a glimpse of another world, another, better way of living and being, how do we move beyond this intimacy to structural change? Unless and until we enact these changes, we are left with a dualism between the possibility of being good, or happy, in private and being much less in public. This encourages more people to retreat into private satisfactions rather than pushing for larger changes.

The possibility of such a retreat is a danger Marx recognized in one of his most famous and perhaps least understood passages: "*Religious* suffering is at the same time an *expression* of real suffering and a *protest* against real suffering. Religion is the sigh of the oppressed creature, the sentiment of a heartless world, and the soul of soulless conditions. It is the *opium* of the people." Marx's point is not that religion is bad in itself but rather that it is a symptom and an expression of bad conditions. Ending suffering requires attention to the material and social conditions that give rise to it. Therefore, he continues, "the abolition of religion as the illusory happiness of men, is a demand for their *real* happiness. The call to abandon their illusions about their condition is a *call to abandon a condition which requires illusions.* The criticism of religion is, therefore, *the embryonic criticism of this vale of tears* of which religion is the halo."[27] Theoretical changes are useless by themselves. Giving up the comfort of religion will not, by itself, end the need for comfort. Expressing environmental values will not stop global warming. Feeling love for our children will not make the world, or even our neighborhood, a better place to be a child. We cannot ask people to do good in a bad system, and simply expressing good values will not change a bad system. More specifically, for Marx, if the modes of production in a capitalist society encourage, even require, people to be alienated from and compete with each other, among other things, moral exhortations to benevolence are meaningless. If our relations to nature are anthropocentric and utilitarian, exhortations to ecocentrism are useless, or worse.

Starting with practice redefines the task of ethics. For a start, ethicists should aim to help people relate morally to each other and to nature. Simply telling them to do better focuses on symptoms while avoiding the underlying causes of immoral ways of acting and relating. Ethics must go to the root, recognizing and changing the conditions that prevent the embodiment of love and the protection of life. As Marx wrote, "It is the task of history . . . once the other-world of truth has vanished, to establish the truth of this world."[28] It is *our* task, perhaps, to establish the truth of interdependence, vulnerability, and humility: not to talk about this truth but to establish it. This task has to begin not in a single, one-step, top-down solution but rather in a range of beginnings, a host of reopenings.[29]

Friendship, nature, and children might all have the capacity to serve as "the soul of soulless conditions." They can provide private pleasures that encourage the indefinite postponement of demands for lasting and collective happiness. The heart of my argument in this book, however, is that personal joys need not simply anesthetize us. Time spent with loved ones or in nature may entail not just a retreat from the vale of tears that is real life but also, as Marx saw, a protest against the suffering it causes. Such pleasures may also provide glimpses of a world that can be, the beginning of social change insofar as they establish a different truth, however small and transient. The question is how these moments of grace can become politically useful. They do so, I argue, by educating our desires—teaching us not to be contented with a little, as Morris exhorted. Our discontent and our educated desires must then be educated again, into effective action.

This task requires that we not only uncover the good and educate desire but also make it possible, structurally, to be good. If the ground of ethics is practice and experience in the world, then in order to construct a new ethic we must transform the world. This suggests a certain ambivalence regarding timing: do we try to change the practical world first or at the same time as we try to change ideas? While there will never be perfect synchronization, on the whole, the changes have to be occurring simultaneously and dialogically. "World and thought co-evolve," as Anthony Weston puts it.[30] There is no set linear or chronological relationship between world and thought. Conditions of life make certain narratives, worldviews, and values possible, but these forms of thought and discourse also shape the world, in a mutual, dialectical transformation of idea and practice. This transformation is open-ended, and we are not ultimately in control—which is part of the moral message of starting with practice. A practice-based ethic, socially and ecologically grounded, necessarily sees the future as open. We start by doing, and, in the words of the Spanish poet Antonio Machado, "the road is made by walking."[31] Not materialism but idealism turns out to be reductive, insofar as the latter cannot imagine an outcome not foretold by its theory. As we begin with practical work in the world, the possibilities for new ethics will emerge.

This calls to mind Marx's eleventh thesis on Feuerbach: "The philosophers have only interpreted the world. The task, however, is to change it."[32] Marx mostly dismissed ethics, at least as usually done in his time and place, because he believed that moralizing would alter nothing important. Values and theories would change, he contended, only when social structures and relations of power changed. This was not a simple dismissal of ideas as mere "superstructure" emerging directly from "real" structures. Marx recognized that the connections between theories and practices were always mutually dependent. As his third thesis on Feuerbach asserts, "The materialist doctrine that men are products of circumstances and upbringing, and that, therefore, changed men are products of other circumstances and changed upbringing, forgets that it is men who change circumstances and that it is essential to educate the educator himself. . . . The coincidence of the changing of circumstances and of human activity can be conceived and rationally understood only as revolutionising practice."[33] In this revolutionising practice, world and thought coevolve. The challenge, of course, is discovering and systematizing the practice that we need here and now.

SEEING ALTERNATIVES

An ethic based on the goods that people live out in their most meaningful and joyful experiences is inherently revolutionary because it challenges dominant ideas and structures. We begin to make this challenge explicit as we construct an ethic based on the values we enact in our most meaningful encounters with other people and with nonhuman nature. We live by a nonutilitarian ethic when we set aside contractual demands and exchange value in favor of mutuality and the pursuit of larger goals. We live by a collective ethic when we experience ourselves not as voluntaristic, self-sufficient monads but as social creatures enmeshed in and joyfully dependent upon a web of relationships and practices over which we do not have ultimate control. The fact that these appear impossible on a larger level suggests the need for sweeping reflection and transformation, if such everyday pleasures are not to remain out of reach.

This reflection must begin by seeing our private pleasures and private suffering as part of larger patterns. Only when individuals view themselves as parts of patterns and connect their motivations and actions to those of others can they recognize that their conditions are heartless, while valuing the comfort and also the education offered by the "heart."[34] This requires balancing involvement and detachment in relation to our personal and local commitments, appreciating the pleasure and comfort they provide while also understanding their connections to much larger patterns and structures. Our militant particularisms can be powerful motivators of human solidarity and political change, for we are most passionate and engaged close to home. However, our particular bonds to places and to individual people and creatures must be connected systematically and rigorously to other issues, so that we understand the larger structures and processes that shape not just our lives but the lives of the human and nonhuman others in our midst.[35] The system, as Williams writes, "for all its local variety, is everywhere recognizable. But the practice of fighting against it has always been entered into, or sometimes deflected, by these other kinds of more particular bonds."[36] We cannot eliminate the tension among different levels of commitment, but we can aim to make this tension productive of social change rather than private retreat. If our particular bonds to people, animals, and places help us connect private and public goods, then we enter into the fight that Williams describes, against a system that is almost universally exploitative.

Our particular bonds provide not only entryways but also concrete examples for the gradual construction of a practice-based ethic, for an approach to moral thinking that begins not with abstractions but with actual experience. This approach does not focus on the values that philosophers elaborate, that religious bodies dictate, or even that ordinary people profess. Instead, it asks about the values that people enact and specifically about the ways that people live by an ethic opposed to excessive individualism, civic disengagement, privatism, and self-interest. Such challenges occur, sometimes, in interracial marriages, in friendships that cross lines of political ideology and sexual orientation, and in many other examples of interpersonal relationships in which adults are able to transcend, resist, or even just ignore their society's first language and the structures and institutions that reinforce it.

We cannot preserve and strengthen what we value—time with our friends and families, nonhuman nature, neighborly communities—unless social conditions make it possible. For work–family issues, the necessary conditions include men who are willing to share housework, communities that value work in home, and policy makers who demand family-friendly reforms. Achieving such major changes even in this one area seems overwhelming, but many European, especially Scandinavian, societies have already achieved most of these conditions. They have managed to combine economic success with long vacations, thirty-five-hour workweeks, livable cities, and child-friendly labor policies. In global comparative studies, Finland, Norway, and Sweden consistently rank highest in both quality of life and environmental sustainability. They combine high life expectancies, low infant and maternal mortality, low rates of employment and poverty, and high rates of education with low levels of air and water pollution and of greenhouse gas emissions. This success is due in part to abundant natural resources and relatively low population densities, but it may owe more to careful planning, government support for mass transit, highly efficient appliances and buildings, and sustainable practices in national industries, especially agriculture, fishing, and forestry.[37] Economic and environmental success also rests on a strong commitment to a common good. Opinion polls in Norway, for example, show many people oppose tax cuts that favor the rich and want more investment in education, hospitals, and care for the elderly.[38] Although other countries cannot simply imitate Scandinavia and achieve the same results, the ability to live well without either overconsuming or creating large disenfranchised groups is not an unrepeatable miracle but rather the result of human decisions to embody shared values.

Another example exists in the North American heartland. The Old Order Amish represent one of the most recognizable alternatives to modern life, a challenge worth taking seriously. The Amish are Anabaptists, heirs to the Radical Reformation stream within Christianity which has insisted that believers follow a single morality in public and private lives. To live as true disciples, the Amish and other Old Order Anabaptists practice a strict separation from the outside world, living in small communities in which all aspects of everyday life reinforce their moral and religious values. This is the reason behind such well-known characteristics of Amish settlements as horse and buggy transportation, use of horses and mules in field work, plain dress, worship in homes, private schooling, rejection of electricity from public utility lines, and prohibition of ownership of televisions and computers.[39] All these markers of difference are important as symbols and vehicles of the distinctive Amish vision of the good life. This life is a collective undertaking by a community of disciples who seek to embody, in collective fashion, the values and characteristics of the reign of God.

While they are human, fallible, and far from perfect, the Amish show the possibility of living collectively by values that counter mainstream culture in almost every respect. These values, and the practices and histories in which they are embedded, generate and nurture a radically different notion of pleasure and happiness from that found in mainstream U.S. society. Amish people define success, and pursue happiness, in homely settings.

They aim, as one scholar puts it, for "the ability to provide food, clothing and shelter for a large family, sufficient profitability to service debt and taxes on the land and an excess to help others in time of need, including economic assistance for the next generation."[40] Other primary goals include having neighbors who farm well, living amidst a supportive, like-minded community, and, especially, raising children in the tradition. These aims and pleasures come together in agricultural practices, as Amish farmers in Illinois told interviewers who asked about the rewards of farming: "First and foremost is the relaxation of being your own boss. . . . Sometimes you can take a day off if you feel like it. The change in seasons give change to your life. In a factory [you have] the same thing day after day. . . . You can come and go as you like to. . . . We can take a day off if we want to for funerals, weddings. You don't have to ask the boss. You can go to help your neighbor . . . [or] spend time with your family."[41] These noninstrumental goods give more lasting pleasure than whatever convenience or money might be gained in a different way of life.

We cannot all live like the Amish, any more than we can all live like Scandinavians. However, we should not dismiss the experiences of either as irrelevant to our lives. What is most relevant might be the way these experiences narrow the gap between aspiration and reality: people's desires are in line with their lives, not because they expect little but because their educated desires have pushed them to create societies in line with their most important values. This is especially clear in the case of the Amish, who have carefully organized their social institutions in order to make possible the life they desire. "The Amish dream," as one scholar puts it, "is attainable for a much higher proportion of its dreamers than is the American dream."[42] Not only do very few people achieve the "American dream" of limitless wealth and consumption, but even when it is attained, affluence rarely "buys happiness," as even its pursuers admit. The mainstream dream also creates all sorts of unhappiness, through excessive consumption of natural resources and the exploitation of poorly paid and treated workers in the United States or overseas, who produce and sell what is consumed. To change this dream, we must reeducate our desires at home, at church (mosque, temple), at school, and at work, through a host of institutions, relationships, and practices that can connect individual values to those of the larger community.

In any society, people's desires are educated in multiple ways and places, and this education mediates the relationship among different spheres and scales of our lives. Very often, however, our desires are educated not to connect but to divide the values of different parts of our lives. This division, while necessary and even salutary in certain cases, all too often diminishes the quality of our social institutions and ultimately, thus, of our personal lives. Some of the values that prevail in our personal lives should, I argue, be extended to larger spheres, in particular relationality, noninstrumental care, and open-endedness.

EMBEDDED RELATIONALITY

The first and perhaps most important value we can learn from our everyday utopias is relationality or community. We are social animals, and in our best moments we do not claim a largely illusory self-sufficiency but rather acknowledge and celebrate our mutual dependence, the ways that our selves are constituted in and through relationships with others. This is crucial to the "already" we experience in friendships, marriage, and childrearing, relations between loving adults and between loving parents and children, at their best. In family life, at least in the best moments, we acknowledge that we can understand and do right by individuals only when we take into account the web of relationships in which they exist. When parenting, we frequently restrict individual rights for the good of others or of the whole. I do not hesitate, and few parents would hesitate, to tell children not to eat all the peaches, keep others awake with loud games, or leave a mess in the communal bathroom. We point easily to larger goods that transcend the self-interest of particular individuals. In its utopian manifestations, this good is experienced not as deprivation but as self-realization, a potentially transcendent experience of being part of a larger whole.

The community we value involves not only other people but also nonhuman others. We are, after all, not only social but also natural beings, and the nonhuman world presents another possible and perhaps necessary site for utopian glimpses. In nature, we experience ourselves as social animals in concrete relations with others, dependent on other creatures and processes for survival as well as pleasure. We also feel ourselves to be part of these larger processes. Richard Louv quotes a young woman who took to the woods after her father died when she was nine: "I really believe that there is something about nature—that when you are in it, it makes you realize that there are far larger things at work than yourself. This helps to put problems in perspective. And it is the only place where the issues facing me do not need immediate attention or resolution. Being in nature can be a way to escape without fully leaving the world."[43] Recognizing ourselves as part of larger communities and processes, natural and social, is a form of transcendence that generates both humility and hope.

The problem, of course, is how to translate this feeling into effective practice. We need to make nature and domestic life into not just havens but sources of protest, criticism, and energy for political struggles. We do so, as I have argued, by making connections and seeing patterns, which means also seeing structures in everyday life. Political and economic institutions, as well "structures of feeling," enable and constrain our most mundane experiences and intimate relationships. Transforming those structures in order to defeat "the system of meanings and values which a capitalist society has generated" and in the process reeducate our desires is an open-ended process, what Williams calls the "long revolution."[44] We will not finish this revolution, but insofar as we start it we will begin embodying the immanent utopias of everyday life.

NONINSTRUMENTAL CARE

In these utopias, we set aside exchange value and contractual duties. In parenting, in the family, in the natural world, we let what Wendell Berry calls the "sympathetic mind" determine our attitudes and actions, rather than the cost–benefit rationality that dominates other areas of our lives, especially work and the public sphere. Our experiences in these spheres provide lived counterexamples and challenges to the exchange value of the dominant world. We are valued and we value others intrinsically. As Aelred puts it, we offer love "from the dignity of its own nature and the feelings of the human heart, so that its fruition and reward is nothing other than itself."[45] We experience a similar kind of love in parenting, in encounters with nature and animals, and in a few other sorts of experiences. In these encounters we find, in Aelred's words, "a foretaste of blessedness thus to love and thus to be loved; thus to help and thus to be helped."[46] It is a foretaste not just of blessedness but of a social reality that we might be able to expand on Earth.

Sometimes we characterize noninstrumental goods as play, exemplified in the joy that children often find in encounters with nature, intimate friendships, and flights of imagination. Play goes deeper than a chance to shrug off the pressures of everyday life and work. Especially in natural places, play helps both children and adults perceive, experience, and cultivate a love of nature, as well as imagination, cooperation, and a host of other qualities.[47] In play, as Donna Haraway explains, we experience joy, which is not known rationally or used instrumentally, but tasted. This joy is something like "an eternal present or suspension of time, a high of 'getting it' together in action." It is not the same as fun. It entails, as Haraway puts it, different bodies coming together and "getting it," "which makes each partner more than one but less than two."[48] Such play is possible not only with other people but also with nonhuman animals, as in the agility trials in which Haraway competes with her Australian shepherd, Cayenne. Such play not only opens up the possibility of mutual response but puts it front and center, by leading us into a qualitatively different world in which what matters is engaging another without concern for costs and benefits or time constraints.

It is telling that our examples of play are often with children or nonhuman animals, who have little interest in the abstract and instrumental values of exchange and use. Marx argued that without money, one can get love only in return for love. The mythical yet useful figure that Haraway calls the "zoological Marx" would add that with animals, one can get love only in return for love. They have no use for abstract or utilitarian measures, and thus no way to distort or alienate our most basic relationships.[49] They are interested, instead, only in "encounter value."[50] Unlike use value and exchange value, encounter value is noninstrumental; it finds worth not in utility but in measures of companionship, joy, and love. These qualities are, at least for me, more readily apparent in relations with nonhuman animals, whose desires are not colonized by the system as are those of even quite young children. This does not mean that nonhuman animals are not shaped by human social, political, and economic institutions, or that they are confined "to the supposedly ahistorical order of nature," as Haraway writes. When nonhuman and human animals engage each other, however, encounter value comes to the fore, as does the social nature of humanness. We experience, in the flesh, the ways that relations constitute humans and other creatures: "actual encounters are what make beings."[51] Not all our encounters are noninstrumental, but those that are often take the shape of play. Play in this sense helps make possible utopian moments that can serve as critical grounds for evaluating and perhaps transforming the aspects of our lives that are dominated by utility and calculation.

OPEN-ENDEDNESS

Utopian experiences are also characterized by openness. In our best interactions with loved ones and nonhuman nature, we are not driven by means–ends calculations. We can let the future unfold, acknowledging our lack of final control over its direction. True relationality, recognition of our social nature, requires this relinquishment of control. When we admit that our identities are constituted in relationship with others, we also recognize that we are not entirely autonomous agents, able to forge our own destinies. The outcome of an afternoon in the woods or a conversation with a child is not (at least not solely) in our hands. The "not yet" suggests a condition of permanent expectation, in which we need to continue "seriously hoping for" what we know is worth hoping for, without knowing exactly what will happen. Encounters with other beings determine us, in a mutual, fluid exchange. We are only part of something larger if its scope is indeterminate.

Tillich described the human condition as "finite freedom," an interplay of agency and constraint. He insisted on the significance and necessity of human engagement in the historical process, at the same time pointing to a power that always surpasses human understanding and action. History moves toward fulfillment of the ethical demand inherent in human nature and origins, but it moves in this direction only through human action; no miracle will achieve the goal without human participation. This action is motivated by a demand for justice, or "expectation," which links human origins and ends, the is and the ought, through historical processes that are always conflictual and ambiguous. As the human link between origin and demand, expectation is both immanent and transcendent, bound to the concrete, but surpassing it. Expectation is "a witness of life to its fundamental openness," to the hope that is necessary for the realization of justice.[52] The fact that history is open-ended does not negate meaning but in fact reflects the deepest meaning of human life.

Accepting and embracing historical openness means rejecting not only the expectation that we will succeed in any given enterprise but all teleological expectation. In theological language, we cannot control God, and often we cannot even know God's will. We do know that God may not always privilege our particular good, or even human goods in general, as theologian James Gustafson insists.[53] Thus we cannot hope that divine grace will always arrange things in our favor. Utopia as we define it is far from inevitable; neither the universe nor our own lives drive toward some foreordained telos.

Rethinking control means rethinking human goodness. According to the "ethic of control" that dominates our culture, as Sharon Welch explains, "to be responsible means that one can ensure that the aim of one's action will be carried out. To act means to determine what will happen through that single action." This definition of responsible and moral action, however, is based on "an intrinsically immoral balance of power."[54] No one should have the power to determine events unilaterally, in our complex, diverse world. And, in fact, no one does. This has always been the human condition, although modernist thought, in both secular and religious varieties, has encouraged the idea that "man" can accomplish anything "he" puts his mind to. If we admit that this is false, that we cannot guarantee that we will reach our desired end, whether we call it utopian or not, then perhaps we can begin to think about and live out ethics in a new way. We uncover "reasons for hoping," as Yoder puts it, "when there is no reason to hope,"[55] at least in the sense of guaranteed outcomes.

We cannot guarantee outcomes both because we cannot control everything and because we do not know everything; our ignorance, as Wes Jackson reminds us, always far outstrips our knowledge.[56] It might seem paradoxical to suggest that embracing our permanent shortfalls in the pursuit of knowledge can provide hope, but I think this is the case. The acknowledgment that we can never be sure about what we know or what will happen next frees us from the cost–benefit calculation that dominates so many styles of moral decision making. Whether or not a desired result is likely no longer becomes a major motivating factor in moral decisions. This is important because illusions of certain knowledge often tempt people to calculate likely causes and effects, which in turn often leads to exhaustion or abandonment of a cause when calculations prove inaccurate.

If we no longer assume that we can know what people will do and what will result from the actions of various parties, including ourselves, moral decisions and actions must find a ground other than Cartesian or Kantian confidence in human reason. For many, religious faith provides such a ground. Such faith can provide a powerful ground of hope detached from arrogance, as John Howard Yoder argues: "The conviction that one's morality and social style are expressive of a transcendent commitment and not just of consequential calculation . . . contributes to the holding power of individuals in the face of short-range conflict and opposition and protects against giving up the battle or 'burning out,' standard temptations to those whose reason for doing good is too closely correlated to manageable projections of effect."[57] We can also look to immanent rather than transcendent grounds of hope, including interpersonal relationships and the more than human world. These human and natural forces are as unpredictable and powerful as any deity. Their spiritual dimension is not hard to uncover: like the reign of God, nature and other people remain always beyond our grasp, our knowing, and our planning.

Founding our moral acts on ignorance and humility reminds us that the future is open, despite what "common sense" (or the powers that be) claims to know. Tillich addresses this in his nuanced argument for a critical utopianism as ground for hope. This utopianism rests on an admission of ultimate ignorance, combined with an unwavering commitment to continue regardless of knowledge or outcome. Confronting the rise of Nazism in his native Germany, Tillich wrote: "We face here the problem of not using the forces of fanaticism and yet of demanding an unconditional commitment against them in the hour of necessity. In committing ourselves, however, we know that we are not committed to something absolute but to something provisional and ambiguous and that it is not to be worshiped but criticized and if necessary, rejected; but in the moment of action we are able to say a total Yes to it."[58]

This "Yes," for Tillich, is a form of "anticipation" that acknowledges ultimate ignorance about that which is believed in. "The thing ultimately referred to in all genuine anticipation remains transcendent; it transcends any concrete fulfillment of human destiny; it transcends the otherworldly utopias of religious fantasy as well as the this-worldly utopias of secular speculation." And, we might add, it transcends all certain knowledge. We can never bring about, Tillich writes, a situation that is exempt from the permanent uncertainties of human existence, but this "does not mean that distorted reality should be left unchanged."[59] We do not know what will happen; we are always, necessarily, ignorant about the consequences and the ultimate context of our acts; and this is never justification for failure to act.

THE OTHER SIDE

In these trying times, we cannot afford to despise small things.[60]

The education of desire that we need must be first and foremost a practical education, which takes place in and through practices of community, of play, of un-self-interested giving and receiving. These practices may seem to be small things, easy to despise or at least to ignore, as we set our sights on far horizons of social change. If we are to begin with practice, however, we have to start with the structures and values embedded in even the most mundane features of everyday life. Adults and young people alike need to experience different pleasures, not just be told about them. We need to discover in the flesh what it feels like to live differently, and learn to desire it. Experiences of noninstrumental, nonmediated, anticonsumerist pleasures can become seductive and powerful enough to redirect lives and, ultimately, societies. Then "what happens in the occasion of interpersonal encounters," as a feminist critic suggests, might be "transformative of social life as well."[61] For this to become possible, paradoxically, we may have to live as though it already were. Even while we live on this side of what Wes Jackson calls "the brick wall of capitalism," we need not only to "imagine life on the other side of the wall [and] . . . plan for the other side"[62] but also to live as though we were already on it. This is what Valentín and Molina managed to do, in their shared cell, which paradoxically became a potent school for love.

A homely example of this is my daily bicycle commute to school with my oldest son on our tandem bicycle. At first it was hard to get us both up thirty minutes earlier in order to ride instead of drive. My son, not a morning person, complained bitterly for a long time. Now, however, that early morning ride is one of the high points of my day, and the same is true for him. It is good exercise; it is ecologically sound; it is a convenient way to avoid the hassles of traffic and parking. Most of all, however, it is fun, for all sorts of reasons: we see hawks on the phone wires and crows and mockingbirds worrying the hawks, we wave at drivers who salute our bicycle built for two, we enjoy a long glide downhill, and once we watched a squirrel swim out of the creek after falling from an overhead branch. And we talk to each other, creating encounter values that become all the more vital as adolescence looms. Without all these sensual, sociable pleasures, I am not sure my worry about global warming would be enough to get me out every morning. I bike not only for myself, but also because I want my children not simply to take bicycling for granted as a default mode of transportation but also to desire its unique joys. This desire cannot be educated in the abstract but only in the flesh, literally. This holds, I think, for all the alternative pleasures and utopian desires toward which we aim: only if people feel them, experience them, will these be compelling and desirable enough to stick with for the long haul.

At their best, our immanent utopias criticize the status quo and also embody, in embryonic form, a more desirable ideal. They embody the productive tension between the "already" and the "not yet" of the reign of God. They constitute the small yet vital presence of the eternal already among us, and at the same time the beginning of something larger that is not yet, and may never be. Despite the lack of guarantees, we need glimpses of the not yet in order to see the possibilities in our already.

NOTES

1. A Presence and a Beginning

1. Manuel Castells, *The City and the Grassroots* (Berkeley: University of California Press, 1983).
2. Paul Tillich, "The Right to Hope," in *Theology of Peace*, ed. Ronald H. Stone (Louisville: Westminster/John Knox Press, 1990), 184.
3. Paul Tillich, *The Courage to Be* (New Haven: Yale University Press, 1952), 181.
4. Tillich, "The Right to Hope," 185–86.
5. Ibid., 185.
6. Ibid., 190.
7. E. P. Thompson, *William Morris: Romantic to Revolutionary* (Stanford: Stanford University Press, 1988), 790–91; quoting Miguel Abensour.
8. Adrienne Rich, "When We Dead Awaken: Writing as Re-vision," in *On Lies, Secrets, and Silence: Selected Prose, 1966–1978* (New York: Norton, 1979), 43.
9. Sharon Welch, *A Feminist Ethic of Risk*, 2nd ed. (Minneapolis: Augsburg Fortress, 1990), 110.
10. John Howard Yoder, *The Priestly Kingdom: Social Ethics as Gospel* (Notre Dame: University of Notre Dame Press, 1984).

11. Joanna Macy, *Mutual Causality in Buddhism and General Systems Theory: The Dharma of Natural Systems* (Albany: State University of New York Press, 1991), 155.

12. Paul Tillich, *The Protestant Era* (Chicago: University of Chicago Press, 1957), 230.

13. Oscar Romero, *Voice of the Voiceless: Four Pastoral Letters and Other Statements* (Maryknoll, N.Y.: Orbis Books, 1995), 133.

14. Robert N. Bellah et al., *Habits of the Heart: Individualism and Commitment in American Life* (Berkeley: University of California Press, 1985), 138, 153, 135.

15. Ibid., 153.

16. John Keane and Paul Mier, "Preface," in Alberto Melucci, *Nomads of the Present: Social Movements and Individual Needs in Contemporary Society*, ed. J. Keane and P. Mier (Philadelphia: Temple University Press, 1989), 6.

17. Melucci, *Nomads of the Present*, 206.

18. Castells, *The City and the Grassroots*.

19. Mary Midgley, *Animals and Why They Matter* (Athens: University of Georgia Press, 1983), 109, 110.

20. Donna J. Haraway, *When Species Meet* (Minneapolis: University of Minnesota Press, 2008), 19.

21. Robert Roy Britt, "Americans Lose Touch, Report Fewer Close Friends," June 23, 2006; http://www.livescience.com/humanbiology/060623_close_friends.html. See also Henry Fountain, "The Lonely American Just Got a Bit Lonelier," *New York Times*, July 2, 2006.

22. Interview with Lovin, quoted in Britt, "Americans Lose Touch." See also Miller McPherson, Lynn Smith-Lovin, and Matthew Brashears, "Social Isolation in America: Changes in Core Discussion Networks over Two Decades," *American Sociological Review* 71, no. 3 (June 2006): 353–75.

23. Castells, *The City and the Grassroots*, 61, 62.

24. Phillip Berryman, *The Religious Roots of Rebellion: Christians in Central American Revolutions* (Maryknoll, N.Y.: Orbis Books, 1984).

25. Bellah et al., *Habits of the Heart*, 74.

26. Robert D. Putnam, *Bowling Alone: The Collapse and Revival of American Community* (New York: Simon and Schuster, 2000), 100–101.

27. Bellah et al., *Habits of the Heart*, 107, 130, 139, 47.

28. Ibid., 80, 6.

29. Nel Noddings, *Caring: A Feminine Approach to Ethics and Moral Education* (Berkeley: University of California Press, 1984).

30. Reinhold Niebuhr, *Moral Man and Immoral Society* (New York: Charles Scribner's Sons, 1932), xi.

31. Niebuhr is drawing on and modifying a long-standing dualism in Christian social thought, especially Saint Augustine's division between the city of God and the city of man, and Martin Luther's distinction between the "worldly" and "godly" kingdoms. Both Augustine and Luther distinguished not so much between personal and private life but between religious and secular realms. In the former, true Christian values and goals shaped human action, but in the former only inferior worldly claims could prevail.

32. Stacey Oliker, *Best Friends and Marriage: Exchange Among Women* (Berkeley: University of California Press, 1989), 2–3.

33. Val Plumwood, *Feminism and the Mastery of Nature* (London: Routledge, 1993), 184.

34. Habermas elaborates his concepts of system and lifeworld most fully in *The Theory of Communicative Action, Volume I* (Boston: Beacon Press, 1984) and *Volume II* (Boston: Beacon Press, 1985).

35. Manuel Puig, *Kiss of the Spider Woman*, trans. Thomas Colchie (New York: Vintage Books, 1978), 202.

36. Castells, *The City and the Grassroots*, 331.

37. Puig, *Kiss of the Spider Woman*, 203.

38. Tillich, *The Protestant Era*, 160.

39. Castells, *The City and the Grassroots*, 331.

40. Anna Peterson, *Being Human: Ethics, Environment, and Our Place in the World* (Berkeley: University of California Press, 2001), 4.

2. Love and Politics

1. Paul Tillich, *Love, Power, and Justice* (New York: Oxford University Press, 1954), 11.

2. María López Vigil, *Primero Dios: Siete años de esperanza (relatos de "Carta a las Iglesias")* (San Salvador: Universidad Centroamericana, 1988), 91.

3. Roger Lancaster, *Life Is Hard: Machismo, Danger, and the Intimacy of Power in Nicaragua* (Berkeley: University of California Press, 1992), 207.

4. See Anna Peterson, *Seeds of the Kingdom: Utopian Communities in the Americas* (New York: Oxford University Press, 2005), especially chap. 3.

5. See Tillich, *Love, Power, and Justice*, 11–12.

6. Melucci, *Nomads of the Present*, 5.

7. Aristotle, *Nichomachean Ethics*, book 8, chap. 3, in *Introduction to Aristotle*, ed. Richard McKeon (New York: Modern Library, 1947), 475.

8. Ibid., book 9, chap. 8, 511.

9. Cicero, *De Amicitia (On Friendship)*, trans. Andrew P. Peabody, no. 6. http://ancienthistory.about.com/library/bl/bl_text_cic_friendship.htm#5.

10. Ibid., no. 22.

11. Aelred of Rievaulx, *Spiritual Friendship*, Cistercian Fathers Series no. 5, trans. Mary Eugenia Laker (Kalamazoo: Cisterian Publications, 1977), 66.

12. Ibid., 60, 107.

13. Ibid., 63.

14. Ibid., 111.

15. Ibid., 129.

16. Paul Wadell, *Friendship and the Moral Life* (Notre Dame: University of Notre Dame Press, 1989), 101, 96, xiii.

17. Ibid., 152.

18. Aelred, *Spiritual Friendship*, 63.

19. Haraway, *When Species Meet*, 67.

20. Wadell, *Friendship and the Moral Life*, 142.

21. Haraway, *When Species Meet*, 46.

22. Wadell, *Friendship and the Moral Life*, 145.

23. Oliker, *Best Friends and Marriage*, 110–11.

24. Ibid., 159.

25. Wadell, *Friendship and the Moral Life*, xvi.

26. I use marriage here to refer to a variety of long-term, committed relationships between two adults who form a household together.

27. Lis Harris, *Rules of Engagement: Four Couples and American Marriage Today* (New York: Simon and Schuster, 1995), 253.

28. Deal Hudson, "5 Arguments Against Priestly Celibacy and How to Refute Them." http://www.catholicity.com/commentary/hudson/celibacy.html.

29. William P. Saunders, "Spirituality of Celibacy," *Catholic Herald*, May 2, 2002. http://www.catholicherald.com/saunders/02ws/ws020502.htm.

30. Richard Schmitt, *Beyond Separateness: The Social Nature of Human Beings—Their Autonomy, Knowledge, and Power* (Boulder: Westview Press, 1995), 44–45.

31. Ibid., 50.

32. The ordinary emotional and logistical burdens of marriage are often accompanied or subsumed by the sharper weight of abuse. For many women (and not a few men), marriage is far from a haven in a heartless world—the outside world, in fact, may be a refuge to which they flee.

33. Harris, *Rules of Engagement*, 253.

34. Maria Root, *Love's Revolution: Interracial Marriage* (Philadelphia: Temple University Press, 2001), 177.

35. Renee C. Romano, *Race Mixing: Black-White Marriage in Postwar America* (Cambridge: Harvard University Press, 2003), 178.

36. Ibid., 291, 295.

37. Paul Ginsborg, *The Politics of Everyday Life: Making Choices, Changing Lives* (New Haven: Yale University Press, 2005), 91.

38. As Kathleen Gerson notes, children experience gender roles and diverse models of selfhood not only in their parents but in encounters with a wide variety of people. The psychoanalytic approaches of feminist scholars like Nancy Chodorow and Dorothy Dinnerstein, which focus on mothering and identification with same-sex parent, thus oversimplify the development of childhood identities and choices. See K. Gerson, *Hard Choices: How Women Decide about Work, Career, and Motherhood* (Berkeley: University of California Press, 1985), 33.

39. Karl Marx, *On the Jewish Question*, in *The Marx-Engels Reader*, ed. Robert Tucker (New York: Norton, 1978), 42.

40. Ibid., 43.

41. Ibid., 46.

42. Midgley, *Animals and Why They Matter*, 31.

43. Niebuhr, *Moral Man and Immoral Society*.

3. Ethics, Parenting, and Childhood

1. Arlie Russell Hochschild, *The Time Bind: When Work Becomes Home and Home Becomes Work* (New York: Holt, 1997), xxviii.

2. U.S. Bureau of Labor Statistics. http://www.bls.gov/opub/working/page16b.htm.

3. Arlie Russell Hochschild with Anne Machung, *The Second Shift* (New York: Penguin, 1989/2003), xxiv–xxv.

4. This topic made the cover of the *New York Times Magazine* on June 15, 2008, with a caption "Will Dad *Ever* Do His Share?" The article itself discussed the trials and occasional successes of couples who aimed for an exactly equal division of parenting duties.

5. Hochschild, *The Second Shift*, 4, 8–9.

6. Ibid., xiii.

7. Christopher Lasch, *Haven in a Heartless World: The Family Besieged* (New York: Basic Books, 1977).

8. Lillian Rubin, *Families on the Fault Line: America's Working Class Speaks About the Family, the Economy, Race, and Ethnicity* (New York: Harper and Row, 1994), 244–45.

9. Hochschild, *The Second Shift*, 10.

10. Hochschild, *The Time Bind*, 11.

11. Richard Louv, *Childhood's Future* (New York: Anchor Books, 1992), 15.

12. Richard Louv, *Last Child in the Woods: Saving Our Children from Nature-Deficit Disorder* (Chapel Hill: Algonquin Books of Chapel Hill, 2005), 123.

13. Richard Louv, *Childhood's Future*, 12–13.

14. Lillian Breslow Rubin, *Worlds of Pain: Life in the Working Class Family* (New York: Basic Books, 1976), 46.

15. Arlie Russell Hochschild, "The Commodity Frontier," in *The Commercialization of Intimate Life: Notes from Home and Work* (Berkeley: University of California Press, 2003), 42–43. See also Hochschild, "Emotional Geography and the Flight Plan of Capitalism," in ibid., 210.

16. Jennifer Nedelsky, "Dilemmas of Passion, Privilege, and Isolation: Reflections on Mothering in a White Middle-Class Nuclear Family," in *Mother Troubles: Rethinking Contemporary Maternal Dilemmas*, ed. Julia E. Hanigsberg and Sara Ruddick (Boston: Beacon Press, 1999), 319–20.

17. Ibid., 328–29.

18. Hochschild, *The Second Shift*, 282.

19. Rubin, *Worlds of Pain*, 160.

20. Hochschild, *The Time Bind*, 49–52.

21. Hochschild, *The Second Shift*, 242.

22. Hochschild, *The Time Bind*, 249.

23. Noddings, *Caring*, 24.

24. Ibid., 3, 4, 5, 82, 83.

25. Carol Gilligan, *In a Different Voice: Psychological Theory and Women's Development* (Cambridge: Harvard University Press, 1982), 105.

26. Ibid., 19, 28, 32, 44.

27. Noddings, *Caring*, 82–83.

28. Sara Ruddick, *Maternal Thinking: Toward a Politics of Peace* (Boston: Beacon Press, 1995), 57.

29. Ibid.

30. Arlene Skolnick, *Embattled Paradise: The American Family in an Age of Uncertainty* (New York: Basic Books, 1991), 32, 195–96.

31. Arlie Hochschild coined the term "emotion work"; see *The Commercialization of Intimate Life*, 94.

32. Raymond Williams, *Resources of Hope: Culture, Democracy, Socialism*, ed. Robin Gable (London: Verso: 1989), 171. See also Nel Noddings, *Starting at Home: Caring and Social Policy* (Berkeley: University of California Press, 2002), 47.

33. Joan Tronto, "Women and Caring: What Can Feminists Learn About Morality from Caring?" in *Justice and Care: Essential Readings in Feminist Ethics*, ed. Virginia Held (Boulder: Westview Press, 1995), 111.

34. Nedelsky, "Dilemmas of Passion," 329.

35. Eric Noe, "Cindy Sheehan: Anti-War Icon," *ABC News*, August 18, 2005. http://abcnews.go.com/GMA/story?id=1045556&page=1.

36. Sam Kornell, "Maternal Instincts" [interview with Cindy Sheehan], *Santa Barbara Independent*, April 20, 2006. http://www.independent.com/news/2006/04/maternal_instincts.html.

37. Willett Kempton, James S. Boster, and Jennifer A. Hartley. *Environmental Values in American Culture* (Cambridge: MIT Press, 1995), 95.

38. Merck Family Fund. 1995. "Yearning for Balance." http://www.globallearningnj.org/global_ata/Yearing_for_balance.htm.

39. Kempton, Boster, and Hartley, *Environmental Values*, 95–96.

40. Ruddick, *Maternal Thinking*, xx.

41. Adrienne Rich, *Of Woman Born: Motherhood as Experience and Institution* (New York: Bantam Books, 1977), 285–86.

42. Jeffrey C. Goldfarb, *The Politics of Small Things: The Power of the Powerless in Dark Times* (Chicago: University of Chicago Press, 2006), 10.

43. Ibid., 44.

44. Ibid., 27

45. Warren Copeland, *Economic Justice: The Social Ethics of U.S. Economic Policy* (Nashville: Abingdon Press, 1988), 98.

46. Ruddick, *Maternal Thinking*, 81.

47. Noddings, *Starting at Home*, 48.

48. Rich, *Of Woman Born*, 285–86.

49. Diana T. Meyers, "Introduction" to part 1, "Family Life and Moral Theory," in *Kindred Matters: Rethinking the Philosophy of the Family*, ed. Diana Tietjens Meyers, Kenneth Kipnis, and Cornelius F. Murphy, Jr. (Ithaca: Cornell University Press, 1993), 13.

50. Tronto, "Women and Caring," 109.

51. Sara Ruddick, "Maternal Thinking," *Feminist Studies* 6, no. 2 (Summer 1980): 359.

52. Thomas H. Murray, *The Worth of a Child* (Berkeley: University of California Press, 1996), 175.

53. Peta Bowden, *Caring: Gender-Sensitive Ethics* (London: Routledge, 1997), 22.

54. Annette Baier, "The Need for More than Justice," in *Justice and Care: Essential Readings in Feminist Ethics*, ed. Virginia Held (Boulder: Westview Press, 1995), 52.

55. Anne Lamott, *Operating Instructions: A Journal of My Son's First Year* (New York: Random House, 1993), 60–61.

56. Viviana Zelizer, *Pricing the Priceless Child: The Changing Social Value of Children* (New York: Basic Books, 1985), 11; quoted in Tobias Hecht, *At Home in the Street: Street Children of Northeast Brazil* (Cambridge: Cambridge University Press, 1998), 80–81.

57. Nedelsky, "Dilemmas of Passion, 310.

58. The increasing commercialization of childhood has received attention from journalists and scholars, including Juliet Schor's book *Born to Buy: The Commercialized Child and the New Consumer Culture* (New York: Scribner's, 2004).

59. Ruddick, *Maternal Thinking*, 34.

60. Susan E. Chase and Mary F. Rogers, *Mothers and Children: Feminist Analyses and Personal Narratives* (New Brunswick, N.J.: Rutgers University Press, 2001), 284.

61. Evelyn Nakano Glenn, "Social Construction of Mothering: A Thematic Overview," in *Mothering: Ideology, Experience, and Agency*, ed. Evelyn Nakano Glenn, Grace Chang, and Linda Rennie Forcey (New York: Routledge, 1994), 14.

62. Interview by author, April 9, 1990, San Salvador.

63. Hecht, *At Home in the Street*, 25, 168.

64. See, for example, María Gravina Telechea, *Que Diga Quincho* (Managua: Editorial Nueva Nicaragua, 1982); and Anna Peterson and Kay Almere Read, "Victims, Heroes, Enemies: Children in Central American Wars," in *Minor Omissions: Children in Latin American History and Society*, ed. Tobias Hecht (Madison: University of Wisconsin Press, 2002).

65. Wadell, *Friendship and the Moral Life*, 142.

66. Bill McKibben, *Maybe One: A Case for Smaller Families* (New York: Penguin, 1999), 200, 196.

67. Ibid., 196, 197, 200.

4. Encountering Nature

1. Gary Paul Nabhan, "A Child's Sense of Wildness," in *The Geography of Childhood: Why Children Need Wild Places*, ed. Gary Paul Nabhan and Stephen Trimble (Boston: Beacon Press, 1994), 12.

2. Louv, *Last Child in the Woods*.

3. "Lines composed a few miles above Tintern Abbey," 1798.

4. Robert Richards argues that romantic views of nature had a strong influence not only on popular conceptions but on biology and Darwinian thought. See *The Romantic Conception of Life: Science and Philosophy in the Age of Goethe* (Chicago: University of Chicago Press, 2002).

5. Henry David Thoreau, *Walden and Civil Disobedience* (New York: Penguin, 1986), 90.

6. John Muir, *My First Summer in the Sierra* (San Francisco: Sierra Club Books, 1988), 80.

7. Paul Tillich, "Nature and Sacrament," in *The Protestant Era* (Chicago: University of Chicago Press, 1957), 111.

8. Henry Beston, *The Outermost House: A Year of Life on the Great Beach of Cape Cod* (New York: Viking, 1962 [1929]), 10.

9. Bron Taylor, "Earth First! and Global Narratives of Popular Ecological Resistance," in *Ecological Resistance Movements*, ed. Bron Tayor (Albany: SUNY Press, 1993), 11–27.

10. Beston, *The Outermost House*, 220–21.

11. Pablo Neruda, "With Quevedo, in Springtime," in *Winter Garden*, trans. William O'Daly (Port Townsend, Wash.: Copper Canyon Press, 1986), 17.

12. Pablo Neruda, "A Dog Has Died," in *Winter Garden*, 61.

13. Pablo Neruda, "The Egoist," in *Winter Garden*, 3.

14. Midgley, *Animals and Why They Matter*, 119.

15. Caroline Knapp, *Pack of Two: The Intricate Bonds Between People and Dogs* (New York: Dial Press, 1998), 11.

16. Ibid., 9.

17. Anthony Weston, *Back to Earth: Tomorrow's Environmentalism* (Philadelphia: Temple University Press, 1994), 33.

18. Wendell Berry, "Preserving Wildness," in *Home Economics* (New York: North Point Press, 1987), 151.

19. Edward O. Wilson, *Biophilia* (Cambridge: Harvard University Press, 1984), 1.

20. Weston, *Back to Earth*, 17; Midgley, *Animals and Why They Matter*, 119.

21. Stephen R. Kellert, "Experiencing Nature: Affective, Cognitive, and Evaluative Development in Children," in *Children and Nature: Psychological, Sociocultural, and Evolutionary Investigations*, ed. Peter H. Kahn, Jr., and Stephen R. Kellert (Cambridge: MIT Press, 2002), 123.

22. Wilson, *In Search of Nature*, 166.

23. Ibid., 190.

24. Louv, *Last Child in the Woods*, 102. The Stephen Kaplan quotation is from Rebecca Clay, "Green Is Good for You," *Monitor on Psychology* 32, no. 4 (April 2001).

25. Louv, *Last Child*, 2.

26. Midgley, *Animals and Why They Matter*, 122.

27. Knapp, *Pack of Two*, 11.

28. Edward O. Wilson, *Naturalist* (Washington, D.C.: Island Press, 2006).

29. Nabhan and Trimble, *Geography of Childhood*, 6, 7.

30. Peter H. Kahn, Jr., "Children's Affiliations with Nature: Structure, Development, and the Problem of Environmental Generational Amnesia," in *Children and Nature*, ed. Kahn and Kellert, 106.

31. Shepard Krech III, *The Ecological Indian: Myth and History* (New York: Norton, 1999).

32. Stephen Kellert, "Concepts of Nature East and West," in *Reinventing Nature? Responses to Postmodern Deconstruction*, ed. Michael E. Soulé and Gary Lease (Washington, D.C.: Island Press, 1995), 116.

33. The ambivalence within all human worldviews does not contradict the biophilia hypothesis, Kellert insists, but in fact reinforces it: "I believe there is a biological basis for all human values of nature," he writes. Both Eastern and

Western conceptions of nature, then, should be seen as indicative of the content, direction, and intensity that culture gives to diverse biologically based values of nature. The assumption of a biological basis for human affinity to nature does not mean, for Kellert, that all attitudes toward nature are equally valid or functionally adaptive. See ibid., 117; see also Stephen Kellert and E. O. Wilson, eds., *The Biophilia Hypothesis* (Washington, D.C.: Island Press, 1993).

34. Alfred, Lord Tennyson, "In Memoriam" (1850).

35. Charles Darwin, *The Origin of Species by Means of Natural Selection, or the Preservation of Favoured Races in the Struggle for Life* (New York: Penguin Books, 1968; first published by John Murray, 1859), 445.

36. Richard Dawkins, *River Out of Eden: A Darwinian View of Life* (New York: Basic Books, 1995),

37. Holmes Rolston III, *Environmental Ethics: Duties to and Values in the Natural World* (Philadelphia: Temple University Press, 1988), 57, 59.

38. James M. Gustafson, *A Sense of the Divine: The Natural Environment from a Theocentric Perspective* (Cleveland: Pilgrim Press, 1994), 44.

39. Darwin, *The Origin of Species*, 129.

40. See Mary Midgley, *Beast and Man: The Roots of Human Nature* (London: Routledge, 1995), 130–33; and Midgley, *Animals and Why They Matter*, 20–21.

41. Beston, *The Outermost House*, 221.

42. John Seed et al., *Thinking Like a Mountain: Towards a Council of All Beings* (Philadelphia: New Society Publishers, 1988), 36.

43. Quoted in Joanna Macy, "The Greening of the Self," in *Dharma Gaia: A Harvest of Essays in Buddhism and Ecology*, ed. Allan Hunt Badiner (Berkeley: Parallax Press, 1990), 62.

44. Plumwood, *Feminism and the Mastery of Nature*, 180.

45. Beston, *The Outermost House*, 25. Beston refers to seabirds as "ocean peoples," 108.

46. Rolston, *Environmental Ethics*, 202.

47. Midgley, *Beast and Man*, 359.

48. Pat Parelli, *Natural Horse*Man*Ship* (Colorado Springs: Western Horseman, 1993), 7.

49. Donna Haraway, *The Companion Species Manifesto: Dogs, People, and Significant Otherness* (Chicago: Prickly Paradigm Press, 2003), 48, 49.

50. Parelli, *Natural Horse*Man*Ship*, 15. Parelli echoes a point made by Mary Midgley, who writes that the thrill of hunting comes from the relationship

between the hunter and the prey animal who is their "opponent—a being like themselves in having its own emotions and interest." This is why, she concludes, shooting a rock is not a substitute. Midgley, *Animals and Why They Matter*, 16.

51. Midgley, *Animals and Why They Matter*, 113.

52. Stephen Webb, *On God and Dogs: A Christian Theology of Compassion for Animals* (Oxford: Oxford University Press, 1998), 104.

53. Vicki Hearne, *Adam's Task: Calling Animals by Name* (New York: Harper, 1994), cited in Weston, *Back to Earth*, 18–19. Hearne was criticized for advocating training methods that struck some as harsh, and she was a strong critic of animal rights movements and philosophies. Donna Haraway, however, praises Hearne's insight and respect for animals' otherness; see Haraway, *The Companion Species Manifesto*, 48–54.

54. Knapp, *Pack of Two*, 6, 4.

55. Haraway, *When Species Meet*, 42ff..

56. Midgley introduces the notion of a mixed community in *Animals and Why They Matter*, where the phrase is the title of chapter 10.

57. Weston, *Back to Earth*, 20, 130, 131.

58. Michael Vincent McGinnis, "Boundary Creatures and Bounded Spaces," in *Bioregionalism*, ed. Michael V. McGinnis (London: Routledge, 1999), 61.

59. Wes Jackson, *Becoming Native to This Place* (Lexington: University Press of Kentucky, 1994), 2–3.

60. Wendell Berry, *The Unsettling of America: Culture and Agriculture* (San Francisco: Sierra Club Books, 1977), 4.

61. Scott Russell Sanders, *Staying Put: Making a Home in a Restless World* (Boston: Beacon Press, 1993).

62. Muir, *My First Summer*, 98.

63. Ronnie D. Lipschutz, "Bioregionalism, Civil Society and Global Environmental Governance," in *Bioregionalism*, ed. McGinnis, 104.

64. Robert L. Thayer, Jr., *Life Place: Bioregional Thought and Practice* (Berkeley: University of California Press, 2003), 125

65. Juliet Schor, *The Over-Spent American: Why We Want What We Don't Need* (New York: Harper Perennial, 1999), and *Born to Buy*. Schor was a cofounder of the Center for a New American Dream (CNAD), a nongovernmental organization whose purpose is to help "Americans consume responsibly to

protect the environment, enhance quality of life, and promote social justice."
http://www.newdream.org.

66. Tom Princen, Michael Maniates, and Ken Conca, "Confronting Consumption," in *Confronting Consumption*, ed. Thomas Princen, Michael Maniates, and Ken Conca (Cambridge: MIT Press, 2002), 16–17.

67. Thomas Princen, "Distancing: Consumption and the Severing of Feedback," in *Confronting Consumption*, ed. Princen, Maniates, and Conca, 123–24.

68. See these related websites: http://www.sierraclub.org/sustainable_consumption and http://www.truecostoffood.org.

69. Thayer, *Life Place*, 126, 128.

70. Frederick Kirschenmann, "The Current State of Agriculture: Does It Have a Future?" in *The Essential Agrarian Reader: The Future of Culture, Community, and the Land*, ed. Norman Wirzba (Lexington: University Press of Kentucky, 2003), 113.

71. Thayer, *Life Place*, 126.

72. Melissa Pasanen, "Eating Local for the Winter," *Burlington Free Press*, January 31, 2006. Nabhan documents his year of eating locally in *Coming Home to Eat: The Pleasures and Politics of Local Foods* (New York: Norton, 2002), and Kingsolver hers in *Animal, Vegetable, Miracle: A Year of Food Life* (San Francisco: Harper Collins, 2007).

73. Norman Wirzba, "Placing the Soul: An Agrarian Philosophical Principle" in *The Essential Agrarian Reader*, ed. Wirzba, 94.

5. Ideas and Practices: Minding the Gap

1. Sections of this chapter were published, in different forms, as "Toward a Materialist Environmental Ethic," *Environmental Ethics* 28, no. 4 (Winter 2006): 375–93; and "Talking the Walk: A Practice-Based Environmental Ethic as Grounds For Hope," in *Ecospirit: Religion, Philosophy and the Earth*, ed. Laurel Kearns and Catherine Keller (New York: Fordham University Press, 2007).

2. Kempton et al., *Environmental Values in American Culture*, 211.

3. See, for example, James Sterngold, "California's New Problem: Sudden Surplus of Energy," *New York Times*, July 19, 2001, and "Conservation Having Little Effect on Gasoline Prices," July 9, 2008, http://www.cnbc.com/id/25606039.

4. "Poll: Conservation Takes Back Seat to Drilling," July 1, 2008. http://www.msnbc.msn.com/id/25482959/.

5. "Survey: Why Pro-Environmental Views Don't Always Translate into Votes," Nicholas Institute for Environmental Policy Solutions, Duke University School of the Environment and Earth Sciences, Durham, N.C. http://www.duke-news.duke.edu/2005/09/nicholaspoll.html.

6. Boston Indicators Project, "Per Capita Consumption of Earth's Resources." http://www.tbf.org/indicators2004/environment/indicators.asp?id=2209&crosscutID=322&crosscutName=Sustainable%20Development.

7. Parts of this section are taken from a paper I cowrote with Sam Snyder: "Bridging the Gap: Minding the Disconnect Between Environmental Values and Ecological Practice" (ms., 2008). More generally, Sam's research and thinking about these issues have been a major influence for my own reflections here.

8. The first three categories come from Michael Brower and Warren Leon, *The Consumers' Guide to Effective Environmental Choices: Practical Advice from the Union of Concerned Scientists* (New York: Three Rivers Press, 1999).

9. James Blake, "Overcoming the Value-Action Gap in Environmental Policy," *Local Environment* 4, no. 3 (1999): 260; see also Doug McKenzie-Mohr and William Smith, *Fostering Sustainable Behavior: An Introduction to Community-Based Social Marketing* (Gabriola Island, B.C.: New Society Publishers, 1999).

10. Kempton et al., *Environmental Values in American Culture.*

11. Princen, Conca, and Maniates, "Confronting Consumption," 16.

12. Princen, "Distancing," 129.

13. See Lene Holm Pederson, "The Dynamics of Green Consumption: A Matter of Visibility," *Journal of Environmental Policy and Planning*, 2, no 3 (2000): 193–210; and Alex Williams, "Buying into the Green Movement," *New York Times*, July 1, 2007.

14. Williams, "Buying into the Green Movement," 8. See also Michael Maniates's critiques of "easy" environmentalism, in "Going Green? Easy Doesn't Do It," *Washington Post*, November 22, 2007.

15. Brower and Leon, *Consumer's Guide*, 4.

16. Williams, "Buying into the Green Movement," 8.

17. Maniates, "Going Green?"

18. Glenda Wall, "Barriers to Individual Environmental Action: The Influence of Attitudes and Social Experiences," *CRSA/RCSA* 32, no. 4 (1995): 469.

19. McKenzie-Mohr and Smith, *Fostering Sustainable Behavior.*

20. Nathaniel Barrett, unpublished statement prepared for Conference on Values and Practices, Gainesville, Florida, April 2007.

21. Welch, *A Feminist Ethic of Risk*, 2.

22. Niebuhr, *Moral Man*, 44.

23. Antonio Gramsci, *Selections from the Prison Notebooks*, ed. and trans. Quintin Hoare and Geoffrey Nowell Smith (New York: International Publishers, 1971), 323ff.

24. David Orr, *Ecological Literacy: Education and the Transition to a Postmodern World* (Albany: State University of New York Press, 1992), 147.

25. Gustavo Gutiérrez, *A Theology of Liberation* (Maryknoll, N.Y.: Orbis Books, 1973), 15, 11.

26. Juan Luis Segundo, *The Liberation of Theology* (Maryknoll, N.Y.: Orbis Books, 1976), 8.

27. Kelly Parker, "Pragmatism and American Environmental Thought," in *Environmental Pragmatism*, ed. Andrew Light and Eric Katz (New York: Routledge, 1996), 21.

28. Karl Marx, "Theses on Feuerbach," in *The Marx-Engels Reader*, ed. Robert Tucker (New York: Norton, 1978), 145.

29. Ibid., 144.

30. Karl Marx, "The Eighteenth Brumaire of Louis Bonaparte," in *The Marx-Engels Reader*, 595.

31. Arun Agrawal, "Environmentality: Community, Intimate Government, and the Making of Environmental Subjects in Kumaon, India," *Current Anthropology* 46, no. 2 (April 2005): 176, 177, 162–63.

32. Niebuhr, *Moral Man*, xi, 28, 29.

33. Ibid., 28 .

34. Weston, "Non-Anthropocentrism in a Thoroughly Anthropocentrized World," *The Trumpeter* 8, no. 3 (1991): 1. http://trumpeter.athabascau.ca/contents/v8.3/weston.html.

35. Thayer, *Lifeplace*, 267.

36. Sam Snyder, "The Rodman Standoff: A Dam Critique of Bioregionalist Politics of Place," presented at First International Conference on Religion and Nature, Gainesville, Florida, April 7, 2006, 4, 7.

37. William R. Jordan III, *The Sunflower Forest: Ecological Restoration and the New Communion with Nature* (Berkeley: University of California Press, 2003), 5.

38. Ibid., 56.

1. Lancaster, *Life Is Hard*, xvi.

2. Tillich, "The Right to Hope," 189.

3. Hochschild, *The Time Bind*, 198.

4. Hochschild, *Commercialization of Intimate Life*, 202.

5. Hochschild, *The Time Bind*, 14.

6. Martin Ryle and Kate Soper, *To Relish the Sublime? Culture and Self-Realization in Postmodern Times* (New York: Verso, 2002), 58–59.

7. Karl Marx, "Economic and Philosophic Manuscripts of 1844," in *The Marx-Engels Reader*, ed. Robert Tucker, 2nd ed. (New York: Norton, 1978), 96.

8. John Howard Yoder, *For the Nations: Essays Public and Evangelical* (Grand Rapids, Mich.: Eerdmans, 1997), 90.

9. Rolston, *Environmental Ethics*, 60.

10. Marx, "Economic and Philosophic Manuscripts of 1844," 77.

11. Tillich, *Love, Power, and Justice*, 77.

12. Paul Tillich, *The Socialist Decision* (Lanham, Md.: University Press of America, 1977), 158.

13. Paul Tillich, "You Are Accepted," in *The Shaking of the Foundations* (New York: Charles Scribner's Sons, 1948), 154–55. See also Tillich, *Love, Power, and Justice*, 158.

14. Tillich, *Love, Power, and Justice*, 71. It also entails grace: "In grace something is overcome; grace occurs 'in spite of' something; grace occurs in spite of separation and estrangement. Grace is the reunion of life with life, the reconciliation of the self with itself. Grace is the acceptance of that which is rejected." "You Are Accepted," 156.

15. Tillich, *The Socialist Decision*, 141.

16. Paul Tillich, *On the Boundary* (New York: Charles Scribner's Sons, 1966), 87–88.

17. Marx, "The Eighteenth Brumaire of Louis Bonaparte," 595.

18. Ruddick, *Maternal Thinking*, xi.

19. Noddings, *Caring*, 112.

20. Ginsborg, *The Politics of Everyday Life*, 7.

21. Noddings, *Starting at Home*, 22.

22. Williams, *Resources of Hope*, 32.

23. Ibid., 242.

24. Ibid., 115.

25. "Sustainability and Politics: An Interview with Wes Jackson," by Robert Jensen, *Counterpunch*, July 10, 2003, 7. http://www.counterpunch.org/jensen07102003 .html. This is not a condemnation of people who shop at Wal-Mart. I recognize that for some people it is, or appears to be, the only choice for needed items like shoes, clothing, and groceries. This does not make it a good choice, just a necessary one.

26. Thompson, *William Morris*, 806.

27. Karl Marx, "Contribution to the Critique of Hegel's *Philosophy of Right*: Introduction," in *The Marx-Engels Reader*, ed. Robert Tucker, 2nd ed. (New York: Norton, 1978), 54.

28. Ibid., 54.

29. Weston, *Back to Earth*, 114.

30. Weston, "Non-Anthropocentrism," 1.

31. "Caminante, no hay camino; se hace camino al andar." Antonio Machado, "Cantares," in *Selected Poems of Antonio Machado*, trans. Betty Jean Craige (Baton Rouge: Louisiana State University Press, 1978).

32. Marx, "Theses on Feuerbach," 145.

33. Ibid., 144.

34. Feminist scholar Barbara Johnson makes a related point: "It is not that now we know that the Holocaust happened because of the actions of individuals, but that it happened because those individuals did not see that they were part of a pattern. No individual could have produced or stopped it on their own, even though it was through the risky and sacrificial actions of individuals that it could be stopped at all." The difference between imagining individuals who could neither produce nor stop the Holocaust on their own and those who were the only means of stopping it at all is "a chasm that I propose can best be captured in ontological terms. Here the failure is not exactly political, nor is it essentially ethical: it is rather a failure of seeing, or imagining, which is directly connected to a basic conceptualization of 'being.'" Barbara Johnson, *Mother Tongues: Sexuality, Trials, Motherhood, Translation* (Cambridge: Harvard University Press, 2003), 3–4; quoted by Elizabeth Wingrove, "Ontology: A Useful Category of Analysis," *Hedgehog Review* 7, no. 2 (Summer 2005): 91.

35. Williams, *Resources of Hope*, 242.

36. Ibid., 318.

37. Lisa Mastany, "Nordic Countries Are World's Sustainability Leaders," *World-Watch* 18, no. 3 (2005): 8. See also Michael Eden, Lena Falkheden, and Bjorn Malbert, "The Built Environment and Sustainable Development: Research Meets Practice in a Scandinavian Context," *Planning Theory and Practice* 1, no. 2 (2000): 260–72; Olav Mosvold Larsen, "Governing Innovation for Sustainable Development: Integration of Environmental and Innovation Policies in Norway," Program for Research and Documentation for a Sustainable Society (Oslo: University of Oslo, 2005); and SusNord, "New Trends in Sustainable Local Governance: Local Climate Planning in Norway" (Oslo: University of Oslo Centre for Development and the Environment, 2005). http://www.prosus.uio.no/susnord/norway/local_authorities/Sustainable%20Local%20Governance/SLG.htm.

38. "Best Place to Live in 2005? Norway." http://msnbc.msn.com/id/9085910/.

39. Donald B. Kraybill and Carl F. Bowman, *On the Backroad to Heaven: Old Order Hutterites, Mennonites, Amish and Brethren* (Baltimore: Johns Hopkins University Press, 2001), 105–6.

40. Victor Stoltzfus, "Reward and Sanction: The Adaptive Continuity of Amish Life," *Mennonite Quarterly Review* 51, no. 4 (October 1977): 311–12.

41. Ibid., 312. See also Peterson, *Seeds of the Kingdom*.

42. Stoltzfus, "Reward and Sanction," 313.

43. Louv, *Last Child in the Woods*, 50.

44. Williams, *Resources of Hope*, 76.

45. Aelred, *Spiritual Friendship*, 60.

46. Ibid., 129.

47. In *Last Child in the Woods*, Louv discusses research that shows that even troubled children are more cooperative and peaceful in nonstructured natural areas. A host of parallel research shows that children with emotional or psychological problems do better when they spend time with animals. Temple Grandin discusses some of this in *Animals in Translation: Using the Mysteries of Autism to Decode Animal Behavior* (New York: Simon and Schuster, 2005).

48. Haraway, *When Species Meet*, 241, 244.

49. Marx, "Economic and Philosophic Manuscripts of 1844," 105.

50. Haraway, *When Species Meet*, chap. 2

51. Ibid., 67; see also 62, 47.

52. Tillich, *The Socialist Decision*, 111; Paul Tillich, *Systematic Theology, Vol. 3* (Chicago: University of Chicago Press, 1963), 390–91.

53. Gustafson, *A Sense of the Divine*.

54. Welch, *A Feminist Ethic of Risk*, 3.

55. Yoder, *The Priestly Kingdom*, 95.

56. Wes Jackson, "Toward an Ignorance-Based Worldview," in *The Virtues of Ignorance: Complexity, Sustainability, and the Limits of Knowledge*, ed. Wes Jackson and Bill Vitek (Lexington: University Press of Kentucky, 2008): 21–36. These paragraphs borrow from my chapter in that book, pp. 119–34.

57. Yoder, *The Priestly Kingdom*, 97.

58. Paul Tillich, "The Political Meaning of Utopia," in *Political Expectation* (New York: Harper and Row, 1971), 178.

59. Paul Tillich, "The Protestant Principle and the Proletarian Situation," in *The Protestant Era*, 172.

60. Rev. W. J. Pope, "The Poultry of the Farm," *JRASE* 2d ser. 18:104–14 (1882, 114); quoted in Joan Thirsk, *Alternative Agriculture, a History: From the Black Death to the Present Day* (Oxford: Oxford University Press, 1997), 262.

61. Susan Frank Parsons, *Feminism and Christian Ethics* (Cambridge: Cambridge University Press, 1996), 215.

62. Jackson, "Sustainability and Politics."

BIBLIOGRAPHY

Abram, David. *The Spell of the Sensuous: Perception and Language in a More-than-Human World*. New York: Pantheon, 1996.

Aelred of Rievaulx. *Spiritual Friendship*. Cistercian Fathers Series Number Five. Translated by Mary Eugenia Laker. Introduction by Douglas Roby. Kalamazoo, Mich.: Cisterian Publications, 1977.

Agrawal, Arun. "Environmentality: Community, Intimate Government, and the Making of Environmental Subjects in Kumaon, India." *Current Anthropology* 46, no. 2 (April 2005): 161–190.

———. *Environmentality: Technologies of Government and the Making of Subjects*. Durham: Duke University Press, 2005.

Aristotle. *Nichomachean Ethics*, book 8, chap. 3, in *Introduction to Aristotle*. Edited by Richard McKeon. New York: Modern Library, 1947.

Baier, Annette. "The Need for More Than Justice." In *Justice and Care: Essential Readings in Feminist Ethics*. Edited by Virginia Held. Boulder: Westview Press, 1995.

Basso, Keith. *Wisdom Sits in Places: Landscape and Language Among the Western Apache*. Albuquerque: University of New Mexico Press, 1996.

Bellah, Robert, Richard Madsen, William M. Sullivan, Ann Swidler, and Steven M. Tipton. *The Good Society*. New York: Vintage, 1992.

184 ———. *Habits of the Heart: Individualism and Commitment in American Life.* Berkeley: University of California Press, 1985.

Berry, Thomas. *The Dream of the Earth.* San Francisco: Sierra Club Books, 1990.

Berry, Wendell. *Home Economics.* New York: North Point Press, 1987.

———. *The Unsettling of America: Culture and Agriculture.* San Francisco: Sierra Club Books, 1977.

Berryman, Phillip. *The Religious Roots of Rebellion: Christians in Central American Revolutions.* Maryknoll, N.Y.: Orbis Books, 1984.

Beston, Henry. *The Outermost House: A Year of Life on the Great Beach of Cape Cod.* New York: Viking Press, 1962 [1929].

"Best Place to Live in 2005? Norway." http://msnbc.msn.com/id/9085910/.

Blake, James. "Overcoming the Value-Action Gap in Environmental Policy." *Local Environment* 4, no. 3 (1999): 257–78.

Bowden, Peta. *Caring: Gender-Sensitive Ethics.* London: Routledge, 1997.

Britt, Robert Roy. "Americans Lose Touch, Report Fewer Close Friends," June 23, 2006. http://www.livescience.com/humanbiology/060623_close_friends.html.

Brower, Michael, and Warren Leon. *The Consumers' Guide to Effective Environmental Choices: Practical Advice from the Union of Concerned Scientists.* New York: Three Rivers Press, 1999.

Callicott, J. Baird. *Earth's Insights: Multicultural Environmental Ethics from the Mediterranean Basin to the Australian Outback.* Berkeley: University of California Press, 1994.

Castells, Manuel. *The City and the Grassroots.* Berkeley: University of California Press, 1983.

Chase, Susan E., and Mary F. Rogers. *Mothers and Children: Feminist Analyses and Personal Narratives.* New Brunswick, N.J.: Rutgers University Press, 2001.

Cheney, Jim. "Postmodern Environmental Ethics: Ethics as Bioregional Narrative." *Environmental Ethics* 11 (Summer 1989): 117–34.

Cheney, Jim, and Anthony Weston. "Environmental Ethics as Environmental Etiquette." *Environmental Ethics* 21, no. 2 (Summer 1999): 115–34.

Chodorow, Nancy. *The Reproduction of Mothering: Psychoanalysis and the Sociology of Gender.* Berkeley: University of California Press, 1978.

Cicero. *De Amicitia (On Friendship).* Translated by Andrew P. Peabody. http://ancienthistory.about.com/library/bl/bl_text_cic_friendship.htm#5.

CODEHUCA [Comisión de Derechos Humanos de Centroamérica]. *Los niños de la década perdida: Investigación y análisis de violaciones de los derechos humanos de la niñez centroamericana (1980–1992)*. San José, Costa Rica: CODEHUCA, n.d.

Copeland, Warren. *Economic Justice: The Social Ethics of U.S. Economic Policy*. Nashville: Abingdon Press, 1988.

Cunningham, Anthony. *The Heart of What Matters: The Role for Literature in Moral Philosophy*. Berkeley: University of California Press, 2001.

Darwin, Charles. *The Origin of Species by Means of Natural Selection, or the Preservation of Favoured Races in the Struggle for Life*. New York: Penguin Books, 1968; first published by John Murray, 1859.

Dawkins, Richard. *River Out of Eden: A Darwinian View of Life*. New York: Basic Books, 1995.

Eden, Michael, Lena Falkheden, and Bjorn Malbert. "The Built Environment and Sustainable Development: Research Meets Practice in a Scandinavian Context." *Planning Theory and Practice*, 1, no. 2 (2000): 260–72.

Fountain, Henry. "The Lonely American Just Got a Bit Lonelier." *New York Times*, July 2, 2006.

Gardner, Howard. *Developmental Psychology: An Introduction*. Boston: Little, Brown, 1982.

Geras, Norman. *The Contract of Mutual Indifference: Political Philosophy After the Holocaust*. London: Verso, 1998.

Gerson, Kathleen. *Hard Choices: How Women Decide About Work, Career, and Motherhood*. Berkeley: University of California Press, 1985.

Gilligan, Carol. *In A Different Voice: Psychological Theory and Women's Development*. Cambridge: Harvard University Press, 1982.

Ginsborg, Paul. *The Politics of Everyday Life: Making Choices, Changing Lives*. New Haven: Yale University Press, 2005.

Glenn, Evelyn Nakano. "Social Construction of Mothering: A Thematic Overview." In *Mothering: Ideology, Experience, and Agency*. Edited by Evelyn Nakano Glenn, Grace Chang, and Linda Rennie Forcey. New York: Routledge, 1994.

Goldfarb, Jeffrey C. *The Politics of Small Things: The Power of the Powerless in Dark Times*. Chicago: University of Chicago Press, 2006

Gopnik, Alison, Andrew N. Meltzoff, and Patricia K. Kuhl. *The Scientist in the Crib: What Early Learning Tells Us About the Mind*. New York: HarperCollins, 1999.

Gramsci, Antonio. *Selections from the Prison Notebooks*. Edited and translated by Quintin Hoare and Geoffrey Nowell Smith. New York: International Publishers, 1971.

Grandin, Temple, with Catherine Johnson. *Animals in Translation: Using the Mysteries of Autism to Decode Animal Behavior.* New York: Simon and Schuster, 2005.

Green, Duncan. *Hidden Lives: Voices of Children in Latin America and the Caribbean.* London: Cassell, 1998.

Gustafson, James M. *A Sense of the Divine: The Natural Environment from a Theocentric Perspective.* Cleveland: Pilgrim Press, 1994.

Gutiérrez, Gustavo. *A Theology of Liberation.* Maryknoll, N.Y.: Orbis Books, 1973.

Habermas, Jurgen. *The Theory of Communicative Action, Volume 1.* Boston: Beacon Press, 1984.

——. *The Theory of Communicative Action, Volume 2.* Boston: Beacon Press, 1985.

Hanigsberg, Julia E., and Sara Ruddick, eds. *Mother Troubles: Rethinking Contemporary Maternal Dilemmas.* Boston: Beacon Press, 1999.

Haraway, Donna. *The Companion Species Manifesto: Dogs, People, and Significant Otherness.* Chicago: Prickly Paradigm Press, 2003.

——. *When Species Meet.* Minneapolis: University of Minnesota Press, 2008.

Harris, Lis. *Rules of Engagement: Four Couples and American Marriage Today.* New York: Simon and Schuster, 1995.

Harvey, David. *Justice, Nature, and the Geography of Difference.* Cambridge: Basil Blackwell, 1996.

Hearne, Vicki. *Adam's Task: Calling Animals by Name.* New York: Harper, 1994.

Hecht, Tobias. *At Home in the Street: Street Children of Northeast Brazil.* Cambridge: Cambridge University Press, 1998.

Heller, Chaia. *Ecology of Everyday Life: Rethinking the Desire for Nature.* Montreal: Black Rose Books, 1999.

Hochschild, Arlie Russell. *The Commercialization of Intimate Life: Notes from Home and Work.* Berkeley: University of California Press, 2003.

——. *The Time Bind: When Work Becomes Home and Home Becomes Work.* New York: Holt, 1997.

Hochschild, Arlie Russell, with Anne Machung. *The Second Shift.* 2nd ed. New York: Penguin, 2003.

Holloway, Sarah L., and Gill Valentine. "Children's Geographies and the New Social Studies of Childhood." In *Children's Geographies: Playing, Living, Learning.* Edited by Sarah L. Holloway and Gill Valentine. London: Routledge, 2000.

Hudson, Deal. "5 Arguments Against Priestly Celibacy and How to Refute Them." http://www.catholicity.com/commentary/hudson/celibacy.html.

Jackson, Wes. *Becoming Native to This Place.* Lexington: University Press of Kentucky, 1994.

——. "Sustainability and Politics: An Interview with Wes Jackson," by Robert Jensen. *Counterpunch,* July 10, 2003. http://www.counterpunch.org/jensen07102003.html.

——. "Toward an Ignorance-Based Worldview." In *The Virtues of Ignorance: Complexity, Sustainability, and the Limits of Knowledge.* Edited by Wes Jackson and Bill Vitek. Lexington: University Press of Kentucky, 2008.

Jetter, Alexis, Annelise Orleck, and Diana Taylor, eds. *The Politics of Motherhood: Activist Voices from Left to Right.* Hanover, N.H.: Dartmouth College/University Press of New England, 1997.

Johnson, Mark. *Moral Imagination: Implications of Cognitive Science for Ethics.* Chicago: University of Chicago Press, 1993.

Jones, Suzanne W. *Race-Mixing: Southern Fiction Since the Sixties.* Baltimore: Johns Hopkins University Press, 2004.

Jordan, William R., III. *The Sunflower Forest: Ecological Restoration and the New Communion with Nature.* Berkeley: University of California Press, 2003.

Kahn, Peter H., Jr. "Children's Affiliations with Nature: Structure, Development, and the Problem of Environmental Generational Amnesia." In *Children and Nature: Psychological, Sociocultural, and Evolutionary Investigations.* Edited by Peter H. Kahn and Stephen R. Kellert. Cambridge: MIT Press, 2002.

Kahn, Peter H., Jr., and Stephen R. Kellert, eds. *Children and Nature: Psychological, Sociocultural, and Evolutionary Investigations.* Cambridge: MIT Press, 2002.

Keane, John, and Paul Mier. "Preface." In *Nomads of the Present: Social Movements and Individual Needs in Contemporary Society.* By Alberto Melucci. Philadelphia: Temple University Press, 1989.

Kellert, Stephen R. "Concepts of Nature East and West." In *Reinventing Nature? Responses to Postmodern Deconstruction.* Edited by Michael E. Soulé and Gary Lease. Washington, D.C.: Island Press, 1995.

——. "Experiencing Nature: Affective, Cognitive, and Evaluative Development in Children." In *Children and Nature: Psychological, Sociocultural, and Evolutionary Investigations.* Edited by Peter H. Kahn and Stephen R. Kellert. Cambridge: MIT Press, 2002.

Kellert, Stephen R., and E. O. Wilson, eds. *The Biophilia Hypothesis.* Washington, D.C.: Island Press, 1993.

Kempton, Willett, James S. Boster, and Jennifer A. Hartley. *Environmental Values in American Culture*. Cambridge: MIT Press, 1995.

Kennedy, Randall. *Interracial Intimacies: Sex, Marriage, Identity, and Adoption*. New York: Pantheon Books, 2003.

Kingsolver, Barbara. *Animal, Vegetable, Miracle: A Year of Food Life*. San Francisco: HarperCollins, 2007.

Kirkpatrick, Frank G. *The Ethics of Community*. Oxford: Blackwell, 2001.

Kirschenmann, Frederick. "The Current State of Agriculture: Does It Have a Future?" In *The Essential Agrarian Reader: The Future of Culture, Community, and the Land*. Edited by Norman Wirzba. Lexington: University Press of Kentucky, 2003.

Knapp, Caroline. *Pack of Two: The Intricate Bonds Between People and Dogs*. New York: Dial Press, 1998.

Komarovsky, Mirra. *Blue-Collar Marriage*. With the collaboration of Jane Phillips. New York: Vintage Books, 1962.

Kong, Lily. "Nature's Dangers, Nature's Pleasures: Urban Children and the Natural World." In *Children's Geographies: Playing, Living, Learning*. Edited by S. Holloway and G. Valentine. London: Routledge, 2000.

Kornell, Sam. "Maternal Instincts: Interview with Cindy Sheehan." *Santa Barbara Independent*, April 20, 2006. http://www.independent.com/news/2006/04/maternal_instincts.html.

Kraybill, Donald B., and Carl F. Bowman. *On the Backroad to Heaven: Old Order Hutterites, Mennonites, Amish and Brethren*. Baltimore: Johns Hopkins University Press, 2001.

Kumar, Amitava. "Teaching in the Republic of Love Letters." In *Poetics/Politics: Radical Aesthetics for the Classroom*. Edited by Amitava Kumar. New York: St. Martin's Press, 1999.

Laitin, David. "Religion, Political Culture, and the Weberian Tradition." *World Politics* 30, no. 4 (July 1978): 563–92.

Lakoff, George. *Don't Think of an Elephant: Know Your Values and Frame the Debate*. White River Junction, Vt.: Chelsea Green Publishing, 2004.

Lamott, Anne. *Operating Instructions: A Journal of My Son's First Year*. New York: Random House, 1993.

Lancaster, Roger. *Life Is Hard: Machismo, Danger, and the Intimacy of Power in Nicaragua*. Berkeley: University of California Press, 1992.

Lara, Maria Pia. *Moral Textures: Feminist Narratives in the Public Sphere*. Berkeley: University of California Press, 1998.

Larsen, Olav Mosvold. "Governing Innovation for Sustainable Development: Integration of Environmental and Innovation Policies in Norway." Program for Research and Documentation for a Sustainable Society. Oslo: University of Oslo, 2005.

Lasch, Christopher. *Haven in a Heartless World: The Family Besieged*. New York: Basic Books, 1977.

Lipschutz, Ronnie D. "Bioregionalism, Civil Society and Global Environmental Governance." In *Bioregionalism*. Edited by Michael Vincent McGinnis. London: Routledge, 1999.

López Vigil, María. *Primero Dios: Siete años de esperanza (relatos de "Carta a las Iglesias")*. San Salvador: Universidad Centroamericana, 1988.

Louv, Richard. *Childhood's Future*. New York: Anchor Books, 1992.

——. *Last Child in the Woods: Saving Our Children from Nature-Deficit Disorder*. Chapel Hill: Algonquin Books, 2005.

Luther, Martin. "The Freedom of a Christian." In *Martin Luther: Selected Writings*. Edited by John Dillenberger. New York: Anchor Books, 1971.

Macy, Joanna. "The Greening of the Self." In *Dharma Gaia: A Harvest of Essays in Buddhism and Ecology*. Edited by Allan Hunt Badiner. Berkeley: Parallax Press, 1990.

——. *Mutual Causality in Buddhism and General Systems Theory: The Dharma of Natural Systems*. Albany: State University of New York Press, 1991.

Maniates, Michael. "Going Green? Easy Doesn't Do It." *Washington Post*, November 22, 2007.

Marin, Patricia. *Infancia y Guerra en El Salvador*. UNICEF: Guatemala, 1988.

Marx, Karl. "Contribution to the Critique of Hegel's *Philosophy of Right*: Introduction." In *The Marx-Engels Reader*. Edited by Robert Tucker. 2nd ed. New York: Norton, 1978.

——. "Economic and Philosophic Manuscripts of 1844." In *The Marx-Engels Reader*. Edited by Robert Tucker. 2nd ed. New York: Norton, 1978.

——. "The Eighteenth Brumaire of Louis Bonaparte." In *The Marx-Engels Reader*. Edited by Robert Tucker. 2nd ed. New York: Norton, 1978.

——. *The German Ideology: Part 1*. In *The Marx-Engels Reader*. Edited by Robert Tucker. 2nd ed. New York: Norton, 1978.

———. *On the Jewish Question*. In *The Marx-Engels Reader*. Edited by Robert Tucker. 2nd ed. New York: Norton, 1978.

———. "Theses on Feuerbach." In *The Marx-Engels Reader*. Edited by Robert Tucker. 2nd ed. New York: Norton, 1978.

Mastany, Lisa. "Nordic Countries Are World's Sustainability Leaders." *World-Watch* 18, no. 3 (2005).

McGinnis, Michael Vincent. "Boundary Creatures and Bounded Spaces." In *Bioregionalism*. Edited by Michael Vincent McGinnis. London: Routledge, 1999.

McKenzie-Mohr, Doug, and William Smith. *Fostering Sustainable Behavior: An Introduction to Community-Based Social Marketing*. Gabriola Island, B.C.: New Society Publishers, 1999.

McKibben, Bill. *Maybe One: A Case for Smaller Families*. New York: Penguin, 1999.

McPherson, Miller, Lynn Smith-Lovin, and Matthew Brashears. "Social Isolation in America: Changes in Core Discussion Networks over Two Decades." *American Sociological Review* 71, no. 3 (June 2006): 353–75.

Melson, Gail F. *Why the Wild Things Are: Animals in the Lives of Children*. Cambridge: Harvard University Press, 2001.

Melucci, Alberto. *Nomads of the Present: Social Movements and Individual Needs in Contemporary Society*. Philadelphia: Temple University Press, 1989.

Merck Family Fund. 1995. "Yearning for Balance." http://www.globallearningnj .org/global_ata/Yearning_for_balance.htm.

Meyers, Diana T. "Introduction" to Part 1, "Family Life and Moral Theory." In *Kindred Matters: Rethinking the Philosophy of the Family*. Edited by Diana Tietjens Meyers, Kenneth Kipnis, and Cornelius F. Murphy, Jr. Ithaca: Cornell University Press, 1993.

Midgley, Mary. *Animals and Why They Matter*. Athens: University of Georgia Press, 1983.

———. *Beast and Man: The Roots of Human Nature*. London and New York: Routledge, 1995. Originally Cornell University Press, 1978.

———. *Can't We Make Moral Judgments?* New York: St. Martin's Press, 1991.

Muir, John. *My First Summer in the Sierra*. San Francisco: Sierra Club Books, 1988.

Murray, Thomas H. *The Worth of a Child*. Berkeley: University of California Press, 1996.

Nabhan, Gary P. *Coming Home to Eat: The Pleasures and Politics of Local Foods*. New York: Norton, 2002.

Nabhan, Gary P., and Stephen Trimble. *The Geography of Childhood: Why Children Need Wild Places*. Boston: Beacon, 1994.

Nedelsky, Jennifer. "Dilemmas of Passion, Privilege, and Isolation: Reflections on Mothering in a White Middle-Class Nuclear Family." In *Mother Troubles: Rethinking Contemporary Maternal Dilemmas*. Edited by Julia E. Hanigsberg and Sara Ruddick. Boston: Beacon Press, 1999.

Nelson, Hilde Lindemann. "Always Connect: Toward a Parental Ethics of Divorce." In *Mother Troubles: Rethinking Contemporary Maternal Dilemmas*. Edited by Julia E. Hanigsberg and Sara Ruddick. Boston: Beacon Press, 1999.

——, ed. *Feminism and Families*. New York: Routledge, 1997.

Neruda, Pablo. *Toward the Splendid City: Nobel Lecture*. New York: Farrar, Strauss, and Giroux, 1972.

——. *Winter Garden*. Translated by William O'Daly. Port Townsend, Wash.: Copper Canyon Press, 1986.

Niebuhr, Reinhold. *Moral Man and Immoral Society*. New York: Charles Scribner's Sons, 1932.

Noddings, Nel. *Caring: A Feminine Approach to Ethics and Moral Education*. Berkeley: University of California Press, 1984.

——. *Starting at Home: Caring and Social Policy*. Berkeley: University of California Press, 2002.

Noe, Eric. "Cindy Sheehan: Anti-War Icon." *ABC News*, August 18, 2005. http://abcnews.go.com/GMA/story?id=1045556&page=1.

Nucci, Larry. "Moral Development and Character Formation." In *Psychology and Educational Practice*. Edited by H. J. Walberg and G. D. Haertel. Berkeley: MacCarchan, 1997.

Oelschlaeger, Max. *Caring for Creation: An Ecumenical Approach to the Environmental Crisis*. New Haven: Yale University Press, 1994.

Okin, Susan Moller. "Families and Feminist Theory: Some Past and Present Issues." In *Feminism and Families*. Edited by Hilde Lindemann Nelson. New York: Routledge, 1997.

Oliker, Stacey J. *Best Friends and Marriage: Exchange Among Women*. Berkeley: University of California Press, 1989.

Oliver, Kelly. *Family Values: Subjects Between Nature and Culture*. New York: Routledge, 1997.

Orr, David. *Ecological Literacy: Education and the Transition to a Postmodern World*. Albany: State University of New York Press, 1992.

Orsi, Robert. *The Madonna of 115th Street: Faith and Community in Italian Harlem, 1880–1950.* New Haven: Yale University Press, 1985.

Parelli, Pat. *Natural Horse*Man*Ship.* Colorado Springs: Western Horseman, 1993.

Parker, Kelly. "Pragmatism and American Environmental Thought." In *Environmental Pragmatism.* Edited by Andrew Light and Eric Katz. New York: Routledge, 1996.

Parsons, Susan Frank. *Feminism and Christian Ethics.* Cambridge: Cambridge University Press, 1996.

Pasanen, Melissa. "Eating Local for the Winter." *Burlington Free Press,* January 31, 2006.

Pederson, Lene Holm. "The Dynamics of Green Consumption: A Matter of Visibility." *Journal of Environmental Policy and Planning* 2, no 3 (2000): 193–210.

Peterson, Anna L. *Being Human: Ethics, Environment, and Our Place in the World.* Berkeley: University of California Press, 2001.

——. "Ignorance and Ethics." In *The Virtues of Ignorance: Complexity, Sustainability, and the Limits of Knowledge.* Edited by Wes Jackson and Bill Vitek. Lexington: University Press of Kentucky, 2008.

——. *Martyrdom and the Politics of Religion: Progressive Catholicism in El Salvador's Civil War.* Albany: State University of New York Press, 1997.

——. *Seeds of the Kingdom: Utopian Communities in the Americas.* Oxford: Oxford University Press, 2005.

——. "Talking The Walk: A Practice-Based Environmental Ethic as Grounds for Hope." In *Ecospirit: Religion, Philosophy and the Earth.* Edited by Laurel Kearns and Catherine Keller. New York: Fordham University Press, 2007.

——. "Toward a Materialist Environmental Ethic." *Environmental Ethics* 28, no. 4 (Winter 2006): 375–93.

Peterson, Anna L., and Kay Almere Read. "Victims, Heroes, Enemies: Children in Central American Wars." In *Minor Omissions: Children in Latin American History and Society.* Edited by Tobias Hecht. Madison: University of Wisconsin Press, 2002.

Peterson, Anna L., and Samuel Snyder. "Bridging the Gap: Minding the Disconnect Between Environmental Values and Ecological Practice." Ms., February 2008.

Plumwood, Val. *Feminism and the Mastery of Nature.* London: Routledge, 1993.

Princen, Tom. "Distancing: Consumption and the Severing of Feedback." In *Confronting Consumption.* Edited by Thomas Princen, Michael Maniates, and Ken Conca. Cambridge: MIT Press, 2002.

Princen, Tom, Michael Maniates, and Ken Conca, "Confronting Consumption." In *Confronting Consumption.* Edited by Thomas Princen, Michael Maniates, and Ken Conca. Cambridge: MIT Press, 2002.

Puig, Manuel. *Kiss of the Spider Woman.* Translated by Thomas Colchie. New York: Vintage Books, 1978.

Putnam, Robert D. *Bowling Alone: The Collapse and Revival of American Community.* New York: Simon and Schuster, 2000.

Raglon, Rebecca, and Marian Scholtmeijer. "Shifting Ground: Metanarratives, Epistemology, and the Stories of Nature." *Environmental Ethics* 18 (Spring 1996): 19–38.

Rich, Adrienne. *Of Woman Born: Motherhood as Experience and Institution.* New York: Bantam Books, 1977.

———. *On Lies, Secrets, and Silence: Selected Prose, 1966–78.* New York: Norton, 1979.

———. "Woman and Bird." In *What Is Found There: Notebooks on Poetry and Politics.* New York: Quality Paperback Book Club, 1994.

Richards, Robert. *The Romantic Conception of Life: Science and Philosophy in the Age of Goethe.* Chicago: University of Chicago Press, 2002.

Rolston, Holmes, III. *Environmental Ethics: Duties to and Values in the Natural World.* Philadelphia: Temple University Press, 1988.

Romano, Renee C. *Race-Mixing: Black-White Marriage in Postwar America.* Cambridge: Harvard University Press, 2003.

Romero, Oscar A. *Voice of the Voiceless: The Four Pastoral Letters and Other Statements.* Maryknoll, N.Y.: Orbis Books, 1985.

Root, Maria. *Love's Revolution: Interracial Marriage.* Philadelphia: Temple University Press, 2001.

Rosenblatt, Roger, ed. *Consuming Desires: Consumption, Culture, and the Pursuit of Happiness.* Washington, D.C.: Island Press, 1999.

Rothman, Barbara Katz. *Recreating Motherhood.* 2nd ed. Rutgers, N.J.: Rutgers University Press, 2000.

Rubin, Lillian Breslow. *Families on the Fault Line: America's Working Class Speaks About the Family, the Economy, Race, and Ethnicity.* New York: Harper and Row, 1994.

———. *Just Friends: The Role of Friendship in Our Lives.* New York: Harper and Row, 1985.

———. *Intimate Strangers: Men and Women Together.* New York: Harper and Row, 1983.

⸺. *Worlds of Pain: Life in the Working Class Family.* New York: Basic Books, 1976.

Ruddick, Sara. "Injustice in Families: Assault and Domination." In *Justice and Care: Essential Readings in Feminist Ethics.* Edited by Virginia Held. Boulder: Westview Press, 1995.

⸺. "Maternal Thinking." *Feminist Studies* 6, no. 2 (Summer 1980): 342–67.

⸺. *Maternal Thinking: Toward a Politics of Peace.* Boston: Beacon Press, 1995.

Ryle, Martin, and Kate Soper. *To Relish the Sublime? Culture and Self-Realization in Postmodern Times.* New York: Verso, 2002.

Sanders, Scott Russell. *Staying Put: Making a Home in a Restless World.* Boston: Beacon Press, 1993.

Saunders, William P. "Spirituality of Celibacy." *Catholic Herald,* May 2, 2002. http://www.catholicherald.com/saunders/02ws/ws020502.htm.

Schmitt, Richard. *Beyond Separateness: The Social Nature of Human Beings—Their Autonomy, Knowledge, and Power.* Boulder: Westview Press, 1995.

Schneider, Dona. *American Childhood: Risks and Realities.* New Brunswick, N.J.: Rutgers University Press, 1995.

Schor, Juliet. *Born to Buy: The Commercialized Child and the New Consumer Culture.* New York: Scribner's, 2004.

⸺. *The Over-Spent American: Why We Want What We Don't Need.* New York: Harper Perennial, 1999.

Seed, John, Joanna Macy, Pat Fleming, and Arne Naess. *Thinking Like a Mountain: Towards a Council of All Beings.* Philadelphia: New Society Publishers, 1988.

Segundo, Juan Luis. *The Liberation of Theology.* Maryknoll, N.Y.: Orbis Books, 1976.

Skolnick, Arlene. *Embattled Paradise: The American Family in an Age of Uncertainty.* New York: Basic Books, 1991.

Snyder, Samuel. "The Rodman Standoff: A Dam Critique of Bioregionalist Politics of Place," First International Conference on Religion and Nature, Gainesville, Florida, April 7, 2006.

Stephens, Sharon, ed. *Children and the Politics of Culture.* Princeton: Princeton University Press, 1995.

Stoltzfus, Victor. "Reward and Sanction: The Adaptive Continuity of Amish Life." *Mennonite Quarterly Review* 51, no. 4 (October 1977): 308–18.

"Survey: Why Pro-Environmental Views Don't Always Translate into Votes." Nicholas Institute for Environmental Policy Solutions, Duke University School of the Environment and Earth Sciences, Durham, N.C. http://www.dukenews.duke.edu/2005/09/nicholaspoll.html.

SusNord. "New Trends in Sustainable Local Governance: Local Climate Planning in Norway." Oslo: University of Oslo Centre for Development and the Environment, 2005. http://www.prosus.uio.no/susnord/norway/local_authorities/Sustainable%20Local%20Governance/SLG.htm.

Taylor, Bron. "Earth First! and Global Narratives of Popular Ecological Resistance." In *Ecological Resistance Movements.* Edited by Bron Tayor. Albany: State University of New York Press, 1993.

Telechea, María Gravina. *Que Diga Quincho.* Managua: Editorial Nueva Nicaragua, 1982.

Thayer, Robert L., Jr. *Life Place: Bioregional Thought and Practice.* Berkeley: University of California Press, 2003.

Thomashow, Mitchell. *Bringing Home the Biosphere.* Cambridge: MIT Press, 2003.

Thompson, E. P. *William Morris: Romantic to Revolutionary.* Stanford: Stanford University Press, 1988.

Thoreau, Henry David. *Walden and Civil Disobedience.* New York: Penguin, 1986.

Thorne, Barrie, with Marilyn Yalom, eds. *Rethinking the Family: Some Feminist Questions.* New York: Longman, 1982.

Tillich, Paul. *The Courage to Be.* New Haven: Yale University Press, 1952.

——. *Love, Power, and Justice.* New York: Oxford University Press, 1954.

——. *On the Boundary.* New York: Charles Scribner's Sons, 1966.

——. *Political Expectation.* Edited by James Luther Adams. New York: Harper and Row, 1971.

——. *The Protestant Era.* Chicago: University of Chicago Press, 1957.

——. "The Right to Hope." In *Theology of Peace.* Edited by Ronald H. Stone. Louisville: Westminster/John Knox Press, 1990.

——. *The Socialist Decision.* Lanham, Md. University Press of America, 1977.

——. *Systematic Theology, Volume 3.* Chicago: University of Chicago Press, 1963.

——. *Theology of Culture.* New York: Oxford University Press, 1964.

——. "You Are Accepted." In *The Shaking of the Foundations.* New York: Charles Scribner's Sons, 1948.

Tronto, Joan. "Women and Caring: What Can Feminists Learn About Morality from Caring?" In *Justice and Care: Essential Readings in Feminist Ethics.* Edited by Virginia Held. Boulder: Westview Press, 1995.

Wadell, Paul. *Friendship and the Moral Life.* Notre Dame: University of Notre Dame Press, 1989.

Wall, Glenda. "Barriers to Individual Environmental Action: The Influence of Attitudes and Social Experiences." *CRSA/RCSA* 32, no. 4 (1995): 465–91.

Walzer, Susan. *Thinking About the Baby: Gender and Transitions into Parenthood.* Philadelphia: Temple University Press, 1998.

Way, Niobe. *Everyday Courage: The Lives and Stories of Urban Teenagers.* New York: New York University Press, 1998.

Webb, Stephen. *On God and Dogs: A Christian Theology of Compassion for Animals.* Oxford: Oxford University Press, 1998.

Wegner, Phillip E. *Imaginary Communities: Utopia, the Nation, and the Spatial Histories of Modernity.* Berkeley: University of California Press, 2002.

Welch, Sharon. *After Empire: The Art and Ethos of Enduring Peace.* Minneapolis: Augsburg Fortress, 2004.

——. *A Feminist Ethic of Risk.* 2nd ed. Minneapolis: Augsburg Fortress, 1990.

Weston, Anthony. *Back to Earth: Tomorrow's Environmentalism.* Philadelphia: Temple University Press, 1994.

——. "Non-Anthropocentrism in a Thoroughly Anthropocentrized World." *The Trumpeter* 8, no. 3 (1991): 2. http://trumpeter.athabascau.ca/contents/v8.3/weston.html.

——. *A Practical Companion to Ethics.* New York: Oxford University Press, 1997.

Whitman, Walt. *Leaves of Grass. The 1892 Edition.* New York: Bantam Books, 1983.

Williams, Alex. "Buying into the Green Movement." *New York Times,* July 1, 2007.

Williams, Patricia J. *Seeing a Color-Blind Future: The Paradox of Race. The 1997 BBC Reith Lectures.* New York: Farrar Straus and Giroux/Noonday Press, 1997.

Williams, Raymond. *Resources of Hope: Culture, Democracy, Socialism.* Edited by Robin Gable. London: Verso, 1989.

Wilson, Edward O. *Biophilia.* Cambridge: Harvard University Press, 1984.

——. *Naturalist.* Washington, D.C.: Island Press, 2006.

Wingrove, Elizabeth. "Ontology: A Useful Category of Analysis." *Hedgehog Review* 7, no. 2 (Summer 2005): 86–92.

Wirzba, Norman. "Introduction: Why Agrarianism Matters—Even to Urbanites." In *The Essential Agrarian Reader: The Future of Culture, Community, and the Land.* Edited by Norman Wirzba. Lexington: University Press of Kentucky, 2003.

——. "Placing the Soul: An Agrarian Philosophical Principle." In *The Essential Agrarian Reader: The Future of Culture, Community, and the Land.* Edited by Norman Wirzba. Lexington: University Press of Kentucky, 2003.

Yalom, Marilyn, and Laura L. Carstensen, eds. *Inside the American Couple: New Thinking, New Challenges*. Berkeley: University of California Press, 2002.

Yoder, John Howard. *For the Nations: Essays Public and Evangelical*. Grand Rapids, Mich.: Eerdmans, 1997.

———. *The Priestly Kingdom: Social Ethics as Gospel*. Notre Dame: University of Notre Dame Press, 1984.

Zelizer, Viviana. *Pricing the Priceless Child: The Changing Social Value of Children*. New York: Basic Books, 1985.

INDEX